JEAN JACQUES ROUSSEAU

JEAN JACQUES ROUSSEAU

by

JULES LEMAITRE

OF THE FRENCH ACADEMY

TRANSLATED BY

JEANNE MAIRET

MADAME CHARLES BIGOT

GYAN

Published by

GYAN

Gyan Publishing House
5, Ansari Road
Daryaganj, New Delhi-110002
Phone: 011-47034999, 9811692060
E-mail: books@gyanbooks.com

Distribution Network
gyanbooks.com
India, USA, Canada, UK, Australia, France

ISBN : 978-81-212-6180-7 (PB)
First Published, 1907

2nd Impression 2021

Printed at: Gyan Press, Delhi.

Jean Jacques Rousseau
Author: Jules Lemaitre

Jean Jacques Rousseau

BY

JULES LEMAÎTRE
OF THE FRENCH ACADEMY

TRANSLATED BY

JEANNE MAIRET
MADAME CHARLES BIGOT

TO THE READER

First.—I may have been mistaken as to certain facts. This is not a "critical biography" of Rousseau: my chief object has been the history of his sentiments.

Second—These are but lectures. In them I have, above all, endeavored to be simple and clear; and the tone is generally that of a somewhat careful conversation.

J. L.

CONTENTS

CHAPTER PAGE

I. The First Six Books of the "Confessions" 1

II. Rousseau in Paris . . . Thérèse 35

III. Discours sur Les Sciences et Les Arts—The Moral Reform of Rousseau 71

IV. Discours sur L'Inégalité—Rousseau at the Hermitage 107

V. Lettre sur Les Spectacles—Rousseau at Montmorency 143

VI. The "Nouvelle Héloïse" 179

VII. Emile 215

VIII. The "Contrat Social"—The "Profession de Foi du Vicaire Savoyard" 253

IX. The "Lettre à L'Archevêque de Paris"—The "Lettres de La Montagne"—Last Years of Rousseau—The Dialogues 293

X. The Rêveries—Recapitulation and Conclusions . . 333

THE FIRST SIX BOOKS OF THE "CONFESSIONS"

CHAPTER I

THE FIRST SIX BOOKS OF THE "CONFESSIONS"

At the risk of being once more accused of impressionistic, personal, and subjective criticism, I must make an avowal. When I chose Jean-Jacques Rousseau as the subject of this course, it was not, at first, from any feeling of extreme kindliness toward the citizen of Geneva.

And yet, in past days, when I nourished more illusions than I do now, I greatly loved him. But I have had experiences, and have looked closely at realities seen formerly only from afar; I have touched as with the hand the consequences of certain ideas dear to Rousseau. And that is why, when I promised to speak of Jean-Jacques, I purposed especially to study in him the father of some of the greatest errors of the eighteenth and nineteenth centuries.

The first thing to be done was to re-read him, or (let us be sincere) to read him seriously and completely. Then there happened to me something unforeseen. While in this long perusal I sought for reasons to condemn him,—and oh! I found such in great abundance,—I felt at the same time, and very keenly, how those ideas had come to him, by what fatality of temperament and circumstances, as the consequence of what reminiscences, of what deceptions, of what regrets, even of what remorse. Then, what there was in him of candor and sincere piety touched me in spite of myself: and I recognized anew that this man, from whom one may think so many public ills had sprung (unwittingly to himself, it is true, and especially after his death) had no doubt been a sinner, and finally a madman, but in no way a bad man, and that, above all, he had been most unhappy.

And then, his was so singular a case! He is unique, even in our literature, and, I believe, in the literature of the world.

This vagrant, this sluggard, this self-taught man who, after thirty years of idle musings, dropped one day into the midst of the brilliant Paris of the eighteenth century, where he seemed a veritable savage, but a real savage, very much more interesting than the one Voltaire painted; who began to publish toward his fortieth year; who in the space of ten years, in the midst of almost incessant physical suffering, wrote three or four books—which are not particularly strong nor rare as to thought, but show a new way of thinking and a sort of vibration unknown till then; who then sank into a slow kind of madness—and who, by those three or four books, caused, after his death, literature and history to be transformed and the life of a people, to whom he did not belong, to deviate: what a prodigious feat to accomplish!

Therefore, I determined to undertake the study of Jean-Jacques Rousseau's works with a pacified soul, avoiding all useless exasperation against what was really a mystery.

I was then bound to familiarize myself with the latest books published on Rousseau. Having done so, it struck me that perhaps a new study might be superfluous. But if one were to listen to such scruples, one would never do anything.

Thereupon, having already recognized the principal ideas which I might develop, I sought a plan. I could, after my own fashion, either show the unity or the incoherence of Rousseau's work—explain, like M. Lanson, that all in Rousseau, even in the "Contrat social," is subject to a single principle; or like Faguet, that all can be made subject to it, with the exception of the "Contrat social";—follow with regard to each of his books, the posthumous blossoming of the errors he had sown therein;—or else show that Jean-Jacques Rousseau, whatever he may have been besides, was at heart, before and after all, a Protestant in whom Protestantism had prematurely brought forth its extreme consequences;—or else again study, in his life and in his books, the story of a soul, of a poor soul, with its very slow but very real moral evolution . . . . And I might, under these different heads, group all that the reading of Rousseau had suggested to me. The simplest plan was, however, at first sight, to relate first his life, then to present his works.

But I quickly came to the conclusion that this usual method, which is suited to nearly all writers, can scarcely perhaps suit Rousseau, because Rousseau is unlike all other writers.

We see the great classics in their works. These works are all objective, and when we have studied them we know all there is to be known about their authors; and the looking into their lives, be these ever so stormy, would add nothing essential to our knowledge of their works. I should say as much of the eighteenth century writers, and of the Encyclopedists themselves. The lives of Diderot, of d'Alembert, of Duclos, were those of all literary men of the day. The life of Voltaire is amusing; but even if we did not know it, his works would be none the less easy to understand and to judge.

As to Montesquieu and Buffon, their biographies touch their books, so to speak, only so far as to show how the leisure and serenity conferred on them by their fortune and position enabled them to cultivate their minds . . .

But Rousseau is the most "subjective" of all these writers. He is a man who rarely spoke but of himself, a man who spent his time "explaining his character." His early works were already a sort of confession. But, besides, he applied himself to write his real "Confessions," and what confessions! The most sincere, perhaps, but certainly the most detailed, the most complacent, the most immodest, no doubt, but, also, apparently the most candid and doubtless the most courageous, and at all events the most singular and the most captivating ever written.

I therefore think that a study of Jean-Jacques Rousseau might be a continual biography, wherein the story of his books would intimately intermingle with the analysis of his "Confessions." And that is what I shall attempt.

I shall to-day follow the "Confessions" of Jean-Jacques Rousseau up to his last departure from the Charmettes. He was then twenty-nine years of age. These are, therefore, really his "years of apprenticeship."

That Rousseau's finest book should have been his confession, the account of his most intimate life and the description of his most secret personality, is in itself a curious fact. If, as has been asserted, romanticism is the exposing of an individuality in literature, then the "Confessions" of Jean-Jacques, at one stroke, founded romanticism and furnished it with an unsurpassed model. And, furthermore, that Jean-Jacques should have conceived the idea of writing this book, that he should have written it as he did, and that he should have considered himself of sufficient interest to other men, that alone throws a vivid light upon his character, for it is a strong proof of the morbid and insane pride which was at the bottom of that character. The "Confessions" are, by their very essence, a book of immodesty: that book, therefore is in truth father to half the literature of the last century.

He begins thus: "I undertake an unexampled enterprise, the execution of which can never be imitated." And mind that this is true. Nothing like it is to be found either before or after him. There is no need to remind you of the religious and even theological nature of Saint Augustin's chaste confessions. Montaigne, in his "Essais," Retz, in his "Mémoires," confess only weaknesses or faults that can put on a good face and do not dishonor a man. But Rousseau confesses, and without attenuation, shameful things, sins, mortal sins. And, according to his own prediction, he had no followers. For no doubt, after him, the flood-gate of that immodest species of "confessions" was open: but neither Chateaubriand in the "Mémoires d'outre-tombe," nor Lamartine, in the "Confidences," nor George Sand, in "l'Histoire de ma vie," nor Renan in the "Souvenirs d'enfance et de jeunesse," had the courage to acknowledge shameful or simply ridiculous secrets (and if you conclude therefrom that the matter was wanting, it is indeed that you are full of candor).

That is why I understand the exaltation of this first page, and this appeal to God, which ends with these words:

"Eternal Being, gather about me the innumerable crowd of my fellows; let them listen to my confession, let them mourn over my unworthiness, let them blush at my misery. Let each one in his turn lay bare his heart at the foot of Thy throne *with the same sincerity:* then let a single one among them say to Thee, if he dare: I was better than that man."

What does this signify? This outcry is meant to astonish us and smacks of the charlatan. But remember whence came Rousseau, where he had lived, to whom he compared himself: and you will perceive that he thus expressed, in reality—with an inversion as to the words—the reflection of Joseph de Maistre: "I do not know what the heart of a rascal may be; I know what is the heart of an honest man: it is horrible."

And besides (I say this because it is true), when Jean-Jacques Rousseau began to write the "Confessions," at Motiers, in 1762, he had become a very good man. Ill health and persecution had developed his religious feelings. He was already in that half-mystical state of mind which became so apparent in his "Dialogues." To my mind, the "Confessions"—work of a proud penitent who sets himself in opposition to all other men, and who appeals to future ages—partake after all, in many a page, of the nature of a religious confession.

That alone would lead me to believe in their truthfulness, which has been rarely contested, except with regard to chronology, and has been corroborated nearly every time that it was possible to compare Jean-Jacques Rousseau's narrative with his own letters, or with those of his correspondents and contemporaries.

It is, however, certain that the "Confessions," which are above all psychological, are also, and in more than one place, inevitably apologetical (especially in the second version). Then, Rousseau drew his confessions from his memory: the first books were written forty, thirty and twenty years after the events had taken place.

And we know how difficult it is to remember, and to what an extent memory deforms things.

But, in the first place, when he tells us of degrading acts, it is scarcely likely that he invented them (unless certain painful avowals were put there to give credence to the rest); but it is probable, on the contrary, that he remembered them clearly, precisely because they were so mortifying. (Ah! have we not, all of us, or nearly all, in our past lives, some of those things of which it may be said "that they cannot be forgotten"; of those cruelly painful reminiscences, which surge up nearly every day, during prolonged solitude, or else which we call to mind on purpose to sober ourselves?) On the whole, I believe that, if the *veracity* of Jean-Jacques may sometimes be at fault, we must, at least, take for granted, his *sincerity*.

Let us add that he possessed, to an eminent degree, the remembrance of places, which helps that of facts and feelings. Here is an example (and where we shall find also, in the vision and in the accent, a certain something unknown before Jean-Jacques, and which may be called, if you will, the dawn of impressionism).

"The least events of that time please me by the fact that they belong to that time. I remember every detail of the place. I see a swallow darting in through the window, a fly alighting on my hand while I recited my lesson; I see the arrangement of the room where we sat; the study of M. Lambercier at our right, an engraving representing all the popes, a barometer, a great calendar, raspberry bushes which, growing in a garden slanting steeply up from the back of the house, shaded the window and sometimes pushed themselves even into the room. I know that the reader has no great need to know all this, but I feel the need of telling him of it . . ." (Book i).

"I feel the need of telling him of it!" O individualism! O romanticism! And again (reminiscences of the Annecy choir, with the worthy M. Nicoloz, whom he calls M. le Maître):

". . . Not only do I remember the time, the place, the persons, but all surrounding objects, the temperature of the air, its odor, its color, a certain local impression felt only there, the vivid remembrance of which carries me back anew. For instance, all that was rehearsed, all that was sung in the choir, all that was done there, the fine and noble garments of the canons, the chasubles of the priests, the miters of the choristers, the faces of the musicians, an old lame carpenter who played the double bass, a little fair-haired abbé who played the violin, the ragged cassock which, after having taken off his sword, M. le Maître put over his lay clothes, and the fine and beautiful surplice with which, when about to enter the choir, he covered his rags; the pride with which I went, holding a *flûte à bec*,[1] to take my place in the tribune for the bit of solo the master had composed expressly for me; the good dinner that awaited us after-

[1] *Flûte à bec*, small flute used at that time, played, not transversely, but horizontally.

wards; the fine appetite with which we did justice to it; this concourse of things vividly retraced, has a hundred times charmed me in retrospection, as much and more than in reality. I have always kept a tender affection for a certain air of the *Conditor alme siderum* in iambics, because one Sunday in Advent I heard, from my bed, this hymn sung before daybreak, on the porch of the cathedral, according to the ritual of that church . . ." etc. (Book iii.)

But I cannot thus read all the "Confessions" to you, and I regret it. I can only analyze them; and how many details, charming, strange, touching or irritating, I leave behind! For greater clearness, and in order to fix your recollections, it seems to me indispensable to give a very brief summary of the principal facts related in those first six books which to-day occupy our attention.

Book I.—Jean-Jacques is born at Geneva, June 28, 1712. His father was a clock-maker; his mother died in giving him birth. His father allows him to read novels when he is seven. He abandons the boy at eight, an affair of honor having forced him to go into exile. From eight to ten Jean-Jacques is put to school at Bossey, in the house of the minister, Lambercier, who instructs him in religion. Here are placed several anecdotes, among them the whipping administered by Mlle Lambercier.

He is taken from Bossey. He remains two or three years at Geneva, with his uncle Bernard. He goes from time to time to Nyon, where his father lives; he falls in love with Mlle Vulson and romps with Mlle Gothon. He is then placed with a clerk of the court so as to become an attorney. He is sent away and goes to an engraver, who ill-treats him. One evening, after a walk in the country, he finds the town gates closed. And the next day he leaves Geneva, to seek his fortune in the world.

Book II.—He prowls in the neighborhood of Geneva, presents himself to the priest of Confignon, who sends him to Mme de Warens, at Annecy. This lady, newly converted, sends him to Turin to the Seminary of the Catechumens. He lets himself be converted, seeks to earn his living at Turin, spends some weeks with the pretty shopkeeper, Mme Bazile; then enters as footman in the house of the Comtesse de Vercellis. Here comes in the story of the ribbon.

Book III.—After five or six weeks spent in idleness and indulging in certain questionable fancies, he becomes servant to the Comte de Gouvon, where he is treated with some consideration. He falls in love with Mlle de Breil, a daughter of the house. The count's son, the Abbé de Gouvan, grows interested in him and teaches him Italian. His future seemed on the point of being secured: but one fine day, in a new fit of vagrancy, he runs away with a comrade picked up in the streets (at about eighteen).

He returns to Annecy, and goes to Mme de Warens; he allows himself to be fed, but he reads and works. He is placed at the Seminary, but does not remain there.

He takes music lessons of the Professor to the Cathedral boy choir, a M. Nicoloz, whom he calls "Monsieur le Maître." He takes a violent fancy to a kind of musical bohemian, Venture. Then, Monsieur le Maître being obliged to leave Annecy, Jean-Jacques accompanies him as far as Lyons, where he abandons his master at a street corner where he is stricken with an epileptic fit, or perhaps with delirium tremens. (This Monsieur le Maître was a good enough sort of a man, but a sad drunkard.) Thereupon, Jean-Jacques returns to Annecy, where he no longer finds Mme de Warens.

Book IV.—He awaits news of Mme de Warens at Annecy. Here we find the country excursion with Mlles Galley and de Graffenried.

Trusted with the care of taking Merceret, maid to Mme de Warens, to Fribourg, he passes by Geneva, sees his father at Nyon (for the first time, I think, for eight or nine years), and goes from Fribourg to Lausanne, where, under the name of Vaussore, he teaches music, without knowing it, and he even gives a concert (at the house of M. de Treytorens). He goes to Vevey (the native place of Mme de Warens), spends the winter of 1731-1732 at Neuchâtel, where he continues to give music lessons. . . . Finally, by dint of teaching, he himself learned his art. Hard life, misery. He becomes acquainted with an archimandrite, who is begging for the "re-establishment of the Holy Sepulchre," goes to Fribourg, to Berne, to Soleure, where M. de Bonac, Ambassador of France, keeps him. Then M. de Bonac sends him to Paris to do some tutoring. Jean-Jacques travels on foot; quarrels with his pupil's father, learns that Mme de Warens has returned to Savoy, and starts back on foot from Paris. After a short sojourn at Lyons, he arrives at Mme de Warens's house; she was then at Chambéry. She finds him a position as clerk of the surveys.

Book V.—He teaches music to young girls. To guard him against the seductions of some of his pupils, Mme de Warens herself becomes his initiator. He submits, and even accepts the rivalry of the gardener Claude Anet. He goes to Besançon in order to take harmony lessons from the Abbé Blanchard; visits a relative in Geneva, and his father at Nyon (second visit); returns to Chambéry; goes several times to Geneva, to Lyons, to Nyon, sometimes for his own pleasure, sometimes on business for Mme de Warens. An accident blinds him for a certain time. Then he falls seriously ill. Mme de Warens cures him, and both go to live at the Charmettes, a country place near Chambéry (end of the summer, 1736).

Book VI.—Life at the Charmettes. Singular illness. During the winter he returns to Chambéry, then, in the spring, to the Charmettes once more. He reads a great deal, seeking to introduce some method in his studies. In April, 1738, he goes to Geneva to receive his share of his mother's inheritance, which he brings back to Mme de Warens. His malady increases. He fancies that he has a polypus on the heart, and goes to Montpellier for a consultation. On the way, he has his adventure with

Mme de Larnage. He remains two months at Montpellier, returns to Mme de Warens and finds his place occupied by the wig-maker, Wentzenried. He does not accept this new rival; spends a year at Lyons, in M. de Mably's household, as tutor to his two children; returns in 1741, to the Charmettes, finds matters in the same condition and Mme de Warens much colder towards him. He invents a new system of musical notation, thinks that he has made his fortune, and starts off for Paris. He is twenty-nine.

This simple outline of facts, the synopsis of the agitations of Rousseau's outer life up to the thirtieth year, shows us the image of a wanderer and of a stray waif. But let us penetrate further, and, under the mere facts, and thanks, partly, to his own commentaries, let us look at the man himself in the complexity of his nature.

Rousseau (and it is well to remember it) was of French and Parisian origin. His family had been established in Geneva since 1529. His great-grandfather and that man's father had been booksellers: a semi-liberal profession, and close upon that of letters.

And here is another essential remark: Rousseau was born a Protestant. His grandfather, on the maternal side, had been a minister. He was a most genuine Protestant: I mean one whose principles were in harmony with those of the Reformation, who was, later, to write the account of Julie's death, the "Profession de foi du vicaire Savoyard," the "Lettres de la montagne."

Further, we find in Jean-Jacques Rousseau a Genevese imbued with the manners and the spirit of his little republic,—and who, in the "Lettre à d'Alembert," most tenderly recalls having, as a child, taken part in the civic festivities of his town. This young Genevese was predestined to write the "Contrat social."

Let us also notice in him the offspring of an adventurous race. His mother, pretty, lively, well-read, and a much-applauded musician, seems, most innocently, to have caused some scandal in Calvin's city. His father, clockmaker and dancing master, light hearted and romantic, was, during a certain time (from 1705 to 1711) clockmaker to the harem in Constantinople. A brother of Jean-Jacques's turned out badly and disappeared. One of his uncles went to seek his fortunes in Persia.

Furthermore, Jean-Jacques had been a poor child, most absurdly brought up, spending whole nights reading novels with his father, brought up on d'Urfe[1] and la Calprenède[2] (with Plutarch, besides, it is true), abandoned by his father at the age of eight, and who, from the age of ten, was not brought up at all, and became, he repeatedly says so himself, a scapegrace, a thief, an utter scamp.

He also was a child, then a youth, then a man, of extraordinary sensitiveness, and of a very lively imagination,—this sensitiveness will cause him to throw himself into the arms of his friends, weeping abundantly; and he will bathe his waistcoat with his tears when he conceives the idea of his "Discours sur les sciences et les arts."

[1] 1568-1625 [2] 1614-1663

This emotional tendency was closely allied to a pride equally extraordinary, to the intuition of his own private delicacy and also of his intellectual superiority. And, by a natural reaction, the wounds inflicted upon his sensitiveness, exasperated his pride and his pride added cruelly to the sufferings of his sensitiveness. And it will be this morbidly sensitive man who will make of sentiment the basis of morality, and who will write the greater part of the "Nouvelle Héloïse" and of "Emile."

And precisely this emotional nature and this pride will explain the ugliest trait of his youth, the "story of the ribbon." It took place at Turin, after the death of that Mme de Vercellis whose flunkey-secretary he had been. In the disorder following that death, Jean-Jacques stole a "narrow ribbon, pink and silver, already shabby." It was discovered and he was asked where he had found it. He was questioned before the whole family. He stammered and at last said that the young cook, Marion, had given it to him. They were confronted; she denied the fact; Jean-Jacques persisted; both were turned away. "I do not know," says Rousseau, "what became of this victim of my calumny; but it is scarcely likely that she could easily have found another place . . . Who knows to what extremities, at her age, despair brought on by calumniated innocence may not have driven her?" (And on this theme we might imagine some story "on the margin of the Confessions," where we might cause Jean-Jacques, later on, to meet in some ill-famed Paris street poor little Marion, driven to prostitution . . .

But this might perhaps seem a little too easy, and I shall not write the story.)

Rousseau's abominable action serves to show the depth of his nature,—sensibility, imagination, pride,—and that, too, thanks to the explanation which he gives of it, and which, I take it, is the very truth:

"Never was wickedness further from me than at this cruel moment [that in which he falsely accused Marion], and when I calumniated that unhappy girl, it is strange, yet true, that my friendship for her was what prompted me. She was present to my mind; I excused myself at the cost of the first object that occurred to me, and I accused her of having done what I myself had meant to do, for my intention was to give her the ribbon . . . When, later, I saw her come forward, my heart was lacerated, but the presence of so many people was stronger than my repentance. I did not fear punishment: *I feared only the shame, but I feared that more than death, more than crime, more than all things in the world.* I should have wished to bury myself in the center of the earth: invincible shame proved stronger than everything else; shame alone caused my impudence, and the more criminal I became, the more fear of acknowledging it rendered me brazen. I only *saw* the horror of being unmasked, publicly denounced, to my face, as a thief, a liar, a calumniator. An overpowering terror took the place of every other feeling."

(Some questions arise with regard to this anecdote.

The object stolen was a "narrow ribbon" and "old," evidently not worth more than a few pennies. The Comte de la Roque, nephew of Mme de Vercellis, attached so little importance to the story that a few weeks later he procured an excellent place for Jean-Jacques . . . Was all this dramatized by Jean-Jacques? It is irritating, but, with him, one can never be sure of anything. What is certain is that he shows a profound repentance . . . He assures us that the wish to unburden himself of this terrible secret, entered for a great deal into his determination to write his "Confessions," and he goes so far as to say, in the first draft of these same "Confessions," that he considers David Hume's calumnies, thirty years later, as a direct punishment for his lie about little Marion.)

Together with this sensitiveness and this pride, there was in Jean-Jacques a deep love of solitude, of indolent musing, of independence and also of wanderings and, in one word, of vagrancy. Vagrancy, with him, took on the proportions of a passion. He adored an unstable life. Apprenticed attorney, engraver, footman, valet, seminarist, clerk of the surveys, music teacher, one may say that, during the long intervals between these various avocations, he returned willingly, and as much as possible, to his life as a wanderer, a tramp. It was his bent. When he ran away from Geneva, at sixteen: "The independence which I fancied I had achieved was the only feeling that swayed me. I entered upon the wide world with serenity." Elsewhere he says that what he most liked in his solitary wanderings were "the view of the country, the liberty of the inn, the absence of all which could make him feel his dependence. It was also laziness and love of musing." He had so lively a taste for this sort of life that, though, thanks to the Abbé of Gouvon, he could have aspired to an honorable position in the diplomatic career (he was not eighteen), he gave up everything to follow a Genevese scamp, called Bascle, to whom he had taken a great fancy, and with whom he wandered through the land exhibiting scientific tricks.

(Let us note another trait of his character: the facility with which he took to people. He was very fond of Bascle; he became equally fond of Venture, the bohemian musician; he also, at first, was fond of Diderot, of Grimm, and of many others. He had a great need of opening his heart and a credulity which caused him to throw himself into people's arms; and this first impulse of credulous emotion was, little by little, superseded by a sensitiveness full of suspicions; for he soon found each of his idols to be inferior to the image his fancy had painted of them; or else his pride feared that the idol did not return his affection, or even turned him into ridicule.)

Let us proceed. It was to these wanderings in one of this world's most beautiful countries, it was to this contemplative and unsettled life, that Rousseau owed his comprehension of nature and his love for it; it caused him to invent, or nearly so, romantic poetry. His "Confessions" are full of charming reminiscences of landscapes, and moreover, at the beginning of Book iii., he already spoke as René was later to speak: " . . . I was ill at ease, absent minded, full of dreams: I wept, I sighed, I longed for a happiness of which I could form no idea, but the privation of which I yet felt . . ."

It is this vagabond who was later to describe the landscapes and write the lyrical passages of the "Nouvelle Héloïse," and the "Rêveries d'un promeneur solitaire."

Jean-Jacques further owed to these bohemian years his intimate knowledge of humble and modest lives,—and also (for twice he was a servant in noble houses) his observations and studies of fashionable lives, and these observations were made in a position so bitterly mortifying, that later, they engendered eloquence. He dwells but little on this intimate suffering, no doubt because these reminiscences were particularly painful to him, more painful even, no doubt, than the remembrance of his shameful acts: but one guesses what must have endured this proud fellow, full of genius, of decent descent, too, grandson of booksellers and of Protestant ministers, when he wore the livery, even when he was dispensed from the tresse and shoulder knot and the livery "seemed almost an ordinary coat." But in spite of his reserve certain traits reveal his rancor.

". . . Toward the end," says he, "Mme de Vercellis spoke only to give me orders. She judged me less according to what I really was than according to what she had made me, and by dint of looking on me as on a footman she prevented me from seeming more than a servant, in her eyes. It seems to me that it was from that moment that I suffered from the malicious working of hidden interests which persisted all through my life and which inspired me with a natural aversion caused by the *apparent order* which produces it."

(All that because, as he says further on, "there were so many flatterers about Mme de Vercellis, whose end was approaching, that it was difficult for her to find the time to remember Jean-Jacques.") Thus he had a grudge against that society because Mme de Vercellis took so little notice of him. Thus again, at the Gouvon-Solar's while waiting at table, upon being questioned by the old count, he explained the old-time motto of the Solars ("*Tel fiert qui ne tue pas*"),[1] and enjoyed the admiration of the company: "That moment was short, but in every way delicious. It was one of those too rare moments which replace things in their natural order and avenge merit, degraded by the outrages of fortune." And I recall also his exclamation, when he entered the Comte de Gouvon's service, "Still a flunkey!" And it is apparent that if, later, the vagrant was to write the admirable "Cinquième rêverie," it was much rather the quondam lackey who was to write the "Discours sur l'inégalité" and who founded equality on the "Contrat social" theory.

And above all that, or, rather under all that, there was the invalid.

[1] *Tel frappe qui ne tue pas.* (He strikes who does not kill.)

It is necessary here to insist somewhat. The pathology of a Bossuet or a Racine has little in common with their sermons or their tragedies: but the pathology of Jean-Jacques is nearly all Jean-Jacques. (His work itself appears in literature like a morbid eruption.)

"I was born," says Jean-Jacques, "sickly and infirm . . . I was born half dead . . . I brought into the world the germ of an infirmity which grew with my years."

This congenital infirmity was a kidney disease which increased after the thirtieth year.

To this was added another infirmity which may be guessed at from these words of Jean-Jacques; they date from the time when he used to go from the Hermitage to Eaubonne to visit Mme d'Houdetot.

"As I walked, I thought of her whom I was going to see; of the affectionate greeting which she would give me; of the kiss which awaited me on my arrival . . . This kiss alone . . . even before receiving it, sent fire into my veins . . . I was forced to stop, to sit down . . . No matter how I managed, I do not think I was ever able to take that walk with impunity."

Add to this a strange illness which suddenly attacked him at the Charmettes and which he describes thus:

"One morning, when I was no worse than usual, while I was setting up a little table, I felt a sudden revulsion in my whole body . . . My arteries began to beat with such violence that not only did I feel their throbs, but I even heard them, and especially those of the carotids. To this was added a great noise in the ears; and this noise was triple or rather quadruple, that is: a deep and confused buzzing, a clearer murmur like that of running water, a very shrill whistling, and the throbbing already mentioned . . . The noise was so tremendous that it took from me my previous delicacy of hearing, and made me, not at all deaf, but hard of hearing, as I have been ever since." (Book v. of the "Confessions.")

He adds that for thirty years, up to the moment of his writing, the throbbing of his arteries and the buzzings *had never left him one minute.* He refers to them again in the sixth book, where he also speaks of his "vapors," of the "tears that he often shed without having any reason to weep," of his "terrors at the sound of a leaf or a bird."

I pass on to his other ills: his nephritic pains, or what he believed to be such, which date from 1750, frequent quinsies, a hernia at forty-five, etc. (not to mention a laboratory accident which, at the Charmettes, blinded him, so he says, during six weeks). In one word, and to keep to his permanent ills: kidney disease, deep-seated neurasthenia, weakness of the arteries, such was his lot.

It is easy to follow the reaction of these physical miseries upon his moral being.

First of all, his neurasthenia furnishes us with the most kindly explanation of the petty thefts of his childhood and early youth, and also of certain acts of impudence and bragging, as for instance when, at Lausanne, he got up and gave a concert without knowing anything about music; or when, during his journey to Montpellier, he passed himself off for an English Jacobite, without knowing a word of English. His neurasthenia permits one to substitute for the unsavory terms of liar and thief, those of "simulator" and of "kleptomaniac."

Then, it may be that his chief infirmity contributed to his taste for solitude and for long and lonely walks through woods and plains.

But most of all, his physical woes acted powerfully on his sensitiveness, on his passions, and consequently, on his books themselves.

The sentimental life of Jean-Jacques is very curious and very sad. His sensual nature awoke when he was ten and was whipped by Mlle Lambercier (who was thirty years of age). It would be impossible for me to enter into the details of what he calls "the dark and loathsome labyrinth of his 'Confessions.'" But it is necessary to hint at the truth. His childhood and adolescence were full of vice; and with all, corrupt and morbidly depraved as he was, he preserved until he was twenty-two, what may be called his innocence. Why? From timidity and for pathological reasons. Thus he fell into the arms of Mme de Warens, vicious and innocent, and his first love adventure was of no very honorable nature. And that is how, save for Mme de Warens and Thérèse, he had but one real love adventure, that with Mme de Larnage. And that is why he resigned himself to Thérèse. And these things explain others, whether in the "Nouvelle Héloïse" or in "Emile."

(Besides, I do not forget that timidity to which we owe the charm of his idyl with Mme Basile, the young Italian shop-woman.)

I have several times referred to Mme de Warens. Hers is a curious psychological case and merits some attention. But you know her. I need not remind you of her Protestant birth, her marriage, her flight to Vevey, after some domestic incident, her appeal to the King of Sardinia, under whose auspices she was converted to Catholicism, and who granted her a pension of two thousand francs. She herself undertook proselytism (as we see by her first meeting with Jean-Jacques), though her Catholicism was extremely lax. She was of a fussy activity, busied herself with chemistry and prepared drugs; she was disorderly, chimerical, credulous with regard to adventurers and inventors, and always had some new scheme on hand. As to love, an old gentleman had taught her that it was of no great consequence, and she had believed him. She was always ready to be kind to her friends, and was quite indifferent as to their social position. With it all, she was of a placid temperament. In one word, she acted in such matters, like a man —somewhat like our George Sand, with less decency, however.

Rousseau loved her deeply; but the nature of this affection is defined by the names they gave each other: "Maman" and "Petit." The first time he saw her she was twenty-eight and he sixteen. He was a poor little lost tramp, and very timid. She was the first woman, beautiful and elegant, and rich (in his eyes) whom he had ever met. And, at once, she was good to him with a simple and maternal kindliness. She withdrew the little wretch from the abyss into which he had fallen. His first impulse toward her, and which was to last a long time—was one of adoration.

We must con over again the account of their first meeting, for it is exquisite:

"It was on a by-way behind her house. . . . As she was about to enter the church, Mme de Warens turned, at the sound of my voice. What surprise this sight caused me! I had imagined an old, pious, ill-favored dame; the good lady of M. de Pontverre, to my mind, could not be otherwise. I saw a face beaming with charm, beautiful blue eyes, full of sweetness, a dazzling complexion and enchanting figure. Nothing escaped the rapid glance of the young proselyte; for instantly I became hers, certain as I was that a religion preached by such a missionary, could only lead to paradise. She smilingly took the letter which I had presented to her with a trembling hand, opened it, glanced over that from M. de Pontverre, took up mine once more and read it to the end, and would have read it over again if her footman had not warned her that it was time to enter. 'Ah! my child,' she said, in a voice that made me thrill, 'you are wandering about the world at a very tender age, and it is really a pity.' Then, without awaiting my answer, she added: 'Go to my house and wait for me; ask for breakfast, after mass I shall have a talk with you.'"

And a little later:

"Hers was a beauty destined to last, because it was more in the expression than in the features; besides hers was in its first flush. She had a caressing and tender air, an angelic smile, a mouth no larger than mine [Jean-Jacques had a small mouth], very fair hair of singular beauty and which she wore so simply dressed that it added to her peculiar charm."

And the lines that follow give us to understand that she was chubby. The pages where Jean-Jacques tells us how Mme de Warens proposed to take him as her lover, in order to shield him from the perils inherent to his age (he was twenty-two and she was thirty-four), and in what a grave and matter-of-fact way she made the proposition, giving him eight days wherein to make up his mind, and how he accepted with no great enthusiasm, but out of gratitude, still calling her "Maman," and how he discovered that he had a rival in the gardener, Claude Anet, and how he accepted this complication, and how Mme de Warens blessed them both, and how Jean-Jacques remained full of respect for Claude Anet; these pages where he eternally speaks of virtue, these pages which might be an anticipated and crude caricature of the far more decent story of Sand between Musset and Pagello, seem to us, to-day, prodigiously comic. And doubtless, in all this, Rousseau was but half responsible (we often notice in him a strange passivity), and doubtless the account of his life at the Charmettes, where his mind was formed, is of a new and fresh savor; and I well know that Rousseau, on several occasions, tried to earn his bread; and when he came into his little inheritance, he handed it over to his friend, and that, at his third or fourth return, when he found his place taken by the wig-maker, Mme de Warens, with ingenuousness proposing a threefold union, he refused; and I do not forget, finally, that some years later, when the poor woman was totally ruined and degraded, he sent her a little money from Paris; it remains proved, however, that the young man, for about ten years, lived almost exclusively on Mme de Warens, that he was under too heavy obligations to her to refuse anything she might require of him, or to insist on fidelity from her; and that thus his first love was neither free nor dignified, nor disinterested, at least in appearance;—and that, in his conception of love, all this led to certain results which we shall note in the study of his works.

Finally—and to complete the enumeration of all the natures that were combined in him,—that, if in Jean-Jacques there was a Protestant by birth, we must not forget that there was also a Catholic.

He became a convert to Catholicism—while yet almost a child, it is true—to obey the beautiful lady of Annecy, and to escape from misery. Perhaps, in later times, he exaggerated (but I know not) his scruples and his hesitations when on the point of deserting his paternal religion. Perhaps, also, in referring to the story of the abominable Moor,—writing about it thirty years later, —he exaggerated, through renewed anti-papalism, the cynicism of the director of the catechumens' seminary, and especially the singular coolness of the ecclesiastic who was there. But after all, I know nothing about it. What surprises me is that, after his conversion, he should have been set adrift with twenty francs in his hand, and that no one should have felt any further concern about him. For what interest would the clergy find in converts, if it were not to create adherents and, consequently, to follow them up? It is true that the most pious institutions can lose all vitality and degenerate so as to forget their very aim.

But, however that may be, one thing is certain: that is that Jean-Jacques was a Catholic during twenty-six years (from 1728 to 1754), and that for the first ten years he lived in a purely Catholic atmosphere. He spent about two months in the great seminary of Annecy, with a view of becoming a priest. At Annecy, at Chambéry, at the Charmettes, he practiced his new religion. He was acquainted with priests and monks, who, on his own evidence, were very good to him. After the laboratory accident, which nearly cost him his sight, he wrote his will with all the terms and according to the formula of Catholic piety, and he made small legacies to nuns, to Capuchins and other monks. When Mme de Warens undertook to have M. de Bernex, former bishop of Annecy, beatified, Jean-Jacques certified in writing a miracle performed by the good bishop (a conflagration was put out by the prayers of the bishop and Mme de Warens!) —"Thoroughly Catholic in those days," says Jean-Jacques, "I was quite sincere." He begins thus the account of a walk with "Maman."

"We started off together and alone, early in the morning, *after mass*, which a Carmelite friar had come to celebrate in a chapel joining the house."

He says in the same book iv.:

"The writings of Port-Royal and of the oratory, being those which I used to read most frequently, nearly made me a Jansenist."

He had a terror of hell:

"But my *confessor*, who was also 'Maman's,' contributed to keep me in the right way."

And speaking of Father Hémet and Father Coppier:

"Their visits used to do me the greatest good: may God do as much for their souls!"

And again we shall see that Jean-Jacques, according to his own account, never had any complaint to make against the Catholic clergy (with the exception of the mandate against "Emile"), but he had many complaints to make against the Protestant ministers.

All I wish to say on this subject is that, in him, the Catholic impress was added to the Protestant impress; that his sensibility was peculiarly Catholic. This I shall explain when the time comes: but why should I not say at once that there is, in his leaning toward confession, and a certain confession, and in the sort of pleasure it procures to him, something like the corruption of a Catholic sensibility,—a disposition which is not rare, it seems, with certain female penitents, to whom auricular confession gives a second taste of their sin, in spite of the shame of avowal?

. . . . .

Such is the man,—oh! with much candor, with kindliness, and even with certain aspirations toward moral reform,—and also with this singularly extenuating circumstance, that it is through himself alone that we know all his turpitudes,—but yet such is the man, vicious in his childhood and early youth, a rebellious vagrant—indolent, weak and a dreamer,—a liar and a thief, (on the last occasion, at the age of twenty-eight, stealing wine at M. de Malbly's),—a Protestant grafted with Catholicism,—a pardonable deserter, but a deserter of country and faith,—many years the lover of a kind-hearted and discredited woman, whose dependent he was—above all, pitifully ill, with unstrung nerves, doomed to madness,—such was the man who, at twenty-nine, sought his fortune in Paris, and who, a few years later, undertook the reformation of Society and set up as a professor of virtue.

ROUSSEAU IN PARIS . . . THÉRÈSE

CHAPTER II

ROUSSEAU IN PARIS . . . THÉRÈSE

I HAVE described the singular young man, full of oddities, of blemishes and of pride, who at twenty-nine years of age went to Paris to seek his fortune (in music or in literature)—until the day when he set up, eight years later, as a reformer of manners and a professor of virtue. But it is well to add that, during those eight years, he never thought of such a thing.

What was this world of letters where the vagrant of Geneva, of the shores of Lake Leman, of Savoy, of Piedmont and of Turin,—the dreamer of the Charmettes and the lover of Mme de Warens,—was to enter? If we put aside the Lord of Ferney, and Montesquieu and Buffon, somewhat disdainful and high-born gentlemen, who most of the time wrote in the seclusion of their homes, that world consisted of a score of authors, who met at divers cafés, and who were familiar guests at the houses of a dozen—not more—farmer-generals, great lords and fine ladies, people who prided themselves upon their liberty of thought, and were fond of patronizing men of letters because they amused them, and also from a feeling akin to snobbism.

The future author of the "Discours sur l'inégalité" and of the "Contrat social," was no exception to the rule, and did not seek to be an exception. And yet, no one was less fitted than he for that worldly life, for conversation, for pleasures as refined as they were futile. He was a plebeian in his tastes and in his mind, really fond of simplicity, besides, extremely timid. He relates the stupid blunders of which he was guilty at the first fine dinners to which he was invited. He repeats incessantly, in fifty passages of his "Confessions" and of his letters (which proves that in his heart he suffered from it) that he was timid and awkward, that he could not keep up a brilliant and witty conversation, and that, in order not to remain silent, he often said foolish things . . .

But, on the other hand, his countenance was interesting, and his eyes extraordinarily full of fire; and from time to time, when he was moved, he would, for a few moments, be eloquent, the very effort he made giving all the more weight to his words. He would then excite great curiosity. And he, noticing this, would persevere, and feeling that he could never be "like the others," a dazzling conversationalist like Diderot, keen and cold, like Grimm, or of a savory bluntness like Duclos, he made up his mind to appear more and more peculiar and "apart," for that may also bring success. But with it all, and this I repeat, until 1749, his ambitions were purely musical and literary.

"I reached Paris," says he, "during the autumn of 1741, with fifteen louis of ready money, my comedy of 'Narcisse' and my musical scheme, as my only resources."

This "musical scheme" was a new system of writing music with numbers (the same system, if I am not mistaken, as the one taken up and perfected by Galin-Paris-Chevé, and so often recommended by Sarcey). He exposed his scheme, without success, before the Academy of Sciences, August 22, 1742. He bore his disappointment pretty well; and as he was rather wanting in initiative, he spent his time reading and playing chess.

But the persons to whom he was recommended, and also his visits to the Academicians, brought him some acquaintances. Besides, he himself says: "A tolerably good-looking young man, who comes to Paris and shows some talent, is always sure of a good reception." (That is no longer quite true.) So, he meets and frequents Fontenelle, Mably, Marivaux, Bernis, the Abbé de Saint-Pierre, Diderot, and, a little later, Grimm.

Soon after the failure of his memoir on music, while he quietly awaited the end of his money, a Jesuit, Father Castel, said to him one day: "I regret to see you waste your time in idleness. Since the learned world and the musicians do not sing in harmony with you, change your key, and turn to the women. You may succeed better with them." Thus spoke the Jesuit. To him, Jean-Jacques owed the acquaintance of Mme de Benzenval, of Mme Dupin, of M. de Francueil, and, through him, of Mme d'Epinay and Mme d'Houdetot.

Jean-Jacques, with M. de Francueil, followed a course of chemistry. He fell dangerously ill, and, in the height of fever, composed melodies and choruses. These inspirations came back to him during his convalescence; he elaborated a theme and began his opera of the "Muses galantes," We are still far from the "Discours sur l'inégalité."

He naturally fell in love—without any danger to her—with Mme Dupin (George Sand's great-grandmother), for he could not see a high-born lady without falling in love with her, and without building castles in the air. In Jean-Jacques there was a sort of Julien Sorel,[1] without strength of will (which, it is true, constitutes a notable difference). He writes:

"She allowed me to visit her. I took advantage, more than discretion warranted, of the permission. I went to her house almost every day. I dined there two or three times a week. I was dying to speak to her, and never dared to do so. Several reasons increased my natural timidity. *The admission into a wealthy house was a door opened to fortune; I would not risk having it shut upon me.* . . . Mme Dupin liked to have about her brilliant people who did her honor, the great, writers, beautiful women. In her drawing-rooms one saw but dukes, ambassadors, the shimmer of orders. The Princesse de Rohan, the Comtesse de Forcalquier, Mme de Mirepoix, Lady Hervey, were counted among her friends. M. de Fontenelle, the Abbé de Saint-Pierre, the Abbé Sollier, M. de Fourment, M. de Bernis, M. de Buffon, M. de Voltaire, belonged to her circle, and dined with her. . . ."

1 Hero of "Rouge et noir." Novel by Stendhal.

Here we find Rousseau in the highest society, and, we must acknowledge, in the most voluptuous and corrupt of worlds, and he enjoyed it. Yes, here we are at a great distance from Jean-Jacques, citizen of Geneva, and the philosophical advocate of nature.

Meanwhile, these fine ladies interested themselves in him, and tried to find him a situation. Toward April or May, 1743, he was sent to Venice as secretary to the French ambassador, M. de Montaigu. He there spent eighteen months. Jean-Jacques dwells complacently on this period of his life.

To tell the truth, he says not a word of the beauty of Venice, since so glowingly and enthusiastically described.

Sébastien Mamerot, a priest of Soissons, wrote in 1454, in the "Passages d'outre mer faits par les Français," [1] a book published in 1518:

"Venice is a beautiful city, half as large as Paris, situated in the sea, surrounded by water, which runs into most of the streets; and the little barges and boats go in and out of these streets; and there are bridges, both large and small, of wood or stone, about fifteen hundred. And it is the most populous city that one can see, for one perceives neither gardens nor empty places. . . . And there are the most beautiful shops and all sorts of goods, and most of the manufactures are of silks and velvets. And there are quantities of fine houses, which are called palaces; . . . and every lord has his boat to go where he lists. And it is said that there are more

[1] "Travels undertaken by Frenchmen beyond the seas.'

boats in Venice than are mules and horses in Paris. And in the precincts of the town there are about a hundred and thirty churches," etc.

And Sébastien Mamerot then duly and minutely describes the mosaics of Saint-Marc.

Now, Jean-Jacques, the grandfather of the romanticists, of whom Chateaubriand was the father, does not even tell us as much. Precisely because he is, in the art of description, a forerunner, he keeps to simple subjects: lakes, forests, hills; and he has no time to expatiate, or to be lyrical. We must not forget either that Venice, toward the middle of the eighteenth century, was a very bustling city, that its palaces were new or cleaned, and by no means menaced ruin, and that it did not therefore show that attraction of decay and deliquescence over which we have learned to grow enthusiastic.

But, above all, while he is telling us of his sojourn in Venice, Jean-Jacques is too full of his important official duties there to care for Saint-Marc, the Bridge of Sighs, the canals, and the gondolas. Obviously, he is proud of having been secretary to the Legation (for he did the work of one), of having once filled an honorable, official post in regulated society. Listen to the tone, the accent of this:

"It was time that I should be at last that which Heaven, who had endowed me richly, that which the education which I had received from the best of women [Mme de Warens had perhaps been something of a secret agent of the King of Sardinia], that which my self-acquired education had made of me. Such did I now become. Left to myself alone, without friends, without counsel, without experience, in a strange land, serving an alien cause in the midst of a crowd of rogues who, for their own interests and to put aside the scandal of good example, tempted me to imitate them: far from doing so, I served France well, France to which I owed nothing, and still more the ambassador, as was but fair, in everything for which I was responsible. Irreproachable in a rather important position, I deserved and obtained the esteem of the Republic, that of the ambassadors with whom we were on good terms, and the affection of the French, established in Venice."

And he enumerates the services he rendered. The tone, the seriousness, the air of profound satisfaction, remind one of Chateaubriand relating his embassy to London. (How closely Chateaubriand, that aristocratic son of Jean-Jacques, resembled him is what we notice more and more as we study them both.)

But, if we are to believe Jean-Jacques, his superior, M. de Montaigu, was a man coarse, avaricious, ignorant, and somewhat out of his mind.[1] He was forced to leave

[1] I have received from M. Auguste de Montaigu a pamphlet entitled: *Démêlés du comte de Montaigu, ambassadeur à Venise, avec son secrétaire, J. J. Rousseau.* (Plon et Nourrit, 1904.) M. Aug. de Montaigu proves, by documents of the Venice archives, that Rousseau's charges against his ambassador were ill-founded, that he was not an irreproachable secretary, that, among other things, he was guilty of smuggling, and that he was dismissed by the Comte de Montaigu.

him without being able to obtain his salary. On his return to Paris he vainly demanded justice from his ambassador. The refusal he met with (it must be added that, though he did the work of an embassy secretary, he was only, in reality, secretary to the ambassador) left in his soul, says he, " a germ of indignation against our stupid civil institutions, where the public weal and true justice are always sacrificed to I know not what apparent order, in truth fatal to all order, and which only add the sanction of public authority to the oppression of the weak, and the iniquity of the powerful."

It was a pity. Had he been able to get along with M. de Montaigu, had he been content to have become a regular official, he might have followed his diplomatic career (and it is likely that his influential lady friends of Paris would have pushed him on rapidly); he would have become more and more enamored of his profession; he would have sent his minister reports, written in admirable style; he would have turned toward political economy, for which he had a taste, but he would have broken down no social barriers; he would not have written the "Inégalité," "Emile," nor the "Contrat," and we should have lost much from a literary point of view, but, from other points of view, it would have been a good thing; and he would not have married Thérèse Levasseur.

But let us finish with the Venetian reminiscences of Jean-Jacques.

In that city of love and pleasure, in that Venice of

Casanova (who was there at the same time as Rousseau), the amorous life of Rousseau was meager. His only real adventure was with a woman called Padoana. A more notorious incident was with Zulietta. I refer you to the text, but I must at least quote the beginning:

"I entered that room of a courtezan as though it had been the sanctuary of love and beauty. . . . I found that instead of the devouring flames I had at first felt, a mortal chill ran in my veins, and, almost fainting, I sat and *wept like a child.*"

There is no mistake here: good or bad, this is perhaps the first time that he wrote words of such sentiment, such accent, such color. And, unless I greatly mistake, in order to obtain this tone, were needed (Rousseau was fifty-five when he wrote this) a whole life of painful timidity in love affairs, of extreme shyness, of sensibility, and of imagination exasperated by this timidity; a half century of ill-health also and of frustrated desires—and above all real genius. Rousseau continues thus:

"Who could have guessed the cause of my tears, and what was passing through my mind at that moment? I said to myself: This creature who is at my mercy is the masterpiece of nature and love; mind, body, both are perfect; she is as good and generous as she is beautiful and amiable; the great, princes even, should be at her feet. Yet, there she is, miserable waif, slave to the public;" etc.

Do you not feel that here is the first and most perfect draft of one of the themes on which the romantic school has fed: the pity, a little solemn and mystical, for the courtezan; the respect for fallen woman, all the more worthy of it and touching for her fall;—oh, surely, this would have been a good sentiment, had one not made some abuse of this substitution of sentiment for reason. A romantic theme, did I say? That is so true, and Jean-Jacques's page on Zulietta was so new, and seemed so insane, that when the "Confessions" became known, La Harpe saw in it one of the surest signs of Rousseau's madness. Romantic theme—which deviates in the narration of Jean-Jacques, for he pretends that a physical defect is the cause of Zulietta's degradation—but an essentially romantic theme in the lines I have quoted. Jean-Jacques near Zulietta, foreshadows Rolla near Marion, and do you not perceive the resemblance between the relatively moderate-toned meditation of Jean-Jacques, and the pitying and wild effusions of Rolla:

O Chaos éternel, prostituer l'enfance! . . .
Pauvreté! Pauvreté! c'est toi la courtisane,
C'est toi qui dans ce lit a poussé cet enfant
Que la Grèce eût jeté sur l'autel de Diane! . . .

And further on:

Jacque était immobile et regardait Marie . . .
Il se sentait frémir d'un frisson inconnu
N'était-ce pas sa sœur, cette prostituée? . . .

Yes, it seems to me that really the inflation, the want

of reason, and what I should call the romantic disproportion between the sentiments and things are already to be found in that episode of Zulietta.

We have now to come to Thérèse.

On his return to Paris, Jean-Jacques, fallen from his ambitions, was very sad and very much unsettled. He once more took up his quarters at the Hôtel Saint-Quentin, rue des Cordiers, near the Sorbonne. The boarders took their meals with the hostess and a young seamstress of twenty-two or three years of age, Thérèse. Her mother, Mme Levasseur, had been a shopkeeper at Orleans, where her husband was clerk of the Mint. Not having prospered, she had given up business, and had come to Paris with her husband and children. (Jean-Jacques, without going into details, tells us that she had "many children.") And now, let us listen to Jean-Jacques:

"The first time I saw this girl at table I was struck by her modest demeanor, and yet more by her bright and gentle glance, *the like of which I never saw.* The table was surrounded by several Irish and Gascon priests and other like folk. Our hostess herself was a woman with a past; I alone spoke and acted with decency. All teased the young girl, and I took her defense. Immediately, jokes were showered on me. Had I felt no liking for this poor girl, pity and the spirit of contradiction would have attracted me to her. I have always loved polite manners and decent talk, especially with the other sex. I became her declared champion, I saw that she was pleased with my attentions, and her glances, brighter from the gratitude she did not dare to express, were all the more eloquent."

In a word, he makes love to her. . . . He begins by telling her that "never will he abandon her, and never will he marry her." She hesitates. At last, one day, "weeping, she confessed that when she was a mere child, from ignorance and from the arts of a seducer, she had committed one single fault." He exclaims joyously: "Is that all?" And they unite their lives. Yet, until 1749, he keeps his room at the hotel, and spends his days with Thérèse and her mother. "Her home became mine." In 1749, only, he settles with her in a small apartment of the Hôtel de Languedoc, rue de Grenelle, and they live there until his removal to the Hermitage.

Let us pause and study Thérèse.

I believe that none of Rousseau's critics or biographers have failed to deplore his meeting with Thérèse: "An attachment unworthy of him," they say, "and that had the sorriest influence on his fate." It seems to me that they exaggerate. Thérèse's family, no doubt, caused him much trouble. On the other hand, Thérèse's fecundity was for Rousseau the cause of his most wicked action. But Thérèse herself, in spite of her faults, seems to me to have brought him more happiness by her gentleness, care, and usefulness than she brought hindrances to his fortunes. And, finally, that he should have formed this attachment is natural enough; he might have fallen into worse hands.

As a girl Thérèse must have been rather pretty. (Indeed, she is not ill-looking in the only portrait that exists of her, and which represents her as a woman of about fifty.) Speaking once of Diderot, with a somewhat amusing spirit of rivalry, Jean-Jacques says:

"He had a Nanette, as I had a Thérèse; this formed between us another bond of sympathy. But the difference was that my Thérèse, *as well favored as his Nanette*, was gentle and amiable . . . whereas the other was a foul-mouthed scold," etc.

Evidently, Thérèse must have been pleasing, since fine ladies petted her. Mme de Boufflers in Montmorency would go and take a bite with her, and the Maréchale de Luxembourg embraced her heartily. Even later, and when Thérèse was over fifty, a young man from Marseilles, M. Eymar, who, in 1774, visited Rousseau, says: "Mme Rousseau was far from resembling the hideous portrait which a celebrated poet painted of her in one of his satires [probably Voltaire in his "Guerre de Genève,"]. I, of course, found her neither young nor beautiful; but she was polite, well-mannered, dressed simply but neatly, and had the appearance of an excellent housekeeper."

At twenty-three Thérèse might have been attractive. This seems certain to me.

What did Rousseau need when he met her? A nurse and a servant, as well as a companion.

Thérèse had had a misfortune? So much the better! "As soon as I understood," says Rousseau, "I uttered a cry of joy." Why? He did not care, for many reasons, to be a first lover—and, as for me, I see clearly why jealousy in love was absent from his life, as it is almost absent from his books.

Thérèse was a seamstress—a "grisette"—ignorant and simple:

> "At first," says he, "I tried to cultivate her mind; I lost my time. . . . Her mind was such as nature had made it; culture and care could do nothing for it. I do not blush to confess that she never read with ease, though she wrote quite decently. . . . She never could tell the months of the year, and knew nothing of figures, though I did my best to give her some notion of them. She knew nothing of money, nor the price of things. While speaking, she would often use one word for another. In olden times, I had composed a dictionary of her sentences for Mme de Luxembourg's amusement, and her blunders had become celebrated in the different circles I frequented."

All that is excellent, and he had found what he needed. He was thirty-three years of age, and he tells us that after thirty his infirmities increased. He required a nurse. He required a companion, inferior to him socially, and in every particular; a daughter of the people, poor, who would owe him everything, who would be neither over-refined nor easily shocked, before whom he need not blush for his physical weaknesses, and who would care for him in every way. And that is why he chose Thérèse.

And he chose her because she was ignorant, and, as he himself says, "stupid." He wanted a companion whom he did not need to entertain; a woman whose simplicity rested and sometimes amused him. . . . Besides, his was no very rare case: we have often seen artists choose an uncultivated and dull companion—as a rest. . . .

Rousseau did not marry Thérèse. In 1755 he gives his (somewhat vague) reasons to Mme de Francueil: "Why did I not marry, will you say? Ask that of your unjust laws, madame. It did not suit me to enter upon an eternal engagement, and no one can prove to me that I should have done so." In 1761 he gives another reason to Mme de Luxembourg: "A public marriage between us would have been impossible on account of the difference of religion." But, in 1745, Rousseau was still a Catholic—this reason, therefore, is of no value. In short, he did not marry Thérèse so that he might be more free, that she should always depend upon him; also, perhaps, so as not to be forced to take her to the houses he frequented.

If he did not marry Thérèse, he certainly cared for her. But he did not really love her. He says in the ninth book:

"What will the reader think when I tell him that from

the first moment when I saw her to this day [about 1769] I never felt for her the least spark of passion, any more than I craved the possession of Mme de Warens? . . ."

But he felt great affection for her—that cannot be disputed. Before describing their first meeting, he says: "There, was awaiting me the only real consolation which Heaven has granted me in my misery, and which alone has made it bearable." This he wrote after twenty-four years of union. A little further he says: "The heart of my Thérèse was that of an angel." In twenty passages of the "Confessions," in something like fifty passages in his letters (and of every period), he speaks of her good qualities, of her virtues, especially of "her kind heart, her affectionate nature, of her unparalled disinterestedness, of her spotless fidelity." However, he says, in a footnote written after 1768: "She was, it is true, less intelligent, easier to deceive than I could have imagined;" but he immediately added: "But as to her nature, it was pure, excellent, guileless, worthy of my esteem, and that she shall have as long as I live." He took great care of her. After his flight from Montmorency he recommended her tenderly to Mme de Luxembourg, and to the superior of a convent. One of his reasons for choosing Motiers-Travers as a residence, was that there was a Catholic church where Thérèse could attend mass. At Motiers again, when he thought himself dying, he left in his will enough for Thérèse to live upon, and he recommended her to a priest who had been kind to her during her journey to Switzerland. . . . And one could quote twenty such acts.

He dwelt on her better qualities. Like many a superior man, living with a simpleton, he said: "She is not clever, but she has a great deal of common sense and a very sure instinct." Jean-Jacques, as an adorer of nature and of instinct, was especially bound to say this. After having spoken of Thérèse's blunders, he adds:

"But this simple and, if you will, stupid person gave excellent advice in trying circumstances. . . . In the presence of very highborn ladies, of the great, of princes, her feelings, her good sense, her answers, and her behavior won for her universal esteem, and for me, compliments on her qualities, which I felt to be sincere."

It must be owned that he also wrote this passage, book ix.:

"The depth of my attachment will be known when, later on, I disclose the wounds, the gashes she inflicted on my heart at a time when my misery was at its worst. Until this moment I never allowed myself to utter a word of complaint to anyone."

But of these "wounds" and "gashes" he says no more. What is undeniable is that he preserved to the end, until his death, his feelings for Thérèse. The Prince de Ligne went to see him in Paris toward 1770, and had a long conversation with him: "His ugly wife or servant," says he

(Thérèse was then nearly fifty), "would interrupt us by some stupid questions about her linen or her soup—he answered her with a gentleness that would have given dignity to a bit of cheese, if he had spoken of it." And Corancez, one of the founders of the *Journal de Paris*, who had married the daughter of a Genevese, friend to Jean-Jacques, Corancez, who knew Jean-Jacques intimately during his last years, says: "He had confidence in no one but her."

On the other hand, Thérèse, without meaning it, certainly did him harm. First of all, there was her mother, who played at being a lady, and who was most grasping. Rousseau says:

"As soon as she saw that by my efforts we were somewhat more prosperous, she caused all her family to fall upon us and share that prosperity. Sisters, sons, daughters, grand-daughters, they all came, with the exception of her eldest daughter, married to the manager of the Angers coaches. All that I could do for Thérèse was turned over by her mother to the famished band."

And further:

"It is singular that Mme Levasseur's youngest child [Thérèse], the only one who had received no portion, should yet have been the only one who took care of her father and mother; and that, after having for years been beaten by her brothers, her sisters, and even her nieces, the poor creature should now be robbed by them, without being able any more to defend herself from their thefts than from their blows."

We must conclude that Thérèse was a good sort of a fool. Only, driven by her mother, she accepted, without telling Jean-Jacques, presents from his rich friends. Later, at the Hermitage, it seems proved that, jealous of Mme d'Houdetot, she was foolish, gossipy, indiscreet. That is not all, for Jean-Jacques, after having praised Thérèse's good sense, says:

"Often, in Switzerland, in England, in France, in the catastrophes into which I fell, *she saw what I did not see myself;* she withdrew me from dangers toward which I was blindly rushing."

Oh! . . . this no doubt means that one day she said, let us suppose: "Don't you see that Mme d'Epinay treats you like a servant?" or, "Don't you understand that your M. Grimm is jealous of you?" Another day at Motiers: "Don't you see that Montmollin connives with the Geneva people?" Another day, much bored at Wootten: "Do you think that Mr. Hume is really such a great friend of yours?" In one word, that she kept his suspicions alive by stupidity, in order to hold him, to play an important part, or because she did not like the cut of this one's countenance, or that such or such had not treated her with sufficient deference. And, as Jean-Jacques had great need of her, he believed in her.

Yes, all that is possible; but, with all that, I am convinced that Thérèse was really devoted to him. And, if during the first years, when she was under obligations to him, when she saw him become celebrated, when fine ladies amused themselves with her chatter, this was easy enough, later, I think that she had some merit. After his retreat to Switzerland, it seems to me that it was Rousseau who was under obligations to her. After 1755 he treats her but as a sister. She might have left him—Rousseau's friends would not have allowed her to starve, and, besides, she could live by her needle. She remained. She followed him in all his exiles. She joined him in Switzerland, then in England; she went with him to Trye, to Bourgoin, to Monquin; she followed him to Paris, to Ermenonville; she was with him when he died. There was a moment of coolness, after a union of twenty-four years, in 1769. It was at Monquin. Jean-Jacques proposed that she should leave him, and in an admirable letter promised to provide for her. Thérèse refused. Thérèse remained.

On the whole they were almost perfectly suited to each other, more so than many regularly married people, for thirty-three years. Rousseau's death alone liberated Thérèse.

Perhaps it may have been that they were united by a crime, by a crime five times repeated, and such a bond is a solemn one.

Rousseau had three children by Thérèse from 1746 to 1750; he had two others between 1750 and 1755. He put all five in the foundling hospital.

Who told us this? Rousseau himself, and Rousseau alone.

Those who spoke or wrote of this during the eighteenth century only knew it through Rousseau. No authority but what is founded, directly or indirectly on the confidences made by Jean-Jacques. (None save an anonymous testimony in the *Journal Encyclopédique*, in 1791. The anonymous writer says that he had been Rousseau's neighbor in the rue de Grenelle Saint-Honoré—therefore between 1749 and 1756,—and that he had heard his barber say that M. Rousseau sent his children to the foundling hospital, and that all the neighbors knew it. This anonymous testimony, thirty-five or forty years after the event, and nine years after the publication of the "Confessions," is of no great weight.)

What am I trying to prove? This:

One feels that at heart, and in spite of all, Jean-Jacques was, on the whole, better than most of his brother-writers of the day. There are in Voltaire's life dark deeds, odious lies, much obsequiousness, and even dishonest acts. And there are shameful secrets in the lives of many others. But, then, five children thrown among foundlings, that is monstrous, however one may look at it; it seems worse —by the very fact that it so strikes the imagination—than the desertion of a seduced girl, about to become a mother. In one word it appears as a crime against nature—against that nature of which Jean-Jacques was the apostle. And, then, Rousseau's friends would greatly like it not to be true.

Formerly, I myself reasoned thus:

No other proof exists than the avowals of Rousseau,

avowals made without necessity, "so that my friends," says he, "should not think me better than I am. I told it to all who knew of my situation, I told it to Diderot, to Grimm, I told it later to Mme d'Epinay, and later still to Mme de Luxembourg, without the slightest necessity, and whereas I might easily have hidden it from everybody." That is a little strange, for, that he should have acknowledged it "without necessity and being able to hide it," means that, from 1747 to 1755, none of his friends, none of the fine ladies who amused themselves with visiting Thérèse, noticed any signs of her position, and that five times over. And, if we believe Rousseau, he tells the story precisely because, had he held his peace, no one would have guessed the truth.

(Thérèse, he informs us, told Mme Dupin, and that might create a difficulty; but we may believe that Thérèse acted as he bade her, and that consequently the confession of Thérèse is no more a proof than that of Jean-Jacques.)

In 1761 Mme de Luxembourg undertook to discover Jean-Jacques's children. She asked him for the dates and the marks of identification. He wrote to her on the subject:

"These five children were deposited at the foundling hospital with so little precaution for future recognition that I have not even noted the dates of the births."

Is that possible? And could Thérèse also have forgotten? . . . He, however, remembered that the first child was born "during the winter of 1746-47, or thereabouts." This one had a mark in his swaddling clothes. (He says in his "Confessions" that "this mark was a figure made over twice on two cards, one of which was placed in the child's swaddling clothes.") For the other children, there was no mark.

Laroche, confidential servant of the Maréchale, made efforts to find the eldest, the one who had a mark, and who, in 1761, if living, would have been fourteen years of age. The efforts were fruitless.

Then, Rousseau wrote to the Maréchale: "The success of your search could no longer give me a satisfaction pure and free from anxiety." (And that was true: Where, in what a state, could he find, if he found him, this boy of fourteen? and could one be absolutely sure that it was he? etc.) "It is too late. Rest content with your first efforts; I beg you not to renew them."

Rousseau, in this part of his "Confessions," written in 1769, names the midwife Gouin. Did he mention her to Mme de Luxembourg in 1761? Or had this midwife died? At any rate, Rousseau knew very well that she would not be living when the "Confessions" were to be given to the public. But all that does not prove that the five children were an invention of Rousseau. And it seems that he would have acted in the same way to Mme de Luxembourg, if the whole thing had been an invention.

And, thereupon, one might venture a hypothesis.

Afflicted with the infirmities you wot of, on that account timid with women, adoring them all—from afar;

with no other tie but that with Thérèse; reserved in a very corrupt world; guessing what his conduct might suggest to malicious people, reading it, perhaps, in the eyes of his friends, men and women—could it not be that one of his worst fears, the one that haunted him, was to pass for impotent? Hence, that answer which might be called triumphant: the fable of the five children, and,—since he could not have shown them, because, on the other hand, the horror of such a confession implied its veracity,—the story of the quintuple recourse to the foundling hospital. Perhaps Rousseau, full of imagination and "simulator," as he was, preferred passing for abominable than for the victim of a mortifying calamity.

The hypothesis is a slight one, I know. There is another. According to Mrs. Macdonald, Thérèse five times made Rousseau believe that she was pregnant; that she had given birth to a child at a midwife's, and that the infant had been deposited at the foundling hospital. Mrs. Macdonald's chief argument is that Rousseau acknowledges never having seen one of the five children. This plot is supposed to have been formed by Grimm and Mme Levasseur. Why? So as to prevent Rousseau from leaving Thérèse.

Such a hypothesis presents strange difficulties, material and moral. Besides, if it suppresses the fact of the birth and the desertion of the children, it does not suppress the consent of Rousseau to the desertion of children of whom he thought himself the father. Therefore it does not exonerate him.

Here comes in another explanation, which is that of Victor Cherbuliez. Yes, Thérèse brought five children into the world, and they were put among the foundlings. But Rousseau was not the father of those children. And, under those circumstances, his conduct was evidently less abominable.

I do not absolutely reject this solution, but, yet, it suffers many objections. According to Tronchin, Rousseau was quite capable of having children. On the other hand, if he had suspected Thérèse, would he have spoken of her "spotless fidelity"?

After reflection my hypothesis (which, besides, is not mine only) satisfies me more fully. But I went to the foundling hospital. In the books for the year 1746 I found a paper[1] bearing these words: "2795—*Marie-Françoise Rousaux*" (this last word is crossed out and over it the name "Rousseau" is correctly written. "A boy November 19th, 1746." Then, in another writing, and with different ink: "*Joseph Cath^{ne} was baptized November 20th* 1746. *Daguerre, priest.*" This paper is pinned to the printed page. And in the register, where are inscribed the entries for the year 1746, I read this: "*Joseph Catherine Rousseau, given to Anne Chevalier, wife of André Petitpas, at Guitry* (*Andelys*), 1*st month,* 6 *francs, paid December* 22*nd,* 46; *January* 21*st*, 1747, 5 *francs.* 2*nd* (*month*) *until January* 14*th*, 1747, *day of the death, one month and* 23 *days.*"

1 This discovery is due to Mrs. Macdonald. I am not aware what her conclusions on the subject may have been.

This is impressing. The mark for recognition has disappeared. But the date accords with Rousseau's indication. "Marie-Françoise," name of the consigner, is also that of mother Levasseur. On the other hand, why should there be the name of Joseph, and, especially, why should the feminine name of Catherine be given to a boy? I do not know. And one should notice also that the name of Rousseau was, and is, very common. Still, the date, the family name, the Christian name of the consigner, form three very curious coincidences.

But, then, if Mme de Luxembourg's confidential servant saw that paper and that register, why did he declare that he had found nothing? Must we see here a charitable lie on Mme de Luxembourg's part, so as not to tell Rousseau of the child's death?

As to the other children, if there remains no trace of them in the registers, it is, perhaps, because the consigner or the administration gave them, as often happened, a false family name. I know nothing about it, you know nothing about, we know nothing about it.

So I perceive that we must admit the story, about which, moreover, none of Rousseau's great admirers during the eighteenth century, except Sébastien Mercier, ever entertained any doubts.[1] Let us now see his own account, and what explanations and excuses he gives us

[1] In a "Collection of melodies, songs, and duets" by Jean-Jacques Rousseau, published by subscription in 1871, we read after the list of subscribers: "The editor thought it due to his delicacy to present this list, to make public the amount of the sum collected, *which he destines to the Foundling-Hospital.*"

successively in his "Confessions," in his letters, and in his "Rêveries." (For he often comes back to the story, and that may equally show a preoccupation to uphold the imposture; or the trouble of a soul, little by little, filled with remorse.)

The first time he mentioned it in his "Confessions" (a little more than twenty years after the event), it was lightly and almost flippantly. He excused himself on the score of his evil frequentations at the *table d'hôte* of Mme La Selle:

"I heard there many amusing anecdotes, and I took to the maxims in vogue, though never, thank Heaven, to the loose morals. Honest girls seduced, husbands deceived, clandestine births; *and he who lavishly peopled the foundling hospital was always the most applauded.* This worked upon me, and I formed my principles on those common to very amiable people, who were with it all honest folk, and I said to myself: 'Since it is the custom of the country in which one lives, one can follow it.' That was the expedient I needed. I adopted it *frankly and without the slightest scruple;* the only objection came from Thérèse, and I had extreme difficulty in forcing upon her this means which alone could save her honor (!). Her mother, *who feared the burden of more brats,* came to my help, and Thérèse yielded."

She was taken to a prudent and sure midwife, called Gouin, where she was delivered. The following year

(1748) repetition of the same trouble and the same expedient, with the exception of the mark, which was neglected. (Therefore even greater indifference.) "No more reflection on my part;[1] no more spontaneous acquiescence on the part of the mother; she obeyed weeping."

In 1760, third child, third consignment (with no mark, therefore with no intention of claiming it in better days). This time he gives as his reason that in trusting his children to a public training, as he was not able to bring them up himself, in destining them to become workmen or peasants, rather than adventurers or seekers after fortune, "he considered that he had done his duty as citizen and father, and looked upon himself as a member of Plato's republic."

In his letter to Mme de Francueil, April 21, 1751,

[1] See in what measure this may excuse Rousseau.—A reader of the *Temps* sends me these observations: ". . . In the most honest and cultivated families the relations between parents and children were less close (during the eighteenth century) than they now are; if the feelings which constitute family life had as much and even more power than ours, they were more simple, less complex and mixed with roughness. . . . It does not seem that public opinion was then moved by what would revolt our conscience. This is proved by the fact that a man of Rousseau's genius, after his avowals, would not, to-day, find a friend willing to take his hand. . . . Whereas all the drawing-rooms were open to the author of the 'Devin' and of the 'Discours.'" But only a few of his friends knew of his fault, and only knew of it *through himself*.) ". . . It is neither just nor human to judge him in the name of a *morality foreign to him*." (Then, what becomes of his mission as moralist? And why did he feel such remorse? And did not the reader of the *Temps* say himself that "the feelings which constitute family life had then as much and even more power than in our days?" After all, judge for yourselves.)

these are his alleged reasons: First, his poverty; second, he shrank from dishonoring Thérèse (which is rather farcical); third, that he could only have provided for his children by becoming dishonest; fourth, that life was not unpleasant at the foundling hospital. These children pass from the hands of the midwife to those of a nurse. Rousseau knows that these children will not be reared delicately—so much the better for them! They will be all the stronger. They will not be gentlemen, but peasants or workmen. They will be happier than their father.

As he writes, he forestalls this objection: "When one cannot care for children, one should not have any. I beg your pardon, madame, nature requires that children should be brought into the world, since the earth produces enough to feed all; but it is the rich, it is your caste, that robs mine of its children's bread." (This was written after the "Discours sur les sciences et les arts.")

Finally, fifth reason, already given: he believed that he was acting like a citizen of Plato's republic.

(He might have added yet this excuse—which I owe to M. Lanson—that in his vagrant life he had unscrupulously made use of charitable institutions.)

Mme de Francueil might have answered that his reasons were not worth a rap. Poverty? Rousseau, when the two elder children were born, was earning nine hundred, then a thousand francs, in the employ of Mme Dupin. He might have earned more, had he not been lazy. The fine ladies, besides, made presents to Thérèse, and would willingly have cared for the children. He says that they would not have been brought up honestly. The reason is a weak one. In December, 1750, he was already celebrated. A little before 1752, probably, he had a lucrative position, that of cashier to the farmer-general, Francueil. And, in 1753, the "Devin du village" brought him in from five to six thousand francs. He might, at least, have brought up the last two children. But no doubt the bent was taken. And then he would not commit any injustice with regard to the three elder ones. Had he not, meanwhile, become the apostle of equality?

As to the happiness reserved to foundlings. . . . That is but a sorry joke.

In the "Neuvième rêverie" (1776, two years before his death) he gives another explanation:

"Their mother would have spoiled them; her family would have made monsters of them. . . . I shudder to think of it; what Mahomet made of Seide would have been a trifle in comparison to what they would have made of them with regard to me."

Finally, let us remember this passage of book ix. of the "Confessions":

"I had no family; Thérèse had one, and that family, whose instincts so differed from hers, was not such that I could make it mine. This was the first cause of my misfortune. How I should have loved to have been the son of her mother! I did my very best, and did not succeed.

In vain I tried to unite our interests: it was impossible. She always had her own, different from mine, alien to mine, and even to those of her daughter, who was already too contrary to mine. She and her other children and her grandchildren became so many leeches, and *the smallest part of the harm they did to Thérèse was to rob her.* The poor girl, *accustomed to yield, even to her nieces,* allowed herself to be fleeced and *governed* without protesting; and I saw with sorrow that emptying my purse and giving her advice did nothing toward helping her. I endeavored to detach her from her mother; she always resisted. I respected her resistance and esteemed her all the more for it; but her refusal turned against her as well as against me. Submissive to her mother and to her kin, she belonged to them more than to me, more than to herself. Their avidity, *however ruinous, was less pernicious than their influence.* In a word, if, thanks to her happy nature, she was not entirely subjugated, she was enough so at least to *prevent,* to a great extent, *the effect of all the maxims I tried to inculcate.* . . . . Then came the children; and *all went from bad to worse.* I shuddered at the thought of trusting them to such a family to be brought up in evil. The risks of an education of foundlings were less dangerous. This reason for my resolution, stronger than all those I dwelt upon in my letter to Mme de Francueil, was, however, the only one I did not dare to give her. I *preferre*d to be less disculpated for so grave a fault, rather than to accuse the family of one I loved."

Whereupon Emile Faguet, who examined the question in the *Journal des Débats* of June 18, 1906, concludes thus:

"Either I greatly mistake, or, for those who can read, this means: Absolutely in the power of a family of bandits, which she always loved more than she did me, Thérèse deprived herself for them, robbed and filched from me for them. You understand full well that this family did not wish Thérèse to bring up children, who would have had their share of the cake, and who might, on the other hand, have detached Thérèse from her kin, thanks to her maternal love. Thérèse's family decreed that Thérèse should not have her children with her. Submissive to them, fearing, perhaps, that the children might some day be murdered by them, Thérèse ordered me to desert them. Partly from love for her, partly so as not to acknowledge that I obeyed her as she obeyed her family, I never would say that it was she who required this sacrifice."

This would prove that Rousseau abandoned five children out of fear of Thérèse, and, especially, of mother Levasseur; in one word, out of weakness, passivity, infirmity of will. This may be true.

He felt the pangs of remorse, at least after 1769. At Moultou (February 14, 1769), he writes:

"It was against her will that she [Thérèse], it was against our will, that she and I *were unable to fulfil a great duty;* but she accomplished many others, worthy of praise."

And he adds this sentence, which I confess I do not exactly understand:

"How many things that ought to be divulged are destined to be buried with me! And what advantages will accrue to my enemies from the *impossibility of speaking to which they have reduced me!*" (?)

And in his admirable letter to Thérèse, when he proposes to leave her: "*There are faults common to us, which we must deplore with tears and expiate.*" Words such as these, in an intimate letter, are to me a better proof of the desertion than the narrative of the "Confessions." And in the letter to Mme de Chenonceaux (January 17, 1770):

"None shall ever see me falsify the holy laws of nature and duty in order to palliate my faults. I prefer expiation to excuses."

(It is true that, later, he returns to his lame excuses.)

Finally, in his letter to M. de Saint-Germain (February 26, 1770), and which is a sort of general confession:

"Bad examples, necessity, the honor of one I loved, caused me to confide my children to an establishment intended for such cases, and prevented me from accomplishing myself the first, the holiest of nature's duties. And, far from seeking excuses, I accuse myself. . . . I did not hide my conduct from my friends, as I did not wish to appear in their eyes better than I was. What advantage these barbarous beings drew from it! With what art they placed it [my conduct] in the worst possible light! . . . As though sin were not the heritage of man, even of the just! My fault was a heavy one, it is true, it was unpardonable, but it was my only one, and I have cruelly suffered for it."

We, perhaps, do not find here "perfect contrition," but still, there is emotion and repentance, as also in the audacious allusions which he makes publicly of his children's desertion, in book i. of "Emile." If the story of the five children deserted is a "simulation," we are bound to confess that Jean-Jacques sustained it with stupefying and miraculous likelihood.

Alas, I well see that we must believe him! . . . And then, however indulgent one may wish to be, it seems, nevertheless, both offensive and comic, after a sinister fashion, that it should have been between two desertions of newborn babes, a little after his return from the austere château of Chenonceaux, where he had composed the light comedy of the "Engagement téméraire" and the light verses on the "Allée de Sylvie" for the pleasure of great ladies; . . . that it should have been in the room of the rue Plâtrière, where he dictated his paragraphs to mother Levasseur who, every morning, lit his fire; that it should have been under these conditions that he wrote his virtuous "Discours,"—oh, how virtuous!—on the corruption of morals by science and art.

DISCOURS SUR LES SCIENCES ET LES ARTS
THE MORAL REFORM OF ROUSSEAU

CHAPTER III

DISCOURS SUR LES SCIENCES ET LES ARTS[1]—THE MORAL REFORM OF ROUSSEAU

I HAVE exhausted, so far as possible, the question of Thérèse and that of the five deserted children.

I have exposed the different explanations given by Rousseau, and those that he did not give; but there is another one which I forgot, and which could be applied to many of his acts.

We possess a long letter, written October 21, 1803, by Joubert to Molé, with regard to Chateaubriand, and which is a marvel of analysis, one might say of psychological anatomy.

Toward the end of the letter, we read:

"There is in the depths of that heart [Chateaubriand's] a kind of goodness and purity which will never permit the poor fellow—I fear—to recognize and to condemn his own foolish actions, because, to the consciousness of his conduct which calls for reflection, he will instinctively oppose the sentiment of its essence, which is excellent."

To my mind, this applies, and most admirably, to Rousseau. And here is a passage of the "Confessions," which

1 "Discourse on science and art."

seems to have been written purposely to illustrate Joubert's remark on Chateaubriand.

It was during Rousseau's journey to Geneva in 1754. He saw Mme de Warens, fallen as low as possible:

"Oh," writes he, "that was the moment for me to have paid my debt. I should have left everything, have clung to her to her last hour, and have shared her fate, whatever it might be. *I did nothing of the kind.* Another attachment absorbed me. I felt mine for her slacken, for lack of any hope of being useful to her. I bewailed her lot and did not follow her. No remorse, during my whole life, proved deeper or more lasting."

(Here, decidedly, he exaggerates, for certainly the remorse about his deserted children was, must have been, or ought to have been, deeper; but he spent his life exaggerating.)

"I deserved thereby," adds he, "the terrible calamities which, since then, have never ceased weighing on me; may they prove to be the expiation of my ingratitude! This ingratitude was in my acts, but my heart was so torn by it that never could that heart be deemed that of an ingrate."

Let us translate: "I may have acted like an ungrateful man, but such I cannot be, since my feelings are good." Or again: "I abandoned my children, but I could not be a bad father, because I am a tender-hearted man."

This is comic stage psychology; it is entirely the logic of Jobelin in "Le plus heureux des trois"[1]: "We have deceived you, Marjavel! . . . *I have no remorse because I repent.*" Thus, Jean-Jacques, convinced of his own goodness, judges himself according to his sentiments, not according to his actions. And this is extremely convenient. Briefly, this is a profane misinterpretation of the pure love doctrine of Molinos and Mme Guyon, a doctrine according to which actions are of no consequence provided that one loves God. So true is it that laic errors all correspond with some form of heresy.

This we must remember when, in "Emile," we meet with the doctrine of sentimental morality and the appeal to conscience.

Meanwhile, let us take up Jean-Jacques where we left him.

He began his life with Thérèse: a simple life, that of the lower classes, which he describes after a most savory fashion.

"If our pleasures could be described, they would provoke a smile by their simplicity; our walks together in the environs of the city, where I prodigally spent eight or ten *sous* at a wayside inn; our little suppers in the embrasure of my window, seated opposite each other on two small chairs perched on a trunk, which just fitted into the space. In that position, the sill was our table, we breathed fresh air, we could see all around us the passers-by, and, though we were on the fourth floor, we could

[1] Comedy by Eugène Labiche.

look down into the street while we ate. Who could describe, who could feel the charm of those meals, consisting only of a big loaf, some cherries and a little cheese, with half a bottle of wine which we shared. Affection, confidence, intimacy, soul effusions, what delicious seasonings! Sometimes we remained there till midnight, having no idea of the time, until the old mother came to warn us."

(Ah! what business had the old woman to interrupt them? . . . But certainly, this simplicity, most sincere with Jean-Jacques, is one of his great charms, which nothing can take from him.)

However, in the midst of many discouragements and many fits of idleness, he sought to make his way, either in the musical world, or in that of letters, most of all in that of the stage: and this was his chief preoccupation between the years 1741 and 1749.

Later on, he will say and repeat that his was a unique case, that he never thought of glory, that he did not take up his pen until he was nearly forty—and to his sorrow. This is not true. At an early age he possessed the gift and the passion of music, and dreamed of being a composer. At an early age also, and in spite of erratic and incomplete studies, he scribbled verse and prose, and he dreamed of being a poet and, above all, a dramatic writer.

When he reached Paris, he brought with him not only "Narcisse," a little comedy in prose after the style of Marivaux, written at twenty, but poems, elegies, love verses and a tragedy on the discovery of the New World. And from 1741 to 1749 he wrote epistles in verse, the "Dissertation sur la musique moderne,"[1] the "Projet concernant de nouveaux signes pour la musique,"[2] a little comedy entitled "Prisonniers de guerre,"[3] the opera of the "Muses galantes,"[4] the "Persifleur,"[5] first and only number of a periodical publication, "l'Allée de Sylvie,"[6] "l'Engagement téméraire,"[7] comedy in three acts, in verse; and others.

In 1745 he had some communication with Voltaire, and retouched for him the "Princesse de Navarre," which reappeared at Versailles under the title of "Fêtes de Ramire." In 1747 his father died; he inherited from him a small sum of money, which he shared with Mme de Warens. The same year he presented, unsuccessfully, his comedy of "Narcisse" at the Italiens.[8]

His dinners with Thérèse, on the trunk, in the embrasure of the window, did not prevent him from frequenting fashionable drawing-rooms. He became, as I said, secretary to Mme Dupin. Francueil presented him to Mme d'Epinay. He became acquainted with Mme d'Houdetot, on the very eve of her marriage. He supped with Mlle Quinault.

1 "Dissertation on modern music."
2 "A scheme concerning a new musical notation."
3 "Prisoners of war."
4 "The gallant Muses."
5 "The quizzer."
6 "Sylvia's alley."
7 "The rash engagement."
8 One of the principal theaters of the day.

And doubtless he often saw Grimm, Diderot, Condillac, dined with them every week at the *Panier fleuri* (a restaurant of the Palais-Royal), knew d'Alembert and the Abbé de Raynal, and was considered as belonging to the party of the "philosophers"; and, doubtless, Diderot had some influence on him, and, doubtless, Jean-Jacques' religion, until then half Protestant, half Catholic, turned to pure deism—a very sincere deism, it is true, very pious, very tender; but still one finds not a vestige either of social revolt, nor even of paradox, in the little verses of the "Allée de Sylvie," nor in the rather meager verses of the "Engagement téméraire," written during an autumn spent in very brilliant society at Chenonceaux, and acted in 1749, at Mme d'Epinay's country place, the Chevrette. The future citizen of Geneva even took part in it. The subject is still in the taste of Marivaux. The "engagement" in question is that of a lover who is bound for a whole day to show no sign of love for his mistress, who, at that price, consents to marry him. And as to the "Allée de Sylvie," it resembles somewhat, in tone and force, with less ease, the "Chartreuse" of Gresset.

In short, Rousseau was a man of rather singular manners, it is true, but one who composed amorous music and little comedies of a gallant turn,—his music was not wanting in originality; his comedies resembled those of many other writers and were even a little worse—a man who seemed to think of nothing but the Opera, or the "Italiens," or the "Comédie Française." And this up to 1749.

But in the month of October, 1749, this is what happened:

A few months earlier Diderot had published his "Lettre sur les aveugles à l'usage de ceux qui voient."[1] It was written after an operation for cataract performed by Réaumur on a patient born blind. Réaumur, in spite of solicitations, had invited but very few on the day when he removed the first bandages. Hence on the first page of the "Lettre," this witticism of Diderot's: "M. de Réaumur consented to lift the veil only before some unimportant eyes." Among those unimportant eyes Mme du Pré de Saint Maur recognized her own. This lady was a friend of Réaumur and also of the Comte d'Argenson. She was wounded to the quick.

It must also be said that certain ideas contained in the "Lettre sur les aveugles," might pass for bold.. Briefly, there were perquisitions made in Diderot's dwelling under the pretext of searching for the manuscript of a tale, "l'Oiseau bleu,"[2] which was supposed to contain allusions to Mme de Pompadour. In reality, the object was to put an embargo on material collected for the "Encyclopédie." Diderot was arrested, July 29, and taken to Vincennes. A month later the castle with its gardens was given to him as prison, and he was allowed to see his friends. Here he remained until the 3d of November.

And now let us listen to Rousseau, then to Marmontel, then to Diderot.

1 "Letters on the blind for the use of those who see."
2 "The bluebird."

And do not complain that I quote too freely, for it is important to know under what circumstances, how and why, and how easily he might not have written, or written otherwise, this first work, this "Discours sur les sciences et les arts,"[1] the work which began his glorious reputation, and which influenced the spirit of all his other books.

". . . Every other day, in spite of very absorbing occupations, I used to go, alone, or with his wife, to spend the afternoon [at Vincennes] with him [Diderot]. The heat that summer [1749] was excessive."

(The question suggested by the *Mercure* was dated October, and October is not a summer month; but that is of small importance. Rousseau wrote of the event twenty years afterwards.)

"Vincennes is two leagues from Paris. As I could not afford a carriage, I walked, at two o'clock in the afternoon, and when I was alone I walked fast so as to reach my destination earlier. The trees of the road, always clipped, according to the fashion of the country, gave but very little shade; and, often, worn out, overcome by the heat and fatigue, I would throw myself down. In order to moderate my step, I decided to carry a book with me. Once, I took up the *Mercure de France*, and glanced over it as I walked. I chanced upon this question proposed by the Academy of Dijon for the prize of the

[1] "Discourse on science and art."

following year: *Si le progrès*[1] *des sciences et des arts a contribué à corrompre ou à épurer les mœurs.*[2]

"At the very instant when I read those words, I saw a new universe and I became a new man . . . When I reached Vincennes my agitation had become almost delirious. This, Diderot noticed. I explained the reason of it, and read him my prosopopœia of Fabricius which I had written in pencil, in the shade of an oak. He exhorted me to give vent to my ideas and to compete for the prize. I did so, and, from that moment, I was lost."

This, he wrote in 1769. In 1762 he had already related the fact in his second letter to M. de Malesherbes, with even greater heat: ". . . If ever anything resembled sudden inspiration, it was the emotion caused by this reading . . ." And he speaks of palpitations, of vertigo, of dizziness like that of intoxication, and, according to him, he threw himself at the foot of a tree in the avenue and spent there half an hour in such a state of agitation that, on getting up, he noticed that his waistcoat was wet with the tears he had unwittingly shed.

All that for the prosopopœia of Fabricius!

Such is Rousseau's narrative. But there is that of Marmontel in his "Mémoires" (book xii.).

1 "Whether the progress of science and art has contributed to corrupt or to purify morals."

2 The real text says: *Si le rétablissement . . .* (*Whether the re-establishment . . .*).

"Here is the fact in all its simplicity, as Diderot told it to me and as I told it to Voltaire.

"I was [it is Diderot who speaks] prisoner at Vincennes. Rousseau visited me. He had made of me his Aristarchus, as he himself said. One day as we were sauntering together he told me that the Academy of Dijon had just proposed an interesting question and that he thought of treating it. The question was: *Le rétablissement des sciences et des arts a-t-il contribué à épurer les mœurs?* 'Which side will you take?' I asked. He answered: 'The affirmative.' 'A truce to such trivialities!' said I; 'all the mediocre spirits will take that side, and you could find nothing but commonplaces; but the other theme presents a new, rich and fertile field to philosophy and eloquence.' 'You are right,' said he, after having thought a moment, 'and I shall follow your advice.' . . . Thus, from that moment," adds Marmontel, "he chose the rôle he was to play and the mask he was to wear."

One must remember, it is true, that Marmontel was informed by one of Rousseau's enemies, who was speaking to another of his enemies.

Then, in the "Essai sur les règnes de Claude et de Néron,"[1] chap. 67, in the course of a most violent diatribe against Jean-Jacques, Diderot merely says:

"When the program of the Dijon Academy appeared, he came *to consult me* about the view he should adopt.

[1] "Essay on the reigns of Claudius and Nero."

'The part you will take,' said I, 'is that which others would reject.' 'You are right,' answered he."

These are the three versions. That of Rousseau is very extravagant in its tone, and doubtless, in his memory, the incident became amplified and embellished. He thought fit that his first book should have been conceived tragically and tumultuously. Of the other two versions, one is that of a malevolent person (and at second hand), the other that of an enemy who, I believe, was sincere. I take neither part. I notice only that the version of Jean-Jacques does not radically differ from that of Diderot. Jean-Jacques himself says: "*Diderot exhorted me to give vent to my ideas and to try for the prize.*" This seems to indicate that Rousseau hesitated. It would be strange, indeed, if the decision on which depended the rest of his work, and of his life, had been the result of mere chance and of a friend's advice. Had he chosen the other side, and proved that science and art were beneficial to morals, or had he chosen a half-way theme (and why not? the author of "Narcisse" and the "Muses galantes," could not, at that time, have been a very violent adversary of art), he would still have obtained the prize, thanks to his admirable style, but his life would probably have been shunted on another track.

And what if he had not read the fatal number of the *Mercure de France?*

I well know how futile are these deductions and hypotheses. But here, a man of genius is at the bar, a man whose influence has been prodigious, a man of vacillating will, and a man of whom it can justly be said, that his works reflected his private life and the incidents of that life, and are, nearly exclusively, "works sprung from circumstances." And the importance of the consequences cause us real emotion when we see them spring from such insignificant causes, causes almost fortuitous, and when we see how all these things hang together and how fatal or providential they really are.

At any rate, this essay of fifty pages, the first conception of which moved the author so as to give him palpitations, and to cause the front of his waistcoat to be wet with his tears, now seems rather insignificant: a school rhapsody, of which I shall give a synopsis.

It consists of two parts.

The first part contains a series of affirmations. "Our souls are corrupted in proportion as science and art approach perfection." This is proved by history (history as it was then taught in the schools. For example, Egypt, Greece, Rome, the Eastern Empire, China itself.)

And here is the counter proof. "Let us oppose to these pictures that of the manners and customs of a small number of nations who, preserved from the contagion of vain knowledge, have by their virtues secured their own happiness and served as models to others." Such were the early Romans. And here comes in the prosopopœia: Oh, Fabricius, what would thy great soul have thought. . . .

"Thus," concludes Rousseau, "luxury, dissipation and slavery have in all times been the punishment of the proud efforts we make to shake off the blessed ignorance in which eternal wisdom placed us."

The second part is an attempt to prove the evil of science and art.

The origin of science is foul. "Astrology was born of superstition (how, he does not say); eloquence was born of ambition, of hatred, of flattery, of lies; geometry sprang from avarice (an allusion to a passage in Herodotus); physical science, from vain curiosity; all, and even morality itself, from human pride." (Thus speaks this modest man.) In a word, "science and art are born of our vices."

But then our vices cannot spring from science and art! Yes; for, in their turn, science and art produce loss of time, because of their uselessness, because of enervating luxury. (Nations deprived of luxury are strong; thus Persia, in the days of Cyrus, the Scyths, ancient Rome, the Franks, the Saxons, the Swiss against Charles the Bold, the Dutch against Philip II.) Science and art engender corruption of taste from the desire to please (here come in some true remarks), the diminution of military virtues, finally the frivolous and dangerous education given to children (here again some judicious remarks).

Philosophers are charlatans. The invention of printing was a great misfortune.

He ends with a contradiction. For he exalts Bacon, Descartes, Newton. He distinguishes between real and false scholars or philosophers, and wishes the former to direct the state: but how are they to be recognized? who will point them out? And then, is science not after all necessarily and universally fatal?

This first discourse is therefore a piece of mere declamation, a rhetorical exercise, where a great lack of logic and some foolishness are discernible. Precision is wanting. Rousseau seems to suppose that the "revival of science and art" (by the diffusion in Italy of the relics of ancient Greece after the taking of Constantinople) was a sudden outburst, which had instantaneously tainted the world's morality, and he does not even ask himself about the previous state of that morality. He does not distinguish between the various sciences and arts, whose corrupt influence could scarcely be identical. He does not consider that the corruption due to science and art could only attack a very few, all the more that by "corruption" he means especially conventionality, worldly prejudices and lies, luxury, effeminacy, the frivolities and artifices of life in drawing-rooms, in a word, the vices and foibles of that very limited world where he himself moved. He does not take into consideration that eighteen millions of peasants and workmen in France were almost totally preserved from such corruption, and that the lower middle classes were but slightly touched by it; that, moreover, good and evil are so inextricably intermingled in the efforts attributable to art and science, that it seems impossible to disentangle them or to prove in any case that the evil is the more powerful. In brief: Rousseau's thesis was a tissue of vague commonplaces, somewhat threadbare even at that time, almost as much so as the opposite theory.

This hobby of Rousseau's (the state of nature's innocence as contrasted with the vices of civilization) was already to be found almost everywhere (for example, in the "Lettres Persanes,"[1] second part of the "Histoire des troglodytes," or in Marivaux's "l'Ile des esclaves,"[2] "l'Ile de la raison,"[3] and was not worthy of much consideration.

(To-day, when there are several thousand of us, writers, of whom two or three hundred are celebrated, it is evident that a work like this first discourse of Jean-Jacques would pass completely unnoticed. The question, besides, which Jean-Jacques here so easily solves, resembles nothing more than those trite questions, useless and impossible to elucidate, that reporters propose to authors, simply because they give rise to endless small-talk.

But, if the commonplace theme is dull, it might have been made more attractive by precise and convincing pictures, for which he had plenty of material; for perhaps high society had never yet been so preverted, if not by "science and art," at least by the over-refinement of the mind, and culture devoted exclusively to accomplishments.

What Rousseau failed to do, Duclos did, exactly at the same time, with great sagacity and some vigor, in his "Considérations sur les mœurs"[4] (1751). First of all,

[1] "Persian letters" by Montesquieu.

[2] "The island of slaves."

[3] "The island of reason."

[4] "Considerations on customs and manners."

Duclos draws a distinction between Paris and the provinces, and even in Paris, he studies only certain centers. And Duclos seizes and defines excellently the *characteristic* vices or faults of this small society: not so much even the looseness of morals (from which I do not suppose that Rousseau considered himself free), but vanity, frivolity, the exaggeration of wit, flippancy and chaff (what we should to-day call "blague,") the dryness and hardness of heart (what Gresset in 1745 represented in the "Méchant,")[1] and all that mixed up with "philosophical" pretence. Nothing or next to nothing of this is seen in Rousseau's "Discours"; he was no observer.

Whence comes then that the effect produced by the "Discours sur les sciences et les arts" should have been such that Garat in his "Mémoire sur M. Suard" could write:

"It was at that very moment that a voice, no longer young and yet quite unknown, arose, not from the depths of deserts or forests, but from the very heart of that society, of those academies, of that philosophy where so much light gave birth and nourished so many hopes. . . . And, in the name of truth, it brings forth an accusation before the whole of humanity, against letters, arts, sciences and society itself . . . And it was not, as has been said, scandal that arose, but admiration and a *sort of terror* that were almost universal."

How can this be explained (if we suppose that Garat did not exaggerate)?

1 "The wicked man."

Because of the accent and style which distinguished this first work of Rousseau's.

There was the accent of the man of letters who had not succeeded, of the invalid who was only at ease in solitude, of the timid man who had often suffered in fine company; the accent of the former vagrant, of the revolted plebeian; in a word, of a man who takes to heart a commonplace, till then deemed inoffensive. Besides, one can say of nearly all that he wrote,—and this is wherein his books appealed to human stupidity,—that, for the first time, a man of genius treated seriously antiquated fancies or jokes.

On the other hand, this commonplace production, all vibrating with this accent, was destined to be read, first of all, by that little minority of privileged people for whom Rousseau's theme was partially true; and besides, he attacked, from the first, a few of that select society's pet idols: philosophy, science, which were all the fashion, and faith in progress. This grave and vehement sermonizing was sure to move and fascinate people who no longer went to hear preaching. Hence the scandal and the kind of terror of which Garat speaks. To a certain extent, such was, in Parisian drawing-rooms, the success of Tolstoï's first evangelical writings.

And then, there was the style. We do not find in it all the qualities which the style of Jean-Jacques was to possess later on, but, in its intensity, it is beautiful; it shows an oratorical swing and the phrase is strongly rhythmical; with its air of novelty, it was opposed to the quick, subtle sentences then in vogue. I must add that we already find there apostrophes, the abuse of certain words such as virtue and nature, the emphasis and the false republican frankness, which so unfortunately characterized, forty years later, the Jacobin and *sans-culottes* eloquence. Jean-Jacques furnished the Revolution with its vocabulary.

How, in the brain of this flat versifier of the "Engagement téméraire," did this prose, so full, so logical, so robust, so grave, form itself?

Let us review, if you will, the story of this self-educated man's readings (I speak only of his French readings).

At six years of age he read, with his father, the "Astrée"[1] and La Calprenède's[2] novels. At seven, Ovid and Fontenelle,[3] but also Plutarch, La Bruyère, Molière and the "Discours sur l'histoire universelle."[4] From twelve to sixteen, a whole circulating library, haphazard. Later, and especially at the Charmettes, while he was learning Latin, he read Le Sage, Abbé Provost, the "Lettres philosophiques" of Voltaire, but also (with Locke and Leibnitz) the works of the Port-Royal writers, Descartes, Malebranche, etc. . . .

With it all, very few contemporary books, but nearly all those of the seventeenth century, devoured in silence, far from Paris. Rousseau, without doubt, owed his literary training to that century, and that is why—and also because he had the gift—when he began to write in prose, he fell naturally into the tone and the

[1] By d'Urfé, toward 1608-1627.

[2] Toward 1640 or 1660.

[3] 1657-1757.

[4] By Bossuet.

very phrases of the seventeenth century writers. I said that his style had an air of novelty: that is the reason of it. He went back further than Marivaux, Fontenelle, Voltaire, even than La Bruyère. He renewed a tradition and it is true that he added something to it because, into a traditional frame he put a new soul.

Therefore, such as it was, Rousseau's discourse, crowned by the Dijon Academy, August 23, 1750, obtained, and from the first, a prodigious success.

Men of great and noble standing published criticisms on it: King Stanislas, with the help of a Jesuit father; Professor Gautier; Bordes, academician of Lyons; Lecat, academician of Rouen; Formey, academician of Berlin; without mentioning Voltaire, d'Alembert, Frederick II., who, as occasion served, gave their opinion of it. Rousseau replied successively to Stanislas, Gautier and Bordes. All these refutations and answers prove but little, either on one side or the other, the question having been proposed too vaguely and being, besides, I think, quite insoluble. But, naturally, in these polemics, Rousseau had the best of it, because he possessed superior talent. He does not notice that the very art of which he wishes to show the pernicious effects, caused him, nevertheless, to be victorious against itself.

And so it happened that Rousseau's answers are better and more interesting than his "Discours." On the one side, forced as he was to meditate more deeply on the subject, to grapple with it, to express its very essence, he cleverly softens, without seeming to do so, what there was rather rough in his first rendering of his easy paradox, thereby making it more acceptable. Thus, in his answer to King Stanislas, after having written:

"What! Should we suppress all these things of which there has been so much abuse? Yes, doubtless, I answer without hesitation, all those that are useless, all whose misuse does more harm than their use can do good."

He adds immediately:

"Let us stop a moment over this last consideration, and let us beware of concluding that we should, to-day, burn all libraries and destroy both universities and academies. All we should gain by it would be to plunge Europe once more into barbarism, and morality would, thereby, gain nothing."

We breathe more freely, we say "Ah! well, well . . ."

On the other hand, while he defends and seeks to force his idea on others, that idea takes hold of him and fructifies. The embryo of his future "Discours sur l'inégalité"[1] is already in his answers to Stanislas and to Bordes. For instance, he writes to Stanislas:

"It is not from science, I am told, but from riches that, in all ages, sprang nobility and luxury. I never said that luxury was the child of science, but that they were born together and that one could not go without the other.

[1] "Discourse on inequality."

This is how I arranged this genealogy. *The first source of all evil is inequality:* from inequality sprang riches . . . from riches, luxury and idleness. From luxury came the fine arts, and from idleness, science."

Another example. The belief in the natural virtue of man is implied, but not formulated, in the "Discours." It is in a note of the "Réponse à Bordes," that Rousseau, for the first time, says: "I believe that man is naturally good."

In the third place, as by degrees he endeavored to define the idea of his first "Discours," the sentiments of which this idea is but the product and expression become deeper and more violent. He takes the offensive, whenever he finds a weak spot. The accent is more full of passion in the answers, and above all in the "Notes," than in the "Discours" itself. Here is a note of his "Réponse à Bordes":

"Luxury feeds a hundred poor in our cities, and kills a hundred thousand in the country. The money that passes from the hands of the rich to those of those artisans who furnish their superfluities, is lost for the subsistence of the laborer, and he has no coat, because others need ribbons. [To tell the truth, I do not see how.] The waste of articles which serve to feed men alone renders luxury odious to humanity. . . . We must have sauces in our kitchens, and that is why so many sick people lack broth. We must have liquors on our tables, and that is why peasants drink water. We must have powder for our wigs, and that is why so many poor have no bread."

Oh! we find that in La Bruyère, and you need not seek long before you find it in Bossuet and in Bourdaloue. But here, it seems to me, is the revolutionary turn of mind and style, what I should call a trumpet blast; there is the terrible sophistical turn: "That is why . . ." That burst of eloquence must have shaken deliciously numbers of dainty women belonging to the nobility and to financial circles.

Finally, this first discourse took possession of its author; by a well-known phenomenon of auto-suggestion, Jean-Jacques modeled himself on his book. He wished to resemble the image which this book gave of him . . . He wished to justify its epigraph:

Barbarus hic ego sum quia non intelligor illis.

He now undertook his moral reform.

One should not forget either his origin or his Protestant antecedents, or his period of Catholic practices and the time when he composed prayers for Mme de Warens. I believe that he never ceased to be concerned with the "inner life." Several times he was taken with an incipient desire of reform, and made attempts and efforts in that direction.

For instance, after his adventure with Mme de Larnage (the only pleasant adventure he ever had), he had promised to pay that lady a visit at Saint-Audiol. When the time came, he hesitated, and tells us why. He had passed himself off to Mme de Larnage as an Englishman, and feared discovery. Then, knowing that Mme de Larnage had a fifteen-year-old daughter, he feared beforehand that he might fall in love with her, seduce her, and "introduce dishonour, dissension, hell itself, into the household." (A singular reason: poor Jean-Jacques was not such a terrible Don Juan as all that!) Finally, he says:

"To all this were added reflections on my situation, on my duty, on the good 'Maman,'[1] so generous, who, already burdened with debts, assumed others on account of my foolish extravagance, and whom I so unworthily deceived. This remorse became so violent as to remain victorious. As I approached Saint-Esprit I determined not to stop at the village of Saint-Audiol, and to pursue my way. I courageously kept to my resolutions, not without many sighs, I confess, but feeling intimate satisfaction in saying: I deserve my own approbation; I have preferred it to my pleasure."

Ah, so much the better! . . . Well, well, poor little Mlle de Larnage had a narrow escape! . . .

And, thereupon, Jean-Jacques fell into deep meditation, swore within himself to "regulate henceforth his conduct according to the laws of virtue . . . and to hearken to no other love than that of duty."

And, in consequence (so true is it that one act of virtue engenders others) when, on his return to Chambéry, he found his place occupied by Wintzenried, the wig-

[1] Mme de Warens.

maker, and that Mme de Warens assured him "that his rights remained the same, even while they were shared," Jean-Jacques, who had accepted the gardener, refused to accept the barber. He threw himself at the feet of Mme de Warens, he "embraced her knees, shedding torrents of tears," and uttered these astounding words: "No, Maman, I love you too deeply to degrade you; your possession is too great a boon to be shared." A fine impulse which Mme de Warens never forgave him.

Oh! Jean-Jacques had had more than one of these noble impulses. But, until then, they had rarely been carried into effect. This time, after the "Discours sur les sciences et les arts," he was really in earnest. He decided to be another man, and for life. This he explains in book viii. of the "Confessions," and more fully in the "Troisième rêverie," where he decidedly idealizes his past and sees himself as he would like to have been. This determination was not merely the result of his own fine sentences in his "Discours," but also of his past religious sentiments which welled up in his heart:

"Born in a family distinguished for morality and piety, brought up later by a minister of the Gospel, full of wisdom and religion, I had, from my tenderest infancy, imbibed principles, maxims, some might say prejudices, which never entirely left me. Still a child, and left to myself . . . forced by necessity, I became a Catholic, but I remained a Christian always [epigram suggested by his Protestant training] and soon, thanks to habit, my *heart grew to be sincerely attached to my new religion.* The instructions, the example of Mme de Warens, consolidated that attachment. The rustic solitude, where I spent the best years of my youth, the study of good books, *made me pious almost after the fashion of Fénelon.*"

And further, to qualify his reform, he makes use of solemn expressions, mostly of a religious character:

"All contributed to detach my affections from the world . . . I left the world and its pomps . . . A great revolution took place in me, another moral world was unveiled before my eyes . . . From this period dates my entire renouncement of the world."

And, from a distance, he believes this.

In reality, his conversion was at first merely exterior. And we shall never know, and no doubt he never knew, what share belonged to his desire to singularize himself and what share belonged to the desire of becoming a better man.

It must be remembered that it was after a "serious illness" (with him, these were innumerable) that he formed this design of conforming his life to his maxims, "paying no heed whatever to the judgments of men," "the noblest design," says he, "or at least, the most useful to virtue that ever mortal conceived."

First of all, he abandoned every sign of politeness, but he is frank enough to give the reason:

"My foolish and sullen timidity, which I could not overcome, arising from my fear of offending decorum, induced me to take the resolution of trampling it under foot; out of shamefacedness, I played the part of a caustic cynic. I affected to despise that politeness of which I was incapable."

And he succeeded pretty well, but not entirely. Mme d'Epinay says of him in her "Mémoires": "He is a flatterer without being polite." A bastard combination; the reverse would have been more worthy of a sage.

He reforms his costume:

"I abandoned," says he, "all gold trimmings and white stockings; I wore a round wig and gave up my sword; I sold my watch, saying to myself, with unspeakable joy, 'I shall henceforth never need to know the time of day.'"

He refused all presents, and on this point showed himself most sensitive. His correspondence shows that he was quite morbid on the subject. It is true that Thérèse continued to receive presents, but on the sly.

He abandoned the excellent post of cashier, which he occupied in the service of the farmer-general Francueil, partly (for he frankly gives both motives) because the work was too absorbing and was displeasing to him; partly because "his principles were incompatible with a situation so at variance with them."

In order to earn his livelihood, he undertook to copy

music (at ten *sous* a page; a little over the usual price). This was not a passing occupation, taken up for a season, in order to astonish his contemporaries; he lived by this work during whole years, and, it would seem, during the remainder of his life, with the exception of the years spent in Switzerland, in England and in the Dauphiny. And certainly, the pleasure of astounding people is here evident, but very certainly also this occupation, which did not absorb him overmuch, was congenial to him, for he was indolent and a good penman.

Notice that poets nearly all have an excellent calligraphy and are very proud of it. The manuscripts of Racine, of Hugo, of Leconte de l'Isle, of Heredia, are admirable. As much may be said of Rousseau. He was in the habit of giving copies of his works to his fair friends. He copied twice—for Mme d'Epinay, for Mme de Luxembourg—the twelve hundred pages of the "Nouvelle Héloïse"; he copied at least three times, the five hundred and forty pages of the "Dialogues." This ex-engraver's apprentice liked to form beautiful letters, especially when they composed sentences of which he was the author. But one can also find pleasure in jotting down fine notes, with beautiful treble clefs, beautiful braces, beautiful quavers, beautiful sharps. . . . The young Marseillais Eymar, in 1774, was in admiration before the perfection of Rousseau's copied music.

This sort of conversion has but little in common with that of Pascal or de Rancé. But no reformation ever achieved so great a society success. Rousseau, the savage,

Rousseau, the impolite, Rousseau without sword or watch, and especially Rousseau, copyist of music, put the fashionable Paris of the day all topsy-turvy. Every fine lady wished for music copied by his hand. If Tolstoï were to settle in Paris, all our fair socialists would go to him for their shoes.

Rousseau thoroughly enjoyed the curiosity aroused by his conversion:

> "My room," says he, "was crowded with people who, under various pretexts, took up my time . . . I could not refuse to see everybody . . . A little more and, like Punch, I might have shown myself at so much a head."

And, at the very moment when he was obtaining this success of edification, and was so well pleased with himself, we are bound to believe (for these things came to pass in 1750 and 1751) that he had already placed, or was going to place, his third and fourth child among the foundlings.

This would tend to prove that his conversion was not, or was not yet, that of the heart. In spite of his love of solitude, he was merely concerned with the impression he produced on others. He says that he shook off the yoke of public opinion, that he despised it; but such disdain proved that he often thought of it. Indiscreet and noisy conversions are apt to be a little wanting in sincerity. At the very time when he examined his conscience, the operation was diverted from its end because, if he questioned himself, it was that he might confess, not to one man only, a man consecrated for that sacred office, but to the public, and that he was less desirous of culling the fruits of his repentance than of noting the effect produced on others by his confession. For this reason, and because if one eye looked within, the other squinted outward, one may say that this hermit, so loquacious about himself, perhaps never thoroughly knew himself, and was always easily persuaded of the goodness of his own nature. Self-love carried to excess prevents self-knowledge, and *vice-versa.* Jean-Jacques had scarcely resolved to be a better man than he believed himself to be better.

This great adversary of science and letters, of arts and of luxury, was more than ever taken up with the world of luxury, of letters, of science and of arts. He grumbled at being drawn into it, but he allowed himself to be persuaded. He continued to write and to compose music. His "Narcisse" was given (without success) at the Comédie Française, in 1752. About that time he composed the "Devin du village." And so flagrant was the contradiction between his maxims and his occupations that he wrote by way of justification the curious preface of "Narcisse," printed in 1753.

First of all, he once more took up his theme. He affirmed that the taste for letters "could spring only from two evil sources: laziness and a desire for notoriety" (such a desire was apparently unknown to himself). As to science, "it was not intended for man in general, he loses his way while seeking for it." Philosophy is fatal to manners and customs. . . . Here, this magnificent affirmation of a traditionist escapes him:

"The least change in customs, were it even in some way favorable, always turns against morals; for *customs are the morality of the people;* when people cease to respect them, they have no rule but their passions, no restraint save that of the law, which can sometimes check the wicked, but can never make them good."

And again, philosophy renders man proud and hard:

. . . "Family ties, love of country become for him empty words: he is neither relative, nor citizen, nor man: he is a philosopher."

Thus, from the healthy part of Rousseau's soul, from his inherited depths, sometimes came glimmers of light.

"But," adds he, "when a nation has been corrupted to a certain point by science and art, it is preferable to keep them . . . For science and art, having hatched vices, are necessary to prevent these from becoming crimes; they destroy virtue, but they leave its shell, and even that is a beautiful thing; they put in its place politeness and decorum; and to the fear of seeming wicked, substitute that of seeming ridiculous."

And further on:

"There is no longer any hope of inducing nations to be virtuous; we should be content with keeping them from evil deeds, they must be amused with trifles so as to prevent crimes."

And again:

"It is necessary to-day to make use of science and art as of a remedy for the evil they have done, as one crushes baleful creatures on the wounds they have made."

If that is the case, we may come to an understanding! And Jean-Jacques can, in all peace of mind, continue to write little comedies and operas.

"Narcisse ou l'amoureux de soi-même" is an insignificant trifle. The "Devin du village" is a great deal better, thanks especially to the music. We here see an old peasant, who is reputed a sorcerer, teach Colette how to win back Colin by exciting his jealousy. It is a beribboned peasant play, closely allied to Favart's light comic operas. One has difficulty in understanding, however, how that pretty spectacle, very conventional and somewhat voluptuous, with its tender music and its dances of stage peasant girls, can remedy the terrible ills caused by science and art. But it is certain that the success of the "Devin" was one of Rousseau's greatest joys.

The "Devin" was first given in 1752, at Fontainebleau, before the court. The eight or ten pages of the "Confessions," where our society hater tells of this representation, are inflated at every line by the complacent vanity of a writer. He had kept his hermit's costume;

his beard and his round wig were "ill-kempt," so he says; the King, the Queen, the royal family, all the noblest lords and high-born dames looked upon him as on some sort of curious animal: what happiness! . . . "I gave myself up fully," says he, "to the pleasure of enjoying my triumph. . . . Those who witnessed this representation cannot have forgotten it, for the effect was unlike any other."

And here is the reverse of the medal—lamentable reverse, alas! The Duc d'Aumont sent word that he was to present himself at the palace the following day, that he would himself introduce him to the King; that there was a question of a pension, and that the King desired to announce the good news in person to the author. And now listen:

"Who would believe that the night that followed so brilliant a day was for me one of anguish and perplexity!"

And here Rousseau explains, with many details, that his infirmity made it necessary for him frequently to absent himself: that the thought of this humiliation was so painful that he was frequently on the point of fainting.

Then, he feared his awkwardness, his want of ready wit, some possible mortifying blunder. "I should have liked," says he, "*without abandoning the austere tone I had adopted*, to show my appreciation of the honor done me by so great a monarch. I ought, in the midst of warm and merited praise, to hide some great and useful verity."

And Jean-Jacques is afraid of not "hitting it off brilliantly." Then he remembers his principles, most opportunely. Should he accept this pension, "farewell to truth, to liberty, to courage. How could he ever, henceforth, speak of independence, of disinterestedness?" In one word, he drew back. And we shall never know, and probably he himself never knew, whether he refused the pension from republican pride, or for fear of his infirmity.

A few months later the "Devin" was given in Paris. Rousseau received a hundred louis from the King, fifty from Mme de Pompadour, fifty from the Opera, five hundred francs from the publisher, Pissot, and various other sums. This success might have turned Jean-Jacques toward the theater and music. He might have become a sort of Grétry or Gossec. He might all his life have resigned himself to mitigate the evils of art by writing comedies and operas. Everything pushed him in that direction, his tastes and his interests. Nothing, besides, need have prevented him from keeping all the benefit of his eccentricities: his round wig, his beard and his freaks would have contributed to his success as flute-player.

But the Dijon Academy was on the watch for him.

The Dijon Academy recalled his attention by propounding this question in the *Mercure* of November, 1753: "*Quelle est l'origine de l'inégalité parmi les hommes? Et est-elle autorisée par la loi naturelle?*" [1]

[1] "What is the origin of inequality among men? And is it sanctioned by the law of nature?"

Evidently the Dijon Academy, proud of its laureate and of the noise he was making in the world, gave out this question for Jean-Jacques' benefit. Moreover, the elements of his pre-supposed answer were already contained in his letters to Stanislas and to Bordes. Jean-Jacques was sure to answer. He could not do otherwise. All was over, he was the prisoner of his assumed part.

I fancy that the Dijon Academy was composed of very worthy people, and very conservative, even though they may have been attacked by the spirit of the day: rich bourgeois, magistrates, retired officers, virtuous ecclesiastics.[1] And it was those worthies who, taking hold of Rousseau once more, forced him, so to speak, to write the most extravagant, the most revolutionary, of all his works, the most pregnant, after the "Contrat social," with future and fatal consequences! . . .

Unless there happened to be, in that honest Dijon Academy, some man of peculiarly perverse mind, of whom we shall never know anything.

[1] Buffon and Piron were members of this Academy, but rarely assisted at its sittings.

DISCOURS SUR L'INÉGALITÉ
ROUSSEAU AT THE HERMITAGE

CHAPTER IV

DISCOURS SUR L'INÉGALITÉ[1]—ROUSSEAU AT THE HERMITAGE

THE question propounded by the Dijon Academy was as follows:

"*Quelle est l'origine de l'inégalité parmi les hommes? Et est-elle autorisée par la loi naturelle?*" [2]

Rousseau's answer, so far as it touches directly on the Academical question is this: First. The origin of inequality is property, established by social life. Second. Inequality is condemned by the law of nature; for men, in the state of nature, are equal, isolated and good—society has corrupted them.

But Rousseau's discourse is simply entitled: *Discours sur l'origine et les fondements de l'inégalité parmi les hommes.*[3] This title sufficiently proves that he did not methodically treat the two questions of the Dijon Academy. He does not answer with definitions and arguments, but with affirmations, descriptions and images. He answers by drawing, according to his fancy, a picture of humanity from the earliest ages, somewhat after the

1 "Discourse on inequality."

2 "What is the origin of inequality among men? And is it sanctioned by the law of nature?"

3 Discourse on the origin and foundations of inequality among men."

fashion of Lucretius in the fifth book of his poem, or of Buffon in his "Septième époque de la nature,"[1] but more developed and in another spirit. His discourse, in short, is a poem: the romance of humanity, innocent, then depraved.

"Let us begin," says Rousseau, "*by putting aside all facts* [how reassuring!], for they have nothing to do with the question. The researches which we may make on the subject should not be taken for historical truths [so much the better!], but only as hypothetical or conditional reasonings, better fitted to light up the nature of things than to show their real origin, after the manner of those which our scientists hold on the formation of the world."

Thus, we are warned; he relates what he supposes, or, perhaps, what he dreams. I was not far wrong when I said, let us read his discourse as though it were a romance. Rousseau continues:

"Oh, man! this is thy history, such as I believe it to be, having read it, not in the books of thy fellowmen, who are liars, but in *Nature*, that never lies."

Very good. But what is "Nature"? We shall return to that point, but I might as well say at once that I believe Jean-Jacques nowhere has given a precise, scientific definition of that mysterious word of which he has made so frenzied a use.

[1] "Seventh epoch of nature."

He proceeds:

"There is an age at which every individual man would like to stop; seek for the age at which thou wouldst desire to see thy species remain."

Let us seek for it. Rousseau then enters into his "first part": the history of primitive humanity until the establishment of property.

"Considering man," says he, "such as he must have sprung from nature's hands . . . I see an animal, less strong than some, less agile than others, but, on the whole, of a superior organization; I see him satisfy his hunger beneath an oak, quench his thirst at the first stream, find his bed at the foot of that tree that gave him food; thus all his wants are satisfied."

He then shows him to us:

"'Imitating the industry of animals' . . . *rising* [he uses the word] to the instinct of beasts . . . uniting in himself the instincts which characterize each animal species . . . nourishing himself equally with most of the aliments which the other animals share among themselves, and, therefore, finding his livelihood more easily than any of them."

These men were necessarily and hereditarily robust. In that particular, they could but degenerate.

"The body of the primitive man, being his only instrument, he used it for every purpose, of which ours, from lack of exercise, is incapable; *and it is our industry which deprives us of the strength and agility which necessity obliged him to acquire.* Had he had an axe, would his arm have broken off such thick branches? Had he had a sling, would he, with his hand, have thrown a stone with such vigor? Had he had a ladder, would he so lightly have climbed a tree? Had he had a horse, would he have run as swiftly?"

Therefore (and I do not exaggerate Rousseau's thought, and only draw from it its most evident consequence), axe, sling, the domestication of the horse, are so many deplorable inventions. Natural man cannot accomplish the slightest progress without deteriorating.

It then pleases Rousseau to affirm that man, in the state of nature, scarcely knew disease or infirmities, and that death nearly always came to him through old age. (Lucretius did not think so. He says that the first men "did not die much more than civilized men" *non nimio plus.* Therefore, mortality among them was quite as great.)

Jean-Jacques pursues:

"Most of our vices are of our own making, and we could have avoided nearly all of them by keeping to a simple manner of life, uniform and *solitary*, such as nature prescribes to us."

"Solitary," for elsewhere he explains that primitive

man did not burden himself permanently with a female, and that when his young ones were capable of getting their own food he abandoned them to their fate. Rousseau continues and insists:

"If nature destined us to a healthy life, I dare almost affirm that the *state of reflection is a state contrary to nature, and that thinking man is a depraved animal.*"

This is a sentence which he must have written with delight, so as to annoy the philosophers and astonish the fine ladies. It is, besides, nothing but an impertinent phrase, rather meaningless, if, on one side, one cannot understand in what way reflection can seriously keep a man from living in good health, and, if, on the other, man could prevent himself from thinking, any more than he could live without eating or drinking, and if the using of his brain were not as natural as the exercise of his limbs! But Jean-Jacques was riding his hobby—off he goes, off he goes! He affirms that at any rate all inventions are, to say the least, useless.

"It is evident that the first man who made clothes and built a shelter gave himself very useless comforts, of which till then he had felt no need, and it is hard to see why, having reached man's estate, he could not continue a kind of life which he had endured from infancy."

Therefore, intellectual inactivity would be the sovereign good. Rousseau acknowledges that a quality *distinguishes* man from the brute: the faculty of perfecting himself. But, if this distinguishes man from the brute, it must necessarily be "natural" to man, that is, in unison with nature, and therefore commendable. But Jean-Jacques does not even formulate this objection, and continues boldly:

"It would be sad were we forced to acknowledge that this *distinctive and almost limitless faculty were the source of all human woes;* that it, with the complicity of time, drags him from the original condition where his days flowed in all tranquillity and innocence."

(How does he know this?) But he goes still further, for his easy paradox is not yet exhausted. He asks himself the secret of man's progress. He answers, "Through speech." But how was speech invented? No one knows. It is almost impossible to imagine it. Rousseau writes some pages on the origin of language, which I think excellent. But listen to his conclusion:

"One sees, at least, by the little care nature has taken to bring men together through mutual wants and the lack of ease in speech, how she has failed to prepare their social sense, and how little she has aided in the establishment of these bonds."

In other words, man, by inventing speech, went against nature's desires, the proof thereof being that speech had given him a deal of trouble. Therefore, after having regretted, in his first discourse, the invention of the printing press, Rousseau here deplores the invention of speech.

This point settled, he affirms anew that men in the state of nature were happy. Having among themselves no sort of moral bonds or common duties, they could be neither good nor evil, and had neither vices nor virtues. They possessed only the sentiment of pity, a natural sentiment. (Did they all possess it? What does he know about it? And, if it was not common to all, then, already there were good and bad men.) But let us listen to him once more:

"Pity, in the state of nature, takes the place of laws, of customs, and of virtue, with this superiority, that no one is tempted to *disobey its gentle voice.* [Really?] It is pity that keeps a robust savage from robbing a feeble child or an infirm old man of food painfully acquired, if he himself hopes to find his sustenance elsewhere." [And what if he has not that hope?]

But the suffering, the violence, the disorders of love? It is all most simple: primitive man was exempted from them. Society, civilization, and laws created these things. . . . Having no idea of beauty, the savage does not choose:

"He listens simply to the temperament bestowed upon him by nature, *and not to a taste which he could not have acquired,* and any woman contents him. Each one peacefully awaits the impulse of nature, yields to it without any preference with more pleasure than fury, and, satisfied, all desire dies within him."

Rousseau then affirms that in the state of nature inequality is much diminished, for men live scattered and have but few wants, and he thus ends his first part:

"After having shown that inequality is scarcely perceptible in the state of nature, and that its influence is barely felt, it remains for me to show its origin and its progress . . . and to consider the different fortunes which may have perfected human reason in deteriorating the species and rendering a being wicked by making him sociable."

And he adds that these, after all (which was not unnecessary), are but "conjectures."

The second part consists in a broad sketch of the political history of humanity. It begins with this effective passage:

"The first man who, having enclosed some land, thought of saying this is mine, and found people simple enough to believe him, was the real founder of civilized society. How many crimes, wars, murders, how many miseries and horrors would have been spared human nature had some man snatched away the stakes, or filled in the ditch, calling out to his neighbors: 'Beware of listening to this impostor!'" etc.

After this roll of the drum, he retraces his steps, takes

up the history of humanity where he had left it, and pursues the lamentable enumeration of the odious progress of civilization: for every step of progress brings its own misery.

"Men, enjoying greater leisure, employed it in the search of comforts. . . . *But* to lose these, brought more distress than their possession had brought pleasure.

"Men learned to choose in love. . . . *But*, jealousy sprang into being with love, and the gentlest of passions was given human blood in sacrifice.

"Men grew accustomed to assemble together. . . . Each one began to observe the others and wished to be observed, and public esteem obtained its value. *But*, later on, each man resented the disdain he encountered, revenge became terrible, men showed themselves sanguinary and cruel."

And so on. (Rousseau here establishes a distinction between the selfishness of man, wild and solitary, a useful and inoffensive self-love, and the egotism of men living in society, and which is disastrous.)

However, Rousseau reaches that stage of human development where he would have wished humanity to stop. It is after the dawn of agriculture and life in tribes, and before the institution of individual property. To tell the truth, it is rather difficult to understand why he judged this to be humanity's best moment, since he had already told us that each pretended "progress" that had brought it thus far was a disaster. . . . However that may be, let us examine his ideal:

". . . Thus, though men had become less hardy and though natural pity had already undergone some change, this period of development of human faculties, indicating a just medium between the indolence of the primitive state and the petulant activity of our self-love . . . must have been its happiest and most durable stage. The more one reflects, the more it seems that this state was the least subject to revolutions, the best for man, and that he could only have left it by some fatal chance. The *example of savages,* whom one has nearly always found at that point, seems to confirm the theory that humanity was created to remain there always, that this state was the veritable youth of the world, and that all later progress which seemed to be a step forward toward the perfection of each individual, was, *in reality, a step toward the decrepitude of the species.*"

And Rousseau continues to tell us what he chooses. Out of the cultivation of the land followed necessarily its division, and, consequently, the establishment of property. From this sprang competition, rivalry. Soon, there were the rich and the poor. The struggle became atrocious. Then, the rich and the shrewd proposed to establish a government and laws "in the interest of all." Then, cities and states sprang up. Then, national wars broke out. Then, nations chose chiefs to defend their independence.

Then, the chief became a tyrant. Declamation on liberty (which man has no right to alienate). Declamation against despotism. Meanwhile, inequality grew and increased, and with it all vices.

And here is the conclusion and summing up of the work—a singularly heavy, and, at times, obscure conclusion:

"It follows from this exposition that inequality, being almost absent from the state of nature, draws its strength and its growth from the development of our faculties and from the progress of the human mind, and at last becomes permanent and legitimate by the establishment of property and law. It follows also that moral inequality, authorized by the only positive right, is contrary to the natural right, each time that it is not in proportion with physical inequality, which means, I take it, whenever a man, socially powerful, is weak in mind or body; distinction which sufficiently determines what one should think with regard to the sort of inequality existing in civilized society, since it is manifestly against *the law of nature,* however it may be defined, that a child should command an old man, that a fool should lead a wise man, and that a handful of people should be overwhelmed with superfluities, while the starving multitude lacks the necessities of life."

Whereupon one might say, "Heredity, of which you indicate a possible drawback, and the inequality of wealth may be against justice, against reason, but not against nature. Sometimes you oppose nature to justice and reason; sometimes you identify one with the other. Then, we fail to understand."

The "Discours sur l'inégalité" contains a hundred and ten long pages. I have analyzed it for you very faithfully, making use, when it was possible, of Rousseau's own phrases, which I have cut down sometimes, only to shorten them, never to change their meaning.

And therefore I say to myself:

Here, then, is one of the most famous productions of the eighteenth century; one which definitely established Rousseau's fame, and which, forty years later, had the greatest influence (with the "Contrat social") on the sensibilities and the imagination of men!

What poverty, however, under its insolent exterior! The whole thesis is founded on the opposition of nature, which should represent what is good, with society, which should represent what is evil; and the author does not even give a definition of the word "nature"! Yet Heaven knows, however, that the word requires to be explained! For Buffon, nature seems to be that assemblage of forces which composes the life of the universe. For Diderot, nature is atheism, it is the opposite of institutions and of law; finally it is pleasure. For Rousseau, it would seem to mean the instincts and the sentiments with which man is born. Yet, the desire to last, not to suffer, to live in society, even the desire to perpetuate one's being, to possess, to distinguish one's self, to rule, are apparently, and always have been, among those instincts. But, in the eyes of Rousseau, even the invention of the sling and the axe, of agriculture and navigation, is a step downward; choice in love is a step downward; the formation of a family is a step downward; social life is a step downward; the notions of good and evil are a step downward. He grants us, it is true, that humanity's best moment was at the beginning of life in tribes, of agricultural and patriarchal civilization; but what he said before takes from him the right to make this concession; and his ideal, whether he will or not (or else his previous declaration was a lie), is that of savages scattered in forests, without clothes, without weapons, neither good nor bad, *solitary*, *stationary*, and who do not think. As if that would have the slightest interest, as if it would be worth while to people the earth! It would be stagnation in this life of half brutes that would be contrary to "nature"!

And why does Jean-Jacques say he prefers it? Because, affirms he, equality is better preserved in the primitive state. In the first place, he knows nothing about it, for muscular inequality, at a time when it cannot be counterbalanced by intelligence, might be the hardest of all. As though, besides, equality—and equality in ignorance and brutishness—should necessarily be the supreme good, that to which all others should be sacrificed! To tell the truth, this cult is very strange in a book which pretends to discover and to honor the intentions of "nature," which seems so evidently to be mother and mistress of inequality at every degree of being.

Notice that it is impossible that, with a man who feels his intellectual superiority so keenly, and who enjoys it with such inordinate pride, this foolish admiration of equality should be sincere. Unless he happened to be in that state of mind of a certain young socialist who, in a public meeting, said to a friend of mine: "What we demand is not that all should be happy, but that all should be as unhappy as we are."

But no, it cannot be that, for Rousseau, on the contrary, is only concerned with our happiness. Simply, he is the slave of his rôle. He is bound to astonish marchionesses, farmer-generals, and philosophers. He is bound to go beyond the "Discours des sciences et des arts." Ah, poor man, how he works over it! His is not the sort of light paradox, so dear to his time. It is a challenge to reason, crude, naked, and without humor, for Rousseau possesses no wit, and is condemned to be serious, even when he is absurd. But one is astounded by such weakness of thought after the great works of the seventeenth century, and even after those of Montesquieu and Buffon. That this book should have made so much noise in the world and have exercised so great an influence is one of the strongest proofs ever given of human stupidity.

But one may also say:

Yes, without its style, its accent, its interior thrill, the "Discours sur l'inégalité" might be a poor production. The endless objections one could make to it seem foolish and superfluous because they are too easy: so easy that, when one is not obtuse, one blushes to put them forth.

It is necessary to take another point of view; to look upon it as a sort of poem, or rather as a vision of a *nabi*, of an amateur prophet, well composed, and written in a didactic and strained style. The exaggeration, the intrepidity, the insolence of the paradox give it a sort of grandeur. The idols of the day, Science, Progress, Philosophy, are methodically buffeted. The work, seen from afar, and thanks to a little complacency, assumes the aspect of a biblical narrative, of a religious myth. Rousseau merely sets backward the period of the fall. The state of grace was the state of nature; original sin is civilization which, engendering inequality, destroyed fraternity. Civilization for our misfortune, plucked the fruit from the tree of knowledge.

Be sure that Rousseau gave himself up to the joy of the dreamer. But observe how, even when he seems to overset and defy the spirit of his age, he is yet influenced by it. To be reactionist to the point of sighing for an ideal which disappeared five or six thousand years before is to be revolutionary, for, in order to return to it, the destruction of all that intervenes becomes necessary. Whether one endeavors to create the golden age or to re-create it, the same move toward the same chimera becomes inevitable. To-day still, the revolutionary dream—the equality before the same porringer, with a *minimum* of effort for each man—is not this a retrograde ideal, such as that of Jean-Jacques?

Besides (and we have already noted this with regard to his first discourse), Jean-Jacques takes good care, in his correspondence, in his "Lettre à d'Alembert," even in the "Contrat social," and, much later, in the third "Dialogue," to soften the absurdity of his paradox. In the "Discours sur l'inégalité," in spite of the exigencies of logic, he never ventures to present as his ideal the solitary life of man similar to the orang-outang; he stops at the pastoral life, the traditional "golden age" of the poets. In very deed his thought is this (Faguet sums it up with extreme clemency): "A conviction that man is, at least, too social; that it would be well to restrain social life to its *minimum*, to return, if not to the isolated family, at least to the tribe, to the clan, to the small city; thus would be lightened the weight of the task, the intensity of effort, and the monstrous inequality among men; thus fictitious wants, glory, luxury, society life, artistic enjoyments would be diminished; thus man would be brought back to a half animal existence, intelligent still, but above all healthy, peaceful, restful, affectionate, which is his natural state, at any rate a state of happiness."

So far, so good. Thus it happens to you, to me, to feel exasperated by what is artificial in our habits and customs; to think that we could easily dispense with the last scientific improvements, since in former days we did very well without them; that very possibly humanity turns its back on its happiness; that industrial civilization is an evil, as are also those monstrous agglomerations of men that form great cities and great nations; that it would be well to return to a natural and rustic life, etc. These are after all fleeting and unimportant impressions.

Add to this that we do not exactly know where nature ends, that many of these developments of humanity that we call artificial were yet natural at their origin, as natural as were primitive instincts and sensations, whence, after all, they sprang.

Only, had Rousseau been content to exhort his countrymen to simplicity, to recommend country life or life in small towns, that would scarcely have struck anyone as very original, and would have made no stir. . . . His ideas would have seemed very humble had he not madly exaggerated them. And that is why he gave his great trumpet blast. But it is really a pity that Rousseau's best friends should constantly be forced, in their commentaries, to distinguish between what he affirmed (and which is often inept), and what he probably thought. They seem to reason thus: "The proof that what he said was not what he meant to say, is that its refutation would be too easy. A delicate mind does not judge him according to what he says; that would be too coarse." So be it. Let one take him as one will (and, alas! later on brutes will take him at his word, and not to refute him), this difference between the thought and the expression is nothing but charlatanism, and it is scarcely possible to call it by another name. And "charlatan" was, indeed, the name given him by the most sensible part of society at that day, such as the group of Mme du Deffand and the Choiseuls.

But it is evident that this charlatanism was one of the determining causes of the success of this "Discours sur l'inégalité." Besides, this discourse is of all Rousseau's works the one most filled with thrilling bitterness, where the revolutionary accent most vibrates. This accent is much rarer in his other books. Whence came this tone?

Rousseau is careful, in his "Confessions," to tell us, three or four times over, that certain incidents of his childhood and youth awoke in him a lifelong hatred of injustice. But I fancy that his reflections were made afterward. The instances he evokes are, the unjust whipping given him by his Uncle Bernard, the story of the peasant who hid his provisions for fear of paying duty, his quarrels with M. de Montaigu; all this is not, perhaps, sufficient to justify a revolutionary vocation. One might add to them his reminiscences of servitude, and the bitterness of his infirmities. But what seems more likely, or quite as likely, is that this harshness was due to the influence of Diderot, who enjoyed the game. Jean-Jacques lets this out in two notes of his "Confessions."

"I do not know how it happened, but all my conversations with Diderot tended to make me more satirical and biting than it was in my character to be."

And again:

"Diderot took advantage of my confidence in him to give to my writings that *hardness*, that *dark tint* which they ceased to show when he no longer directed me."

However that may be, what, in the "Discours sur

l'inégalité" certainly most impressed fashionable society, and what acted most strongly forty years later, were probably the emphatic and violent commonplaces such as the following (I indicate only the beginning, and, as it were, the prelude):

On liberty:

"As a wild charger shakes his mane, paws the earth and struggles desperately at the approach of the bit, while a tamed horse accepts patiently the whip and the spur, so the barbarous man does not bend his head to the yoke that civilized man accepts without a murmur; he prefers the most stormy liberty to peaceful servitude."

On the rich:

"I can finally prove that, if we see a handful of the mighty and of the rich at the pinnacle of honors and fortune, while the multitude crawls in obscurity and in misery, it is that the former enjoy the things lavished upon them only when the latter are deprived of them, and that, without changing anything in their state, they would cease to be happy if the people ceased to be miserable."

On tyrants:

"It is from the depths of these disorders and these revolutions that despotism, raising by degrees its hideous head, and devouring all that is good and healthy in every part of the State, would end by trampling under foot law and the people, and by establishing its throne on the ruins of the republic."

And, finally, in these pages quite devoid of the *esprit de finesse* we see everywhere that stupid cult of equality, which we shall find anew in the "Contrat social," and which carries with it a great power of persuasion, because it answers less to the sentiment of justice than to the instincts of envy. In a word, one already sees, in this second discourse (and better than in the first) that it is evidently Rousseau who was destined to give its accent to the Revolution, and who will furnish the men of '93 with a stock of stereotyped phrases and commonplaces, sowers of hates as blind as the commonplaces were brutal and summary. . . .

This time the Dijon Academy did not crown Rousseau's discourse, however "advanced" it might be; this was not the work it had expected.

The years which followed were, I fancy, among the least unhappy of Jean-Jacques' life. He enjoyed the conviction that he was good, and, besides, he was famous. He remembered his little native place, Geneva, where they were beginning to be proud of him. He dedicated his "Discours sur l'inégalité" to the "Republic of Geneva." He no longer possessed a Catholic's faith; it is a question whether he ever really did possess it. Convinced that a man should believe in God, and, for the rest, follow the religion of his country, he went to Geneva in order publicly to resume the Protestant faith, and to take up once more his title of citizen; and he knew the joy of returning in triumph to a city whence, a vagabond of sixteen, he had run away six and twenty years before.

On his way to Geneva he passed through Chambéry, and once more saw Mme de Warens:

". . . I saw her again," says he, "in what a situation! Great Heavens! What degradation! What remained of her pristine virtue? . . . I reiterated forcibly and in vain my entreaties, which I had already several times made in my letters, that she should come and live quietly with me, anxious as I was to devote *my days and those of Thérèse* to her happiness."

What a charming picture! And, further on, he describes this little scene, which proves that Thérèse was also a woman "full of feeling":

"During my stay in Geneva Mme de Warens went to Chablais, and paid me a visit at Grange-Canal. She was short of money to complete her journey. I had not with me the necessary sum; an hour later, I sent it by Thérèse. Poor 'Maman'! Let me relate a touching action of hers. Of all her jewels only a little ring was left; she took it from her finger and slipped it on that of Thérèse, who instantly returned it to hers, kissing that noble hand, and bathing it with her tears."

I cannot tell you whether this is grotesque or touching, because I do not know. But in the "Nouvelle Héloïse" we shall again find this hodge-podge of moral ideas, and this sort of beatified security in equivocal situations.

Rousseau was, as I have said, well received in Geneva. He felt at home. He found once more within himself his early Protestant and republican principles. He returned well satisfied. It was about that time (1755) that he began to treat Thérèse like a sister. He enjoyed his heroism; he enjoyed his eccentricities; he enjoyed the beauty of the mask which he himself no longer distinguished from his own face; he lived in a state of moral enthusiasm which lasted "at least four years," says he at first, or "nearly six years," as he says on the following page.

Listen to this magnificent outburst:

"Until then I had been good; henceforth, I became virtuous, or, at least, enraptured with virtue. . . . [Oh, but that is not the same thing! And how ill such raptures and virtue go together! Boileau, a thoroughly honest man, merely declares himself a 'friend of virtue,' and that is already saying a good deal.] This rapture began in my head, but soon passed into my heart. The noblest pride arose from the ruins of uprooted vanity. I played no part, I became such as I appeared, and, during at least four years, while this effervescence lasted in all its force, there was nothing grand or beautiful capable of filling a man's heart of which I was not capable *between Heaven and myself*. From this sprang my sudden eloquence, and the really celestial fire which burned within me was communicated to my first books.

"I was really transformed; my friends, my acquaintances scarcely recognized me. I was no longer that timid man, more shamefaced than modest, who dared neither present himself nor speak, whom a light word disconcerted, who blushed under a woman's glance. Audacious, proud, fearless, I displayed an assurance, all the firmer that it was simple and filled my soul rather than my outward man. The contempt *born of my profound meditations* for the manners, the maxims, and the prejudices of my day, rendered me insensible to the mockeries of those who were subject to them, and I crushed their small jokes with my sentences, as I crushed an insect between my fingers. . . . What a change! *All Paris* repeated the bitter and stinging sarcasms of that same man who, two years before and ten years after, never knew how to find what he ought to say, or the words with which to say it."

Great Scott! What a man! And what will he do, this terrible writer of the two discourses, this despiser of the manners, of the maxims, and of the prejudices of civilization, this fanatic of virtue, of sincerity, and independence, and, finally, this lover of solitude, and this worshiper of nature? He might live in the recovered austere little native land, he might accept the place of librarian offered him by his virtuous countrymen. It would have been the very thing for him. The ex-friend of the fat Warens, the lover of Thérèse, forgetful of his five probable infanticides, might have taught morality to the whole world, at the very foot of Calvin's pulpit. Ah, yes, but he would then have been too far from Paris and from that fine society he so despised. "All Paris" could not then "repeat his bitter and stinging sarcasms." At least, if both the neighborhood of a great city and solitude were necessary to him, the environs of Paris, at that season, were charming and still quite rural. He might have hired a cottage with a garden, the rent of which he could have paid out of his own resources, and he would have been in his own home, and have been beholden to no one. Such would have been a wise course and full of common sense.

But, among the fine ladies whom he still frequented—and who yet practiced the maxims, exhibited the manners, and led the lives he most detested—there was one, Mme de la Live d'Epinay, a little brunette, given to discussion, strong-minded, fond of scribbling, and of a sensual temperament, wife of one of those farmers-general whose very occupation must have seemed infamous to the writer of the two discourses. He often visited her at the château of the Chevrette, where were assembled the most brilliant and frivolous company, and he even took a part in his own comedy of the "Engagement téméraire." This ardent little woman was curious on the subject of Rousseau. After their first meetings, she says of him in her "Mémoires":

"He is given to flattery without being polite, or, at least, without wishing to be so. [I have already quoted this incisive saying.] He appears ignorant of society manners; but it is easy to see that he is prodigiously intelligent. He is of a dark complexion, and his eyes, full of fire, illumine his countenance. When he is speaking, and one looks at him, he seems handsome; but when one remembers him, it is always as ugly. [It is true that, when she wrote her "Mémoires," she hated him.] It is said that his health is bad, and that he is subject to sufferings which he hides with care, from I know not what principle of vanity; it is probably this which from time to time, gives him so wild a look. . . . It is whispered that his story is as strange as his person, and that is saying a good deal."

And further:

"You cannot imagine what pleasure I found in conversing with him."

In one word, Mme d'Epinay took to Jean-Jacques. It was, it would appear, especially out of curiosity and vanity. She wanted to have her "great man." She already called him "My bear."

One day as they were walking together, they went as far as the reservoir of the park waters, close to the forest of Montmorency; here, there was a pretty vegetable garden and a small tumbledown building called the Hermitage. "Ah, madame," had exclaimed Rousseau, "what a delightful spot, the very refuge for me!" Mme d'Epinay said nothing. But a little later, as they took the same walk, instead of the ruined hovel, there was a cottage almost entirely new: "My bear, here is your home; you chose it, and friendship offers it to you." "I do not think," says Rousseau, "that in the course of my life I was ever more greatly or more delightfully moved—I wet with my tears the bountiful hand of my friend."

Mme d'Epinay tells us that the house contained five rooms (very decently furnished by her), a kitchen, a cellar, a vegetable garden of an acre, a spring, and the forest by way of garden. Jean-Jacques paid no rent. He gave the gardener his wages, but with money handed him by Mme d'Epinay for the purpose. Only, several times, he was forced to advance the sum. No matter. The great enemy of social inequalities, and the man who pretended jealously to guard his independence, remained, even financially, the debtor, one might almost say the parasite, of a farmer-general's wife.

On the other hand, the little world, the coterie of Mme d'Epinay showed, as would have said Rousseau of any other such coterie, the worst possible morality. M. d'Epinay was eternally in the society of ballet dancers. After having been the mistress of Francueil, Mme d'Epinay was about to take Grimm as lover. Her sister-in-law, Mme d'Houdetot, was the mistress of Saint-Lambert. Her cousin, Mlle d'Ette, was the mistress of Valory, etc., etc. It was in the intimacy of this society, as elegant and refined as it was vicious, that was about to live the declaimer against the corrupt influence of science and art, the man who proclaimed himself "intoxicated with virtue," the man who had written, as you may remember, that, ". . . We need powder for our wigs, that is why so many poor have no bread."

He took up his abode at the Hermitage April 9, 1756, with Thérèse and mother Levasseur, after having been over-persuaded, so says he. But, nevertheless, he there took up his abode.

Why? Because, if he was proud, he was also vain; because he was strangely weak; because he never had any will power; because he dreamed his life instead of living it; because he dreamed of what he was himself, instead of knowing himself, and because he possessed the gift of not seeing reality as it was.

So he settled at the Hermitage. In which he was wrong. He there knew many tribulations (greatly through his own fault), and it was there that the monomania of persecution developed in him most alarmingly.

On Rousseau's twenty months' sojourn at the Hermitage, we can consult the ninth book of the "Confessions," the "Mémoires" of Mme d'Epinay, and those of Marmontel *passim*, and especially the beginning of book viii., in which Marmontel is Diderot's mouthpiece.

After reading all this, one's brain is somewhat muddled. I must add that the "Mémoires" of Mme d'Epinay are "romanced," and to be taken with a grain of salt, and that Marmontel, when he reports that which he does not know at first hand, inspires me with a good deal of distrust.

But here is the gist of the story, and what I think is true:

When Rousseau arrived in Paris, and later, after his return from Venice, he had been very well received in the literary world. The encyclopedists saw a recruit in him; then, knowing him to be ill, supersensitive, and very touchy, they were disposed to handle him gently. Perhaps, among themselves, they made a little fun of his eccentricities. But, I think, they were by no means ill-intentioned. Here is a page by Marmontel which seems to give the "keynote":

"It was there[1] that I became acquainted with Diderot, Grimm, and Jean-Jacques Rousseau, before he played the savage. . . . Grimm invited us to dinner every week, and at this men's dinner perfect liberty reigned; but it was a condiment of which Rousseau took but sparingly. . . . He had not yet shown his colors, as he did later, and announced no ambition to form a sect. Either his pride was not yet born, or he hid it under the appearance of timid politeness, a politeness which went even to obsequiousness and humility. But, beneath his shrinking reserve, one saw mistrust; his uneasy glances took in everything with an attention full of suspicion. He was, nevertheless, welcomed, as he was known to have a self-love, anxious, sensitive, easily wounded, *he was cared for, handled with the same attention and the same delicacy with which a pretty woman, as capricious as vain, and to whom one was paying court*, might have been treated.

[1] At d'Holbach's, toward 1750.

He was then working at the music of the "Devin du village," and he would sing us the airs he had composed, accompanying himself on the harpsichord. We were delighted with them. We were equally delighted with the firm, living, and profound way in which he wrote his first essay. Nothing, I must say, could have been more sincere than our goodwill toward his person, or our appreciation of his talents. . . ."

(We feel that this must be true. We have seen that sort of thing. We have all been particularly kind to some talented, but ill-tempered, brother writer.)

Such was, it would seem, the state of mind of his friends when Jean-Jacques went to the Hermitage.

Rousseau says that immediately after the "Devin du village," all were jealous of him, because they would have been incapable of writing a comic opera. He also says that they were angry on account of his moral reform, and they could not forgive him for being virtuous. That is scarcely likely. His sudden reputation may have disturbed them momentarily, but I think that they only turned against him later on, when he had exasperated them by his suspicions and ill-humor, and especially after he had clearly and solemnly declared himself the adversary of the philosophers' party.

But, it may be that, before this, they teased him at times, like d'Holbach, who took pleasure in irritating him, because at such moments only was he truly eloquent, that they certainly had not, as yet, any evil feelings toward him.

I fancy that they merely said: "Here is a strange fellow, full of talent. His brain will not stand the strain of a whole winter of solitude. And, then, what society for him is that of Thérèse and her mother! If we could only detach him from Thérèse, or, at least, get him back to Paris!"

As it happened, mother Levasseur was seventy years of age and helpless. They took it upon themselves to say that it was dangerous to force this old woman to spend the winter in complete isolation, far from all help. They fancied that Thérèse would, doubtless, follow her mother, and that Rousseau himself would return to Paris, which would be a good thing for him mentally, and where he could have some society outside of that of the two feminine "bosses."

But they went about it blunderingly. They had secret interviews with the women, of which Rousseau got wind. With him, Diderot, as was his wont, showed himself indiscreet and despotic. Jean-Jacques was cruelly wounded. Henceforth he believed in a plot hatched by his friends (Grimm, Diderot, d'Holbach) to render him odious. Once, (it was always with the view of forcing him to return to Paris during the winter), Diderot wrote to him:

"The Scholar[1] probably wrote to you that, on the fortifications, twenty beggars were dying of hunger, for lack of the farthing that you used to give them. This is a specimen of our chatter."

[1] This was the nickname given to Mme d'Epinay's son.

The joke was friendly and kind, since it was an allusion to the charitable habits of Jean-Jacques. But he was incapable of taking a joke. He received it most ungraciously, and answered with rude clumsiness:

"There is here a respectable, good old man who, after having spent his life working, is now unable to do anything, and is dying of hunger in his old age. *My conscience* is more at peace with the penny I give him every Monday, than with the hundred farthings which I might have distributed among the ragamuffins of the fortifications. . . . In the country one learns to love and serve humanity; in town one only learns to despise it."

Diderot, having by chance said in his "Entretiens sur le fils naturel,"[1] "The evil alone wish for solitude." Rousseau took this for himself, and cried out as though he were being murdered. Ah, he was not easy to get along with!

The other episode of his sojourn at the Hermitage was his passion for Mme d'Houdetot. The studies on this subject abound. The last is the clear and solid book of M. Eugène Ritter, "J. J. Rousseau et Madame d'Houdetot." But here is, I think, all that is necessary to know, and what seems to me the truth.

During the absence at the army of her lover, Saint-Lambert, Mme d'Houdetot, sister-in-law to Mme d'Epinay, thirty years of age, dark-complexioned, with fine hair, cross-eyed and pitted, agreeable in spite of all, free,

[1] "Talks about the natural son."

gay, very good-natured, visited Rousseau at his Hermitage (the first day she was bespattered with mud). On his side he went to see her at the Château d'Eaubonne. He took fire, persuaded that for the first time he was really in love, and that it was a great passion. He tells us of his "tender delirium," and of his "erotic transports." He wrote burning letters to her. She amused herself with his advances, which she repulsed easily enough.

Meanwhile, the little coterie of the Chevrette suspected something. At table Rousseau was teased with sly allusions. Mme d'Epinay was a little jealous. Besides, she hated Mme d'Houdetot. She gossiped with Thérèse, whom Jean-Jacques, as I have said, treated merely as a sister, and who, probably, also suffered from this adventure. Thérèse stole Mme d'Houdetot's letters, and showed them to Mme d'Epinay.

Then, Saint-Lambert was warned, either by an anonymous letter from Thérèse, or simply (according to M. Ritter) by an indiscretion on the part of Grimm. Saint-Lambert was a philosopher, a man who did not take things tragically. Besides, he did not fear Jean-Jacques. Nevertheless, on his return, he turned the cold shoulder on him, and so did Mme d'Houdetot; whereupon (charming detail), Jean-Jacques complained to Saint-Lambert himself. All that he gained by this vain excitement was, as he informs us himself, an aggravation of his physical woes.

Thereupon, Mme d'Epinay, who was to go to Geneva to consult Tronchin, said one day to Rousseau: "Will you not accompany me, my bear?" Rousseau had not the least desire to do so. He had already perceived that he had forged chains for himself. How many times had he been called to the Chevrette at the very moment when he wished to write, or to dream in the woods, or simply to remain at home! Diderot, as usual, indiscreet and impetuous—this buzzing Diderot, whose very style takes liberties with one and seems to slap one on the thigh—ordered him to pay his debt to his benefactress by accompanying her. Grimm—that thrifty and crafty German lover of Mme d'Epinay—pushed him in the same direction. Rousseau answered by a long letter, explanatory, blundering, and proud, from which I cull this delicious passage:

". . . Mme d'Epinay, often alone in the country, wished me to keep her company. That is why she liked to have me on hand. . . . One must be poor, without a valet, hate constraint, possess my soul, to guess what it is to live in the house of others. Yet I lived two years in hers, reduced to servitude while listening to the finest speeches on liberty, served by twenty lackeys, and every morning cleaning my own shoes, burdened by sorry indigestion, and ever sighing for my own porringer. . . ."

This he should have understood earlier. As soon as he had seen the truth he ought to have left, at no matter what cost. But he remained because Mme d'Houdetot, who feared gossip, begged him to do so. He waited until, through the influence of that evil beast, Grimm, Mme d'Epinay, already in Geneva, ordered him to leave.

On December 15, 1757, in the heart of winter and in a snowstorm, he moved—much too late for his own dignity. Where did he go? To Paris, where one can very well live alone? To some cottage of the environs, the proprietor of which might have been some honest stranger, to whom he would have been under no obligation? No, but to Montlouis, near Montmorency, into a house rented to him by M. Mathas, steward of the Prince de Condé, and close to the castle of the Maréchal and Mme de Luxembourg, whose debtor he will be, whether he will or not, and who will do him a great deal of harm without meaning it. How, now! one would say that this friend of the savages, this man of so intolerant an independence, could not do without the company and the protection of the great.

It is, therefore, at Montmorency that we shall find him again—at Montmorency, where he will continue to grow more virtuous, as he grows more insane.

LETTRE SUR LES SPECTACLES

ROUSSEAU AT MONTMORENCY

CHAPTER V

LETTRE SUR LES SPECTACLES[1]—ROUSSEAU AT MONTMORENCY

We therefore find Rousseau, in the dead of winter, settled in the cottage of M. Mathas, fiscal steward of the Prince de Condé. I think that there, at least, he paid a small rent.

"M. Mathas caused a little house, which he possessed in his garden of Montlouis at Montmorency, to be offered to me. I accepted with eagerness and gratitude. The bargain was made."

First of all, Rousseau fell very ill. As usual, he tells us about it with intentional precision in its unsavory details. In this, I think there is a sort of bravado and bitter coquetry.

"Scarcely was I settled in my new dwelling than I felt sharp and frequent attacks of my old disorder. I was soon in a cruel state. My friend, Dr. Thierry, came . . . with all the paraphernalia of infirmity and old age,[2] which made me bitterly realize that one cannot, with impunity, keep a young heart in a body that has ceased to be young. The fine season did not give me back my

[1] Letter on the theater.

[2] He was, however, only forty-six.

strength; and I passed the whole of 1758 in a state of languor, which made me think that I was nearing the end of my career."

And here is a still more pitiful letter addressed to an unnamed doctor (probably Thierry), and dated May 10, 1758 (which proves that Jean-Jacques is sometimes mistaken as to dates, since previously he placed the illness four months earlier).

"The lime water having produced no effect, I have left it off; milk having completely stopped natural functions, . . . I have been equally forced to give that up. I have a swelling which disappears when I lie down and is again visible the moment I stand up. . . . I feel a dull, and not very acute pain, which, for the last four years, has never left me. . . . I ask for no consultation. I expect and want for no sort of relief from men, but only from Him who knows how to console us for the woes of to-day by the hope of a better life."

I am careful to note, as I go on, his maladies and his infirmities, because we must never forget that, all his life, he was really ill and infirm, after a most cruel and mortifying fashion. This should teach us indulgence in the very moments when we are most tempted to feel irritated against him. And it explains many things in him: his vagaries, his ill-humors, and his taste for solitude, and even the diversion he sought in the mechanical occupation as copyist; the excess of his pride, the conviction of his own genius which was a compensation to physical misery; his impassioned desire to be an abstemious hermit; the refuge he sought in dreams; and, also, it renders his religious sentiments truer and more touching, and almost heroic in their persistent optimism.

He recovered from this crisis, as from many others. And he had the relief of getting rid of mother Levasseur. Before leaving the Hermitage, he had packed her off to Paris, with some money, and the promise that he would pay for her rent with her children or elsewhere, and never let her want for bread as long as he himself had any. (It must be added that, according to Mme d'Epinay, Grimm and Diderot had already undertaken to give Mme Levasseur a small annuity.)

Soon after his removal to Montlouis, he received the volume of the encyclopedia containing d'Alembert's essay on Geneva. In this essay, "written in connivance with the most important Genevese," and where Voltaire's hand was visible, d'Alembert advised the establishing of a theater at Geneva.

Rousseau's blood was immediately at boiling pitch. He felt that Voltaire had a finger in this pie; Voltaire, magnificently settled at the gates of Geneva, who invited its principal citizens to assist at representations on his little stage, and who had evidently undertaken to corrupt the city of Calvin. And that city was also Rousseau's. Four years earlier he had been welcomed there, after the most flattering fashion. He, therefore, determined to defend

Geneva's virtue, and he wrote his "Lettre sur les spectacles."

The relations of Rousseau and Voltaire dated from the time (you remember) when Rousseau arranged the "Princesse de Navarre," under the title of the "Fêtes de Ramire." They had afterwards met in a few Paris drawing-rooms; and it was perfectly clear that they had never been able to "hit it off."

Then, in 1756, Rousseau one day received Voltaire's poem of the "Désastre de Lisbonne" (the town was half destroyed by an earthquake and conflagration—thirty thousand human beings had been crushed or burned). Voltaire wrote two hundred and fifty elegant and flowing verses on this subject, in a comparatively respectful attitude toward religion, where he refused to acknowledge that all "was for the best," even as Leibnitz and Pope understood the words, and concluded that one should not say: "All is well," but "Some day, all will be well."

This pessimism, however mitigated, seemed odious to Rousseau, and then (this is really admirable) Rousseau, poor, infirm, ill, wrote a long letter to the author, which contains already several of the principal elements of the "Profession de foi du vicaire Savoyard,"[1] and where he proves that "of all human ills, there is not one for which nature is responsible, and which cannot be ascribed to the abuse of his faculties by man, rather than to nature itself." He even declares expressly that the destruction of Lisbon and its inhabitants was still the fault of man, because it was the fault of civilization. He points out

[1] In Rousseau's "Emile."

that nature had nothing to do with the building of twenty thousand houses of six or seven stories, and that, had the inhabitants been scattered and more lightly sheltered, the damage would have been much less great, indeed perhaps insignificant. "All would have fled at the first shock, and the following day the inhabitants would have been sixty miles away, as gay as though nothing had happened."

Voltaire sent Rousseau a few lines, saying that, being ill and also nursing other sick people, he would put off his answer. That answer was to be the delightful and perverse "Candide" (1759).

In a page of his "Confessions" Rousseau tells us more wittily than was his wont:

"Struck by the thought of this poor man[1] crushed as it were under the weight of prosperity and glory, yet declaiming against the miseries of life, and ever finding that all went wrong, I formed the mad project of causing him to reflect, and to prove to him that all went well. Voltaire, who seemingly always believed in God, never really believed but in the devil, since his supposed god was a wicked being who, according to him, found pleasure only in doing harm. The self-evident absurdity of this doctrine is especially revolting in a man on whom all sorts of favors had been showered, who, in the midst of happiness, sought to drive his fellow-beings to despair by the horrible and cruel image of all the calamities from which he himself was exempt."

[1] Voltaire.

We here see the abyss which separates the two men. Even outside of all literary rivalry, Voltaire represents exactly all that Rousseau most hates: social life in all that is most artificial and corrupt; irony and impiety; Voltaire, amiable and witty; Rousseau, disagreeable and virtuous; Voltaire, rich and aristocratic; Rousseau, poor and lowborn; Voltaire, witty and frivolous; Rousseau, grave and even solemn; Voltaire, realistic in politics, and asking only for moderate reforms; Rousseau, republican of Utopia; Voltaire, impious; Rousseau, religious; Voltaire, a friend of order above all things—but seeking to ruin, at least in the upper classes, religion, the support of order; Rousseau, a menace to that order, yet defending religious sentiment; so that each of them, succeeding in the negative part of his task, will shower on the one side blows on religion, and on the other, on social order, blows which, for my part, I deplore with simplicity.

But let us return to the "Lettre sur les spectacles," or "Lettre à d'Alembert." It is among the best known of Rousseau's works. It never fails to figure in the required course of study for the "licence" and "agrégation." Heaven knows the number of dissertations which have been composed by worthy young men on the "paradox of the Misanthrope." And that is why I shall merely sum up very briefly the "Lettre sur les spectacles." Here it is:

Dramatic art is of all arts the most artificial, that in which there is most pretense and simulation, since the writer pretends to give a direct representation of life, and the actor plays the part of a personage whom he is not in reality, and bends his body and his soul to this pretense. In one word the deception is complete. Man is here as far as possible from the state of nature. The theater is the last flower of civilization. On that alone Rousseau might condemn it. But he chooses to go into details.

Tragedy is evil. The spectator uselessly spends on it his stock of tears and pity, and none are left for real woes. Or else he admires fine scoundrels, and grows familiar with horrors.

Comedy is evil. Its morality is not that one should not be vicious, but that one should not be ridiculous. It preserves conventionality and worldly prejudices. It teaches the ways of the world, which are so many lies. It speaks of nothing but love and gallantry. It consents to the reign of woman. It lowers morality and effeminates the heart.

One could invoke Molière. Ah, yes! let us speak of him. His theater is a school of vice. In it, goodness and simplicity are eternally turned into ridicule. In it, the foolish are victimized by the wicked. In it, the rights of fathers over their children, husbands over their wives, masters over their servants, are flaunted, etc.

For example, see the "Misanthrope" itself, his masterpiece. This comedy, better than any other, shows us Moliére's true aim when he composed his plays. His object is not to form an honest man, but a man of the world.

"In consequence," writes Rousseau, "he did not seek to correct vice, but foibles, and in vice itself he found an instrument well adapted to that end. Hence, wishing to expose to public laughter all the faults which are the reverse of an amiable man's qualities, the qualities of a society man, it remained to him to put on the stage that which the world least pardons, the mockery of virtue—that is what he did in the 'Misanthrope.'"

There are two things which cannot be denied: First, that Alceste, in the play, is a man of a truly high character, sincere, estimable, veritably an honest man; and, in the second place, that the author makes of him a ridiculous personage. (Read between the lines: therefore the author ridiculizes virtue.) This is enough to render Molière inexcusable.

This is a syllogism. But, like many syllogisms, it is lame. One might say (and thousands of candidates to the "Licence ès lettres" [1] have repeated it for the last hundred years) that, doubtless, Alceste is virtuous, but that he is also sometimes absolutely ridiculous; but that he is not ridiculous because of his virtue. He is only ridiculous because certain indignations of his are excessive in their form and out of proportion with their object. But that proves nothing, for in truth Rousseau will not acknowledge that Alceste can appear ridiculous, even in his exaggerations. What am I saying? He does not acknowledge that Alceste exaggerates.

He will not allow us to smile at Alceste, even when we

[1] University degree in France.

love him. He does not admit that turn and attitude of the mind which make us at times jest with what we esteem, and which we, in spite of all, continue to esteem. He knows all about that attitude. His best friends adopted it with regard to himself, Jean-Jacques. They loved him and held him in high esteem, even while they, imperceptibly, made fun of him. And Jean-Jacques, therefore, came to the conclusion that they were hypocrites, that they hated him, and conspired against him. In reality, Jean-Jacques saw himself complacently in Alceste. But that Alceste should be ridiculous, and consequently also Jean-Jacques, Jean-Jacques cannot admit. Or, if it be so, then his contemporaries are very infamous.

Let us note here a rather curious example of the diversity of human judgments. Rousseau accused the dramatic works of Molière of immorality about, as in our days, did Brunetière (and also Faguet, and before them Louis Veuillot), but for very different reasons—at least verbally!

Molière appeared criminal in Rousseau's eyes because his ideal for the stage was the society man. But on the contrary Molière troubled Brunetière because he had been a disciple of "nature." So that we do not know whether to blame Molière for having adored nature or for having disdained it. Evidently "nature" was not quite the same in the eyes of Jean-Jacques and in those of our contemporary: Excellent for one, it is not worth the devil, or rather it is the devil himself, for the other. . . . Oh, Nature! what then art thou? We should so like to know.

But if thou art all things, as seems likely, we shall never be any the wiser. At any rate, Rousseau, who spoke of thee so constantly, ought, one fine day, to have given us a definition of thee.

Let us continue this very summary synopsis of the "Lettre sur les spectacles."

Therefore, "the stage," which can do nothing to correct manners, can do much to corrupt them.

Actors and actresses are by their very profession corrupted and degraded by the stage. They are forced to disguise their real being, and, besides, it is for women a veritable prostitution. And all this is sometimes true, and all that is not always so. And here Rousseau agrees with Bossuet, who had agreed with Pascal, as to the effects of the dramatic representation of love.

"And yet," pursues Rousseau, "the theater may be comparatively of minor consequence in the frightful corruption of large cities. But what a pernicious pleasure for small towns!"

And he calls to mind his native land, he evokes the pastoral, idylic, simple, and perfect life of the "Montagnons," a tribe in the environs of Neuchâtel. After which he explains in how many ways and from how many points of view (moral, social, civic, and economic), the establishment of a theater in Geneva—small town of twenty thousand souls—would harm Geneva. And here he seems to me not far wrong.

"Better for Geneva," says he, "its little 'societies,' its traditional coteries: meetings of men, and meetings of women [for Rousseau deems it well that, as a general thing, the two sexes should live apart]. In the women's circles there will be some gossip and scandal, but in these circles, women, so to speak, will act as the moral police of the town; in the men's circles there will be a good deal of drinking, but in all innocence." Here we come upon a eulogy of wine which is graceful and quite touching, coming from one who took principally milk or water, and who never drank more than his half bottle of wine.

"But how!" exclaims Rousseau, "should there be no performances in a republic?" On the contrary, they should be numerous. The Genevese are not yet virtuous enough for Rousseau to propose to them the nude dances of the Spartan young girls; and this he regrets. But there are reviews, public prizes, the champions of the gun, of the cannon, of aquatic sports. Such festivities should be multiplied.

"But do not let us adopt those exclusive spectacles which shut up a small number of people in an obscure *lair;* that keep them *timorous* and motionless, in silence and idleness; that show nothing but walls, but iron spikes, but soldiers, but sorry images of servitude and *inequality.* [What means here the word inequality? Ah! but this is in truth a phrase of '93!]

"No, favored nation, these are not your festivities.

It is in the open air, it is under the blue sky that you should assemble and give yourselves up to the sweet expressions of your happiness . . . Your pleasures should not be effeminate or mercenary; let nothing which resembles constraint and interest poison them; let them be free and generous like yourselves; let the sun shine on your innocent representations; in your hearts will shine that which is most worthy to brighten them."

All that for some kind of agricultural county fair with a brass band and firemen—festivities of which I say no harm, and in which I have mingled, not without pleasure, but where, as one well knows, the important thing is to drink.

For the winter time, Rousseau imagines other amusements. He proposes especially balls for marriageable young men and young women, which might be presided over by a magistrate of the Council.

"I should like within the hall a convenient and honorable enclosure to be erected, destined to the old of both sexes, who, having already given citizens to the mother-country, might see their grandchildren preparing to do likewise."

And thereupon, he grows singularly lyrical:

"I should allow no one to enter without saluting this tribunal; all the young couples should, before beginning a dance and after having finished it, make a low bow, so as to accustom youth to respect old age. I am certain that this agreeable reunion of the two extremes of human life would present a touching aspect, and that more than once tears would flow from a tender-hearted spectator. . . . I should like, every year, at the last ball, that the young girl who at this ball and all the others had shown herself most praiseworthy and modest, and had been approved by all, might be crowned by the magistrate and honored with the title of queen of the ball, for the rest of the year. I should like her at the close of this same assembly to be led home escorted," etc., etc.

Hold there! and equality, what about equality?

O Sparta! O Lycurgus! O Plutarch! O presence of the magistrate, there where he had no business to be! O publicity and regulations of intimate sentiments and family scenes! . . .

As Rousseau, by his two first discourses, will give the Revolution its vocabulary, by the "Lettre sur les spectacles," he will give the Revolution its festivities—as by the "Contrat social" he will give it its state conception.

As to the real meaning of the "Lettre sur les spectacles," I believe, as does Rousseau, that the stage can do little or nothing for the purifying of manners; but can it do much to corrupt them? I do not know, neither does any one else. Oh, how many *distinguo* would be necessary! Generally, the stage only succeeds by dint of putting itself in unison with the morality of its public: and it is nearly always thus that it proceeds. It is on a level with the spectators themselves. Rousseau, who believed that things are evil in proportion as they recede from the state of nature, considers the theater as the most dangerous of amusements, because it is the most artificial. But this judgment rests on the supposed excellence of that mysterious "state of nature."

The theater is a pleasure taken in common and in public. Now, it seems proved that men assembled only accept manners and morality of medium worth. It is therefore probable that the stage neither improves nor corrupts morality. These things have been said a hundred times, and better than I can say them.

At all events, the condemnation uttered by Rousseau seems very severe, if we consider the theater of his time, the theater before 1758. It might seem better justified when we think of certain modern plays; and even as to these, one can scarcely say that they deprave the public, since they merely put themselves on the level of that public's depravation. But the plays given in Rousseau's time? the theater before 1758? I do not speak of Corneille, of Racine, of Molière, nor even of Regnard. The pleasure of listening to the three first-named is perhaps as laudable as drunkenness or popular dances; and one must be Jean-Jacques to take tragically the immorality of the "Légataire." But can one affirm that the tragedies of Campistron, of Lagrange-Chancel, of Longepierre, of Lafosse, of Dauchet, of Duché, of Lamotte, of Lefranc de Pompignan, of Lanoue, of Marmontel, of Crébillon—and of Voltaire himself—were so very dangerous? And the comedies of Lesage, of Legrand, of Dufresny, of Dancourt, of Destouches, of Marivaux, of Gresset? You will not find in them a successful adultery, and the courtezan is as yet only alluded to, thanks to decent periphrases.

One thing is to be noticed: the moment Jean-Jacques chose to fulminate against the theater is the most inoffensive and weakest period of comedy in France. After Lesage, Dancourt, Marivaux, who had zest, comedy drags along in insipid portraits, in minute satires of manners and especially in little love intrigues. It is gallant and insignificant. It is true that love is often the theme, and a light sensuality is at least exhibited. But one does not understand exactly why Rousseau rebels against this, and here we find one of his habitual contradictions and equivocations.

Pascal, and Bossuet, and Bourdaloue, and many other Christian doctors, had analyzed and denounced the corrupting and enervating power of comedy. They did so in the name of a dogma. The "passion of love," they called "concupiscence." But he, Jean-Jacques, in the name of what did he condemn the too soft impressions the theater can give? In the name of nature, from which, so he affirms, the stage leads us away? Yet it seems that love, and desire, and voluptuousness spring from nature, since, certainly, according to the pulpit, to "fight nature," often means to "fight against the seduction of the senses." Of what nature, then, does Rousseau speak? Never, never shall we know.

(In truth, it is not in the name of "nature" that he condemns the stage, but in that of his old inherited Protestantism.)

With it all, the "Lettre sur les spectacles" is still pleasant reading. It is very Genevese and very Protestant, but of a smiling Geneva and of a relaxed Protestantism. It is far from the mad and somber exaggeration of the "Discours sur l'inégalité." All is not paradoxical in it, and even the paradoxes contain something of reason. It is, besides, of all Rousseau's books, the one which cost him the least effort. (He says that it took him just three weeks to write it.) He wanders off in twenty digressions; as far as he is able to do so, he frolics. One feels that it was written between two parts of the "Nouvelle Héloïse." . . .

The work had great success and brought forth answers, among them one from Marmontel and one from d'Alembert.

Marmontel's answer is a sensible and rather superficial refutation, an honest professor's production. But d'Alembert's answer is clever and has a keen edge; it is full of those malicious insinuations which in our day are called *rosseries.* I shall not go out of my way to cull them. One, however, I must quote—an atrocious one if, as I believe, it is an allusion to the desertion of his children by Rousseau. And it must be so, for, if we read the page which precedes it, it is easy to see that the dart was prepared beforehand, that it was intended and premeditated. Here it is: d'Alembert had just taken Rousseau to task for having adopted and defended in his "Lettre," the prejudice of the day concerning the education of women. Thereupon he exclaims:

"Philosophers, it is your duty to destroy so fatal a prejudice: it behooves *those among you who have felt the sweetness or sorrow of being fathers*, to be the first to shake off the yoke of a barbarous custom, by giving the same education to your daughters as to your other children. . . . We have often seen you, for very slight motives, *out of vanity or ill-humor*, tilt against the ideas of your time: for what higher motive could you brave them, *than for the weal of what is dearest to you, in order to render life less bitter to those who hold it from you?* . . ."

(Notice that d'Alembert must have known of the desertion of the children, since Rousseau confessed it a few years previously to Grimm, to Diderot, to Mme d'Epinay, to Mme de Francueil, etc.)

I pass over other less venomous insinuations. But d'Alembert could not fail to contrast the author of the "Devin" to the author of the "Lettre sur les spectacles," and this he does very wittily:

"Most of our Christian orators, when they attacked comedy, condemned that of which they were ignorant: you, yourself, on the contrary, have studied, analyzed, composed, in order better to judge of its effects, the dangerous poison from which you seek to preserve us; and you condemn our plays with the greater advantage of not only having seen them, but of having composed some. . . . Oh! I am well aware that theatrical representations, according to you, are necessary in a city as corrupt as that in which you dwelt so long; and evidently it was for its perverse inhabitants, for certainly it was not for your native country that you wrote them: that is to say, my dear sir, that you treated us like those poor, dying beasts whose agony one shortens out of sheer pity. Others, without your help, might have taken that trouble; and might not your delicacy toward us deserve to be blamed? I fear that it may be all the more so that the talent you displayed on the lyric stage and your happy efforts as musician and as poet are as likely to give partisans to the stage as your eloquence to deprive it of them. The pleasure we have in reading you will not hinder that of hearing you; and you will, for a long time to come, feel the pangs of seeing the 'Devin du village' destroy all the good which your writings against the stage might have produced."

This is a very pretty bit of satire, and which must have maddened Rousseau. And no doubt he could answer, and he had already almost answered in the preface to "Narcisse: "I have written for the stage, but this could do no further harm to beings as corrupt as you; and besides, I have given up writing comedies. And then, even if I have been false to my principles, is that a reason why I should not proclaim them?" But yet, it remains averred, that this man, who condemned the stage, composed comedies, and the very kind of artificial and gallant comedies which he so bitterly condemned: but yet, he wrote the "Devin," which by its music, its dances, its exhibitions of beautiful young women, must have inclined to sensuality, and have enervated the heart somewhat more, perhaps, than the "Misanthrope"; but yet, he wrote the "Discours contre les arts" at the very moment when he was writing for the stage; the "Lettre à d'Alembert" just after having done so; the "Discours sur l'inégalité," while he was dependent on the great, and his treatise on "Education," a few years after having abandoned his fifth child. . . . And all that is awkward, and I know not whether any other human life was ever spent in such contradictions and divisions against its own convictions. And if Jean-Jacques was but faintly aware of this, it is, as I believe, that he came into the world somewhat daft.

But let us join him in his cottage of Montlouis.

During the first months his life there was peaceful enough. He became acquainted with his neighbors, quite intimate with Father Berthier, an Oratorian—and especially with M. Maltor, curate of Groslay, another good priest who was very kind to him. Besides, according to his own account, Jean-Jacques never met any but amiable priests.

However, Mme d'Epinay regretted having treated him so harshly. Saint-Lambert and Mme d'Houdetot had forgotten their grudge. They invited him to dinner at Paris. All passed off most amicably. Jean-Jacques was himself astonished that this meeting should have left him so calm. He came to the conclusion that Saint-Lambert was admirable. He already saw Mme d'Houdetot between Saint-Lambert and himself, as he was to see Julie d'Etanges between Wolmar and Saint-Preux.

He became acquainted with Malesherbes, who was of great use to him in the printing of the "Nouvelle Héloïse" (it was published in 1760 by Rey, of Amsterdam) and who pointed out himself the necessary corrections which might enable the work to appear freely in France. Malesherbes offered him a position as contributor to the "Journal des Savants." Rousseau refused. It was impossible for him to write on a given day and on a given subject. "One fancied," says he, "that I could make a business of writing, like other authors, whereas, I was never able to write, except under the impulse of emotion."

He began "Emile," immediately after the "Nouvelle Héloïse."

He had visitors from Paris, but not over-numerous; just enough to make him appreciate his solitude. However, for the twentieth time he made plans for definitive seclusion and retirement. He was determined, says he, to give up entirely high society, the composing of books, all literary occupation, and to remain for the rest of his days shut up in that narrow and peaceful sphere for which he felt he was born.

He was especially weary of living in the society of worldly people and under their roof. He remembered the irksomeness and annoyances which he had known at the Chevrette, or at Eaubonne, and he gives us, thereupon, many details with most amusing frankness. . . .

"Living with rich people, without having, like them, a costly establishment, I was forced to imitate them in many ways; and small expenses, which were nothing in their eyes, were for me as ruinous as they were indispensable. . . . Alone, without a valet, I was at the mercy of their servants, whose good graces I was forced to court, so as not to suffer too many privations. . . . Paris women, who are so intelligent, are quite at sea on such a subject, and by dint of wishing to save my purse, they ruined me. Did I sup far from home, the hostess, instead of allowing me to send for a cab, caused her horses to be harnessed to take me back; she was delighted to save me from spending twenty-four *sous* for my cab; as to the crown I had to give the coachman and footman, she never thought of these. If a lady wrote to me from Paris to the Hermitage or to Montmorency, so as to spare me the four *sous* of postage her letter would have cost me, she would send it by one of her servants, who would come on foot, would reach me dripping with perspiration, to whom I would give his dinner, and a crown, which surely he had richly earned. Did she invite me to spend a week or two with her in the country, she would say to herself: it will be an economy for the poor fellow, whose food, during that time, will cost him nothing. She did not reflect that, while I was with her, I did no work, that the expenses of my household, of my rent, of my linen and clothes continued; that I paid my barber double price, and that I should not have spent as much at home as I did with her. . . . I can affirm that I certainly spent twenty-five crowns at Mme d'Houdetot's at Eaubonne, where I slept but four or five times, and more than a hundred *pistoles*, both at Epinay and at the Chevrette, during the five or six years of my intimacy. These expenses were inevitable to a man of my sort, who never knew how to look out for himself nor to manage, and who hated the sight of a servant who waits on one unwillingly and grudgingly."

. . . No, no, he will never more frequent the great! Having at last retrieved his liberty, he will keep it. This time, his perpetual design of moral reform seemed genuine. One would say that he was ripe for the "inner life." The publisher, Rey, urged him to write the "Memoirs of his life." He mocked the "false simplicity" of Montaigne, who was careful only to confess amiable defects "whereas I felt—I, who have always believed myself to be, on the whole, the best of men—that there is not a human soul, however pure it may be, that does not hide some odious vice." And the end of the phrase would seem to convey some self-knowledge and some humility, were there not so much pride—or perhaps only much bravado—in its beginning. It matters not, he never appeared more reasonable and seemed determined to live henceforth in his corner.

But in the beginning of the summer the Maréchal and the Duchesse de Luxembourg took possession of their castle, which was near the cottage of Montlouis, and all his plans of retirement fell to the ground. The Duke and

Duchess were hospitably inclined toward him, and almost instantly he once more took up his chains; less heavy chains, it is true, than those of the Chevrette. Jean-Jacques imposed his conditions: he was only to be received in private: he was not to be forced to accept supper invitations. It would seem, besides, that M. and Mme de Luxembourg showed themselves far more discreet with him than Mme d'Epinay had done. But, all the same, he was no longer quite free. Our would-be savage could never help longing for liberty, nor could he help abdicating it into aristocratic hands. And so many backslidings lead us to think that, in reality, he was fond of that servitude.

It is true that this time he had fallen upon people who did not make him feel it overmuch.

The Maréchal de Luxembourg was an excellent man, cordial and simple-mannered. He at once made Rousseau's conquest by his good humor. He called him "my dear friend." Jean-Jacques took to adoring him, for he always began by adoration. Then, in spite of all, the Maréchal's high rank told upon him. From his letters it is evident that he thought of that rank much more than did the good Maréchal himself. And, with it all, Jean-Jacques wished to keep the appearance of a free man, whom greatness did not dazzle. Hence, a good deal of fuss. He writes to the Maréchal:

"Your kindness places me in a state of perplexity through the desire to prove myself worthy of it. I can well understand that one should with cold respect reject the attentions of the great whom one does not esteem; but how, without too much familiarity, shall I behave to you, sir, whom my heart honors, with you, whose intimacy I should seek *were you my equal?* Having desired to live only with my friends, I know but one language, that of friendship, of familiarity. I am aware that I ought to modify that language, considering *my estate and yours:* I know that my respect for your person does not exempt me from that due to *your rank*. . . . I eternally fear to be at fault either with you or with myself, to be familiar or cringing. . . ."

And so it goes on. Great Heavens! what a to-do, and how heavily expressed! In another letter:

"Ah! Monsieur le Maréchal, you cannot know how sweet it is to see that *inequality* is not incompatible with friendship, and that a *greater than oneself* can be one's friend."

Again! He spends his time dinging into the good man's ears that he is marshal and duke. (Ah! how different is this to the pretty attitude, so thoroughly at ease, of Voltaire with great lords!)

One day, the Genevese Coindet came to show the Maréchal some sketches for the illustration of the "Nouvelle Héloïse." The Maréchal kept him to dinner; and, as Coindet was obliged to return early to Paris, he said to the party: "Let us accompany M. Coindet on the road to Saint-Denis." The Maréchal had no idea that he was accomplishing a sublime act. But, after having told the incident, Jean-Jacques adds: "As for me, I was so moved that I could not utter a word. I followed behind, weeping like a child, and longing to kiss the footprints of the good Maréchal."

This bespeaks a kind heart, but it is too much, decidedly, it is too much! . . .

As to the Duchesse, you know her. Besenval, speaking of her when she was Duchesse de Boufflers, describes her as a monster of debauchery, drunkenness and wickedness. Of that, one is free to believe what one chooses. It is true that Besenval adds: "I know, of her, but one good trait, and that is the way she brought up her granddaughter, the Duchesse de Lauzun. That, one is bound to confess, was the perfection of an education, for she became the most perfect woman ever known." (As to the Maréchal, Besenval describes him as very commonplace.)

The Duchesse was fifty-one years of age when Rousseau was admitted into a sort of intimacy with her. Before her marriage the Maréchal had been publicly her lover. She was still beautiful, very intelligent, with a sharp wit, which was beginning to soften. After her husband's death (1764) she became, it seems, thoroughly kind, a kindness made of long experience. Under Louis XVI. she was considered as an oracle of good manners and urbanity, as one capable of maintaining the rules of "the best society." "Mme Geoffrin was a sort of oracle of taste, and Mme de Luxembourg of *the tone and usages of the world.*" Thus speaks the Prince de Ligne. Mme de Luxembourg was intelligent to the last, for she died in 1787.

The part she played in the world showed a bright mind, much tact and suppleness. She had no difficulty in winning Jean-Jacques, and she was kinder to him than had been the restless and teasing Mme d'Epinay, who, besides, was a second-class great lady. With the sensitive Jean-Jacques, Mme de Luxembourg was all simplicity, all serenity, all tolerance; she showed an admiration for him which seemed quite involuntary, and took care not to show over much of her own wit. The agreeable portrait he traces of her ends with these words: "I fancied, even at my first visit, that I did not displease her."

No, he did not displease her. His strangeness, his reputation as a "bear" full of genius, his curious talent (and then, in all times, fine ladies have liked to monopolize some celebrated man) were all in his favor. Besides, it must be confessed that, personally, he was not only interesting, but that he possessed real charm: for we see that enthusiastic admirers of his books did not feel their enthusiasm diminished when they came to know him —or coldness only came after a long period.

Here, then, once more, Rousseau had become a captive and under the patronage of a great lord and a great lady. He consented to live in a lovely little château in the park of Montmorency, while his cottage of Montlouis was being repaired. He went every day to the castle: in the morning, for dinner, during the afternoon, often, he remained to supper. "I scarcely left her," said he, speaking of the Duchesse. Before she was up, every morning, he would read the manuscript of the "Nouvelle Héloïse" to her: and that took time. He copied the whole for her in his beautiful handwriting at "so much a page." When he had finished reading the "Nouvelle Héloïse," he began "Emile."

"Mme de Luxembourg greatly took to 'Julie,' and to its author; she spoke but of me, was busied with me alone, said charming things to me all day long, embraced me ten times a day. She always wanted my chair next to hers; when some lords wanted my seat, she would tell them it was mine, and send them elsewhere."

The cottage of Montlouis repaired, he took possession of it once more, but he had the right, whenever he chose, to enjoy the delightful little château. Whether there or at Montlouis, M. and Mme de Luxembourg took their guests to him. They were always of the highest nobility. For, and there is no mistake about it, Rousseau was infinitely more run after by those people than was ever Voltaire. And Thérèse gave them dainty things to eat, and the fine ladies embraced Thérèse, after having partaken of her strawberries and cream.

Jean-Jacques was in the seventh heaven. But he is careful to inform us that so much brilliancy did not dazzle him, and that, in the midst of so much glory, he remained simple. (The same rather silly note is to be found later in Chateaubriand.)

"I call upon all those who knew me at that period," says Jean-Jacques, rather solemnly, "to say whether they ever noticed that I was dazzled by this success; whether they ever saw me less calm in my manner, less friendly with humble folk, less familiar with my neighbors," etc.

He praises himself for sometimes having supped with his neighbor, the mason, Pilleu, after having dined with the Luxembourgs. He never gets over his wonder at this.

Therefore, he was never happier. But he was destined to pay for that happiness, and that very soon.

And the lords and ladies who applauded him, who petted and embraced him, also paid for it—later.

The "Nouvelle Héloïse," printed at Amsterdam, appeared in France at the beginning of 1761, with prodigious success. "Emile" was ready a few months later. Out of prudence, Rousseau wished to have it printed and published, like "Julie," only in a foreign country. But, taking his interests to heart more than he did himself, Mme de Luxembourg and Malesherbes insisted that "Emile" should be, in due form, published in France at the same time as in Holland. Malesherbes offered to make the necessary corrections himself. And, as the printing lagged and Rousseau knew nothing of what was happening, he was wild with anxiety. But still, Malesherbes, censor of the press in France, Mme de Luxembourg, and the Prince de Conti, who had taken everything upon themselves, were responsible for all. . . .

The publication was eternally delayed, and Rousseau

once more fell ill. He fancied he was suffering from stone. The Maréchal had him examined by the celebrated Brother Côme. (Rousseau, I repeat, never received anything but kindness from Catholic priests and monks.) Brother Côme reassured Rousseau, and told him there was nothing of the sort, that he would doubtless suffer greatly, but live long.

And still "Emile" did not appear! . . . At last it came out in May, 1762. But alarming rumors were abroad. During the night of June 8, while Rousseau, according to his custom, was reading the Bible before going to sleep, he was warned that he had been condemned to arrest and that he must fly. He did not resist. Tender farewells. Mme de Luxembourg, Mme de Boufflers, Mme de Mirepoix, who were present, embraced him, weeping. The good Duke took him to a traveling coach that was in readiness.

Why was Rousseau condemned? Because the Parliament, having decided upon the expulsion of the Jesuits, wished to give pious persons some small compensation by falling upon a deist philosopher. "The seesaw of politics." In those days liberty of the press did not exist. We possess liberty of the press, but we have no liberty of conscience, no liberty of association, no liberty of education. One cannot have everything.

So poor Rousseau took to flight. This flight condemned him to eight years more of wandering and to confirmed madness.

Mme de Luxembourg, the Prince de Conti, and Malesherbes were answerable toward Jean-Jacques for this cruel mishap. And they must have been sorely troubled. Evidently, it had not depended upon them to prevent the Parliament's decree. At least, they might have foreseen it. I am quite of that opinion. But, when the thing was accomplished, what could they do? Nothing, save to advise Rousseau to fly, to give him time to do so and to provide the means. And so they did; and, probably, that was what the Parliament desired.

Rousseau could not defend himself without compromising Mme de Luxembourg, the Prince de Conti and Malesherbes. So, he did not defend himself. He behaved like a thoroughly honorable man. On this occasion, his powerful friends were beholden to him. They were bound to fidelity and even to gratitude. And they were faithful and grateful, yes—but perhaps not enough so, and for too short a time. But absence, time, the growing suspicions of Jean-Jacques, may serve as excuses.

And after all, it was his fault!

Listen to this paragraph, which, one feels, was written with real pleasure:

". . . That terrace was my drawing-room wherein I received M. and Mme de Luxembourg, the Duc de Villeroy, the Prince de Tingry, the Marquis d'Armentières, the Duchesse de Montmorency, the Duchesse de Boufflers, the Comtesse de Valentinois, the Comtesse de Boufflers, and other persons of the same rank (among them he might have added the Prince de Conti) who, from the castle, deigned to make the pilgrimage of Montlouis, *up a steep and fatiguing path.*"

Bless me! This takes the shine off the Hermitage. But what business had Jean-Jacques in such society?

These fine people, it is true, had exquisite manners and none, better than they, could turn a compliment. But, it must be confessed, these lords and ladies were privileged persons. They represented all that Rousseau, in his first works, pretended to abhor: worldly lies and corruption and most insolent inequality. This luxury, this refinement, this " inimitable life," could only remind Jean-Jacques of the prodigious mass of injustice and misery which it presupposed, and on which it fed. And yet one can say that life had become impossible to him without these extravagant aristocrats and these scandals of inequality. . . . A poor skeptic may frequent everybody: but not an apostle!

We are but weak creatures, and we should try to understand every sort of contradiction. But some contradictions are really too flagrant, too shameless, and really, with a little honesty and good taste, they might have been avoided. I dislike to see Rousseau at the Luxembourgs' as much as I dislike a socialist with millions, a high-born anarchist, or a priest who plays at being facetious and emancipated.

But they, on their side,—those princes, those dukes, and duchesses, and marchionesses, in a day when such titles meant something—what had they in common with Jean-

Jacques? Simply to live, to remain what they were, they had need of the social and political order of the day, they had need of the Church. That they should be interested in the public good, that they should, politically speaking, agree with Voltaire, with Montesquieu, later with Turgot, that one can understand. But this eccentric, half-mad being menaced them directly in all they held most dear! He menaced refined life; he menaced, from afar, property itself and all existing order, and the Church, and traditional and national education. . . . And they found him strange, but sympathetic, and they overwhelmed him with caresses. Did they, generously and disinterestedly, go the lengths of seeking self-destruction? No; but having no longer any faith, they did not understand. They were *snobs*, such as we have seen in our day. They boasted of liberty and free thought. They fancied, moreover, that they were merely applauding certain amusing and bizarre sentences. They never guessed that, thirty years later, the coarsest of those sentences, after having entered the brains of lawyers, attorneys, and professors, would filter into inferior brains and find their fruition in blind acts.

The excellent and virtuous Malesherbes, who gave himself so much trouble to get "Julie" and "Emile" printed, was to be sent to the scaffold by blackguards, intoxicated by the doctrines of Jean-Jacques.

In 1760 Amélie de Boufflers, granddaughter of Mme de Luxembourg and future Duchesse de Lauzun, was eleven years of age. "She had a pure face, and a maidenly timidity. . . ." One day, Rousseau met her alone on the staircase of the little château. . . . Not knowing what to say to her, he asked for a kiss which, in the innocence of her heart, she gave him. Thirty-three years later, the Duchesse de Lauzun, the purest and gentlest among the well-known women of the eighteenth century, was condemned to death by men who were the most fervent of Rousseau's adorers.

And if one recalls the mysterious and fatal chain of effects and causes, would it be mere declamation to say: Was not that kiss, given to little Amélie de Boufflers by Jean-Jacques—he who likewise knew not—already the kiss of the guillotine?

THE "NOUVELLE HÉLOÏSE"

CHAPTER VI

THE "NOUVELLE HÉLOÏSE"

THOSE who insist on attributing all the books of Rousseau to a single theory, assure us that the meaning of the "Nouvelle Héloïse" is this: "If we cannot return to the state of nature, corrupted by society, each of us can, even in the present state of civilization, re-create natural man within himself." And they think that Rousseau was bound, after the "Discours sur l'inégalité" and the "Lettre sur les spectacles," to write the "Nouvelle Héloïse," as he was bound later, necessarily, to write "Emile" and the "Contrat social."

They may be right, but I am not so sure of it. It seems to me, (and we have seen it so far) that Rousseau's books do not all flow from the same premeditated system (whatever he may say, later on, in his "Dialogues"), but that they sprang from circumstances—I mean the circumstances of his own life. The same temperament, the same sort of sensitiveness and, in general, the same sentiments and the same dreams can be found, more or less, in all his works; that was inevitable. His books arose out of the same deep and turbid source: but I do not see that they grew out logically, one from the other. (I shall speak of this again in my conclusions.)

Let us see how was born "Julie" or the "Nouvelle

Héloïse." He tells us all about it, profusely and a little confusedly, in book ix. of his "Confessions."

It was during the month of June. He was at the Hermitage. He took long rambles in the woods. He mused. It seemed to him that "fate owed him something which it had never given him." What? Friendship, love; love most of all. "How was it that with inflammable senses, with a heart full of love, I should never, at least once, have burned for any particular object?" He recalled all the women who had moved him in his youth, "Mlle Galley, Mlle de Graffenried, Mlle de Breil, Mme Basile, Mme de Larnage, my pretty pupils, and even the sprightly Zulietta." (He squarely forgets Mme de Warens.)

Alas! In vain did he conjure up his love reminiscences. All that was very meager, and he knew it well. These were but sketches of adventures. "I have spent my life," says he, somewhere, "full of desire, and silent near those I most loved."

Oh! if he could but know real love! But Jean-Jacques was then forty-five years of age; it was too late; besides, he would not hurt Thérèse's feelings.

"Then," says he, "the impossibility of attaining to reality threw me into the land of dreams; seeing no being worthy of my delirious passion, I placed one in an ideal world, which my creative imagination soon peopled with beings according to my own heart. . . . I evoked two friends. . . . One I made a brunette, the other fair; one lively, the other gentle; one virtuous, the other weak, *but so touching in her weakness that virtue seemed to have gained by it.* (Evidently!) I gave to one a lover whose tender friend the other one became, and even something more. . . . In love with my two charming models, I identified myself as much as possible with the lover and the friend; but I made him amiable and young, *giving him moreover the virtues and the faults which I felt in myself.*"

After which he chose a home for them; he first thought of the Borromeo islands, and finally placed them at Vevey, on his own dear lake. He then began to write, says he, without method, merely in order to "give vent to the desire for love, which he had never satisfied, and which he felt was devouring him." He affirms that the first two parts of "Julie" were written after that fashion, "*without any real plan,* and even without guessing that he might one day be tempted to make of it a regular work."

He looked upon his sketched-in novel so little in the light of a development or an application of his doctrine, that he regarded it, on the contrary, as a sort of refutation of his public rôle.

"After the severe principles which I had just so noisily advocated . . . after so many biting invectives against effeminate books, impregnated with love and softness, what could be more unexpected, more *shocking,* than to see me suddenly place myself among the authors of those books I had so roughly censured? I felt this inconsistency in all its force."

This would tend to prove that Rousseau had conceived the first two parts of "Julie" merely as a love story, and that the moralizing intentions only came to him afterward.

Meanwhile he met Mme d'Houdetot again, both at the Chevrette and at the Hermitage. Immediately, his ideal was realized in her. He saw Julie through her. What an occasion to put into practice the exalted sentiments which he wished to express in his book! In their secret trystings, in their burning conversations (on his part, at least) while Mme d'Houdetot diverted herself during Saint-Lambert's absence, Jean-Jacques was, in reality, working up his novel. And that explains that he should have so easily consoled himself for the sudden end of this great passion. It was nothing but literature.

However, what, till then, he had written of "Julie," haphazard, and without any plot, did not even constitute a story. But, "by dint," says he, "of turning over and over again my dreams in my mind, I formed a sort of plan, of which one has seen the result." And then he tells us that he had, in his novel, two objects. The first was to show to a corrupt generation, by putting oneself on its level, how one can recover from a fall, and that the error of a moment can become the source of sublime acts. "If Julie had always been virtuous," will he say later, in his "Seconde préface," "she would teach us fewer things, for to whom could she serve as a model?" And his second object is to unite believers and atheists in reciprocal esteem; to teach to the latter that one can have faith in God without being a hypocrite, and to believers, that a man may be incredulous without, for that, being a rascal. Julie, pious, is an example to the philosophers, and Wolmar, atheist, is one to the intolerant. The rest, and especially the call to a simple life, to rural and family life, and to the purity of the domestic hearth, was evidently added afterward.

This is what Rousseau says in book ix. of the "Confessions." It is plausible. But I believe that the novel of "Julie" had a still simpler origin.

All that I shall accept of his narrative is that the idea of "Julie" came to him in the springtime, among flowers and trees, during months of sentimental excitement, and that, above all, it was his own imagined romance.

In these strolls through the woods he remembered his vagrant youth, which was thus transfigured in his eyes. Now, one of his most frequent dreams at that time—and which he realized with Mme d'Houdetot more or less, and too late, at forty-five—was to be loved by some beautiful aristocrat. A fugitive from Geneva, wandering through Savoy and Piedmont, he could scarcely come upon a castle or country house, without indulging in this dream:

"I entered with confidence upon the great world . . . It will soon resound with my praise . . . In showing myself, I was about to stir the universe . . . But so much I did not need . . . A single manor bounded my ambition: a favorite with its lord and lady, the daughter's lover, friend of her father, and protector of the neighbors, I was content; I needed nothing more."

And a little later, at Turin:

"My hostess told me that she had found for me a place, and that a high-born lady wished to see me. At this, I sincerely believed myself to be launched in great adventures, for *I always came back to this.*"

But, above all, he recalls Mlle de Breil, at the Gouvons', where he was footman:

"Mlle de Breil was a young girl about my age, well-formed, rather tall, white-skinned, with very black hair and, though a brunette, showing in her countenance that gentleness of fair women, which my heart could not resist. The court dress, so favorable to young ladies, showed off her pretty figure, displayed her bosom and her shoulders, and rendered her complexion still more dazzling, from the mourning which she still wore. One might say that it was not a servant's right to notice these things [a painful sentence] . . . At table, I watched for every occasion to distinguish myself. If her footman, for a moment, left her chair, at once I took his place: from a distance, opposite to her, I sought in her eyes what she needed, and seized the instant wherein to change her plate. What would I not have given to induce her to give me an order, to look at me, to say a single word to me! But she never did; I suffered the mortification of being nothing to her; she ignored my presence."

Once, however, and yet another time, he attracted her attention, and under very flattering circumstances for him: "She glanced at me. That look, however transient, thrilled me with delight." And the second time:

"That moment was short, but in every sense delicious. . . . A few minutes later Mlle de Breil, lifting her eyes to mine, asked in a tone as gracious as it was timid for some water. One guesses that I did not allow her to wait; but on nearing her, I was seized with such a fit of trembling that, having over-filled the glass, a part of the water was spilt on her plate and even on her. Her brother thoughtlessly asked me what made me tremble so. This question added to my confusion, and Mlle de Breil blushed up to her eyes."

Ruy Blas . . . it is truly Ruy Blas, Ruy Blas still under his real name and not disguised as Don César. . . . But no doubt the mother noticed something and spoke to the young girl. In vain Jean-Jacques waited whenever he could, in the entrance hall of Mme de Breil; he obtained no further recognition from the daughter. And on two occasions Mme de Breil very curtly asked him "if he had no work to do." "I was forced," says he, "to give up this dear hall." And he terminates by saying: "Thus ended the romance."

Well, it is clear to my mind that the two first parts of the "Nouvelle Héloïse" are the conclusion of that romance, the romance of all his youth, and that they are nothing more, and that he conceived them and, at first wrote them, for his own pleasure, without thinking of what was to follow.

Jean-Jacques must be loved by her whom in the "Confessions" he calls "the young lady of the manor"; he must make her his: afterward, come what will. And this is the way in which things came to pass in his mind.

Personages: himself, Jean-Jacques, under the name of Saint-Preux; Julie d'Étanges; the Baron d'Étanges, her father, a gentleman full of prejudices (that becomes evident in the course of the story); the Baronne d'Étanges, an indolent and insignificant mother (in order to facilitate and explain certain facts). Then, as secondary personages: the sprightly Claire, by way of contrast with the tender Julie; the energetic and cold Lord Edward, the foil to Saint-Preux, ardent and weak. Background: the landscape Jean-Jacques best knows and loves: the shores of Lake Geneva.

The novel was written in form of letters, for greater ease, so that the author might be prolix at will, and because the oratorical or lyrical form (discourse or outpourings) was most natural to him. The novel somewhat recalls "Clarissa Harlowe" of Richardson, and a little, a very little, "Marianne" of Marivaux.[1] Add to this, if you wish, vague and distant reminiscences of the seven-

[1] 1688-1763.

teenth century romances which, with his father, he read in his childhood.

But in order that Julie's seduction might be possible, the author places Saint-Preux somewhat higher in the social scale than Jean-Jacques was himself, at Turin. Saint-Preux belonged to the middle classes, was of uncertain parentage, well-educated, intelligent, besides, alone in the world, like Ruy Blas, Didier,[1] and their romantic brethren. Just enough of a plebeian to cause social prejudices to oppose his marriage with Julie. On the other hand, Julie had been brought up by a servant who was a rather cynical gossip. In the absence of her husband the Baronne d'Étanges, singularly imprudent, had asked Saint-Preux to give Julie some lessons. Saint-Preux was twenty years of age, Julie eighteen. One guesses the result.

It came pretty rapidly. After some long letters and a somewhat short resistance, Julie, with the help of a friend, the lively Claire, one evening meets Saint-Preux in a grove, kisses him, and flies. After which (and here I simply copy the headings of some chapters) "she requires her lover to absent himself for a short time, and sends him enough money for him to return to his own country and to see to his affairs. The lover submits, but through pride sends back the money. Indignation of Julie at the refusal of her lover. She sends him double the amount. Her lover accepts the sum and leaves." Well, and what then? Julie's arguments are conclusive,

[1] Hero of Victor Hugo's "Marion Delorme."

I assure you; and then, had not Jean-Jacques in the past, and without any embarrassment, been dependent on Mme de Warens? . . . And why does he provoke this unexpected complication, if not because he remembers?

During the absence of Saint-Preux, Baron d'Étanges returns. When the merits of Saint-Preux are dwelt upon in his presence, he declares that he will never give his daughter to a plebeian, but that he destines her for a nobleman, a friend of his. Julie falls ill, secretly calls back Saint-Preux and—" loses her innocence."

She grants a second meeting to her lover. But then she puts it off and forces Saint-Preux to absent himself for two days, for an act of charity which it is needless to explain. Providence rewards them for their sacrifice, for the absence of Saint-Preux saves them from a serious danger.

And Julie, in her turn, rewards him by granting a night meeting. I pass over several episodes. Then Julie has a miscarriage, all this, most secretly. Then Lord Edward, friendly to Saint-Preux, having advised Julie's father to let her marry her professor, the Baron, furious, indulges in a terrible outburst against his wife and daughter; and the subtle Claire manages to send off Saint-Preux to Paris. Before that, Julie swears to him that though, without her father's consent, she will never marry him, yet she will never belong to another, without the consent of Saint-Preux.

And here we have the story—so often written since—of the teacher and the young aristocrat. I have only mentioned the essential facts; in this prolix "Julie," that comprises twelve hundred pages, there are, perhaps, four hundred that concern the story itself; of these, I have analyzed about a third.

This part is, and by far, the most wearisome (with the exception of the digressions: Saint-Preux's journey in the Valais and his letters from Paris). Yet, in all probability it is the part of his book which Rousseau wrote with most ardor. It is of this first volume of "Héloïse" that Mme d'Epinay said in her "Mémoires: "After dinner we read Rousseau's work. I was so out of sorts that I was not satisfied. It is wonderfully well written, but it is too much arranged, and seems to me without life and heat. The personages never say what they ought to say. It is always the author who speaks." And so, or nearly so, thought Mme du Deffand and Mme de Choiseul, and even Diderot (who was then still Rousseau's friend). Of all Rousseau's works this volume is, with certain passages of "Emile," that of which it is easiest to make fun. The animation is all wordy. Three displeasing things (at least) are noticeable in it: the abuse of the word virtue, and the constantly equivocal sense given to the word; the indelicacy of the sentiments; the definitive introduction of the deplorably maudlin style which became that of "men of heart."

First—It is extraordinary that a young man and a girl, who act as did Saint-Preux and Julie, and who think of nothing else, should so eternally talk of virtue. They say somewhere that, in spite of their fault, they, for all the rest, remain virtuous and have not lost their right to love virtue. Evidently: but their fault is not only the result of human weakness, toward which one might be indulgent; it implies a somewhat cowardly abuse of confidence, Saint-Preux being Julie's professor: this, they seem to ignore entirely. This renders still more unpleasant their eternal apostrophes to virtue and gives them an appearance either of hypocrisy or of equally unfortunate unconsciousness. . . . And this mania of putting virtue where it is quite out of place is most distressing. This is imputable to Rousseau and the eighteenth century. *Nothing like it is to be found during the seventeenth century, nor in ancient times.*

In reality, this is the great contradiction of all Rousseau's life, and I have already alluded to it. Saint-Preux and Julie believe themselves to be virtuous because they "adore" virtue, and feel that their hearts are overflowing with "the milk of human kindness." They resemble their father: noble sentiments, fine speeches, and an ugly life (at least up to the fortieth year).

Second—In the second place, Julie is singularly wanting in moral delicacy. She seems far too well instructed; she calls a spade a spade. She says clumsily, "My virtue . . . my innocence . . . my dishonor . . ." She speaks of conquered "desires," of the "pleasures of vice . . ." It is quite delicious to see her write to her lover while giving him a "rendezvous" in the summerhouse. "Oh! nature! . . . There, we shall find ourselves under its auspices and *listen only to its laws.*"

But, here again, she was but the image of her father. Her immodesty is that of Rousseau.

Third—Finally, in the first two parts of "Julie," more, even, than elsewhere, we find the frightful expansion of sentimental phraseology. This style implies a sort of conventionality which always, on every occasion, presupposes that natural sentiments, family affections, maternal, paternal, filial, conjugal love, friendship, pity, humanity, can only be expressed convulsively, in noble words, solemn, emphatic, punctuated by exclamations, apostrophes, suspensions, shudders, silences. . . . To tell the truth, this style had come into existence before Jean-Jacques. It was to be found in the novels of Abbé Prévost,[1] still more in Diderot's works. But Jean-Jacques, in the first third of "Julie," made of it a triumphant and stupefying use. Here are a few examples of that style, really taken at random, for they are to be found on every page.

Julie had met her father, after his absence (she could not have loved him over-much, from what we have seen):

"Oh, you, whom I most love, after the author of my days," writes she, to Saint-Preux, "why do your letters, your quarrels, come to sadden my soul? . . . You would have me think of you incessantly; but, tell me, could you love an unnatural daughter, in whom the fire of love could obliterate the rights of kinship, and whom the complaints of a lover could render insensible to a father's caresses!"

[1] 1697-1763.

And here is a family picture:

". . . I pretended that I was slipping; in order to steady myself, I threw my arms about my father's neck; my face touched his venerable face, and, instantly, it was covered with my kisses and my tears; mingling with them were those that flowed from his eyes, and I knew that his great sorrow had given way; my mother joined her transports to ours. Sweet and peaceful innocence, which alone was wanting to my heart, to make this scene of nature the most delicious moment of my life!" etc., etc.

As to me, I believe that this emphatic and tear-stained style was sincere with Rousseau; that this unnatural style, with him, was natural. Why? Because he was ill, a prey to nervous maladies; because, in the real sense of the word, he was morbidly sensitive; because he, himself, on the least provocation, was eternally bursting into tears. But alas! he had imitators, and that was horrible.

In Louis XVI.'s time, and still more, under the Revolution, nearly all literature was infested by this Rousseau-like sentimentality. It in no way came from the heart: it was especially a strained effort to appear penetrated with altruistic emotions, because this was supposed to be honorable. A great deal of artifice and vanity, therefore, and consequently very little real kindness, entered into it, since the preoccupation of seeming to be, in the eyes of others and in one's own eyes, in a praiseworthy attitude, was the very reverse of real goodness, which presupposes forgetfulness of self, or at least, the effort to forget oneself. And that is why their "sentimentality" by no means prevented the revolutionaries from being pitiless. Then, this sentimentality, being a fashion, and, consequently, being adopted by the most mediocre of creatures, quickly assumed an appearance of inexpressible stupidity. And finally, as this sentimentality was supposed to be noble, it assumed what idiots thought to be a "noble style," that is, the most emphatic, the most foolish phraseology possible—a nameless jargon. And thus some of the writers of the second half of the eighteenth century seem more removed from us, stranger, more barbarous, than the "précieux" or the "burlesques" of the seventeenth century or the pedants of the sixteenth. In order to understand this, glance over the plays of Sébastien Mercier,[1] or the love letters or even the family correspondence of certain "Conventionnels," or certain forgotten novels of the Terror. Rousseau not only made the Revolution heir to his political vocabulary, his festivities and his State conception, but he also left it a ridiculous style.

We have come to the end of the first period of the loves between the schoolmaster and the young aristocrat. It is glacial (it was merely the child of Jean-Jacques' brain, an artificial love, booky and the result of will, as was his own passion for Mme d'Houdetot); and it is sometimes ridiculous and often wearisome. And I am well pleased to be done with it: for what follows is very beautiful, a little mad, but always interesting.

[1] 1740-1814.

The two lovers being separated, one in Paris, the other at Vevey, Rousseau asks himself what he is going to do with Julie. Remember that, just then, his artificial love for Mme d'Houdetot had greatly subsided. I doubt whether he ever for a moment thought of marrying, after some incidents, Saint-Preux to his pupil; such an ending would have seemed too flat. No, but at that point he remembered his rôle as reformer of manners and professor of virtue. And why should we say his "rôle"? He was not modest, he did not know himself thoroughly, but he had come to be sincere in his plan of reform, and of inner perfection. His own life, when we see it in its entirety, appears to us like an evolution, like an effort, often full of illusions, but still a striving after virtue, a kind of slow uprising from his pristine mire, like an ascension which his madness, ever creeping on, will not arrest; quite the reverse.

And then (of that I am persuaded) he thought of merging Julie's existence into his own. Julie also was an unfortunate and weak being, who had stumbled at life's threshold. Well, her life, like Rousseau's, must be the story of a moral evolution, of a "conversion" (that is the real term). And even he will become convinced (afterwards, I fancy) that he only made Julie sin in order to convert her.

"I feel two men in me," says Saint Paul in his Epistle to the Romans. As I have already told you, there were many more than two men in Jean-Jacques. There was the vagabond teeming with desires, the never-satisfied lover, the quondam lackey, in love with the daughter of the house—this is the man who wrote the first two parts of "Julie." The advocate of nature and simple life will describe life in the Clarens house. The proud and romantic dreamer will tell us of the complicated household: Wolmar-Saint-Preux-Julie-Claire. Meanwhile, it is the Genevese, the Protestant, mellowed by Catholicism, the deeply religious man, who "converted" Julie d'Étanges.

He converted her by giving her M. de Wolmar as husband.

The intrigue is cleverly managed so as to force us to accept this marriage. Mme d'Étanges dies; she dies of her husband's hardness, and, especially, of her daughter's fault, and of the secret thereof which she guards, and which weighs on her. Julie, in despair, causes Saint-Preux to release her from her promise. After a decent time—and with the consent of Saint-Preux absent, and who really could not refuse it—she resigns herself to marry M. de Wolmar, that friend whom her father had destined for her. She makes up her mind because, when she had been promised to Wolmar, he was rich, and he is now ruined; she goes to the altar like a victim.

Here, Rousseau has an admirable thought. (It is, perhaps, the portion of his work where the traditional depths of his nature, often in contradiction with his revolutionary soul, most unexpectedly comes to the surface.) The marriage ceremony acts on Julie's serious character after the fashion of a sacrament, like the visible sign of something deep, sacred, necessary, in harmony with the destinies and interests of humanity. The wedding ceremony causes Julie to understand marriage.

This, she had not foreseen:

"At that very moment," she writes to Saint-Preux, "when I was about to swear eternal fidelity to another, my heart swore to you an eternal love, and I was led to the temple like a stained victim that must defile the sacrifice to which it is doomed."

But, mourning as she was and prepared by sorrow, she felt, once in the church, a sort of emotion such as she had never before experienced. . . . Then, the tempered light, the deep silence of the spectators, the family assembled . . . all that gave to what was to take place a solemnity which excited attention and respect:

"The purity, the dignity, the holiness of marriage, so powerfully expressed by the words of Scripture, its chaste and sublime duties, so important to the happiness, the order, the peace, the duration of humanity, so sweet to accept for themselves: all that caused me such an impression that I felt a sudden interior revolution. An unknown power seemed suddenly to allay the disorder of my affections, and to redress them according to the law of duty and of nature."

And again:

"It seemed to me that I was born anew, that I was about to begin another life."

Then, when she returned to the house:

"Instantly, penetrated with a lively sense of the danger from which I had been delivered, and of the honorable and safe state in which I felt myself re-established, I prostrated myself, I lifted my hands in supplication to Heaven, I invoked the Being who sustains or destroys, when He chooses, by our own strength, the liberty He grants us. 'I desire,' said I, 'the good which Thou willest, and of which Thou alone art the source. I promise to love the mate Thou hast given me. I promise to be faithful, because fidelity is the first tie of the family, and of society. I promise to be chaste, because chastity is the first of virtues, and strengthens all the others. I accept all that touches the order of nature which Thou hast established, and the law of reason which I hold from Thee. I put my heart in Thy keeping and my desires in Thy hand. That all my affections may be in harmony with Thy will; and do not permit the error of a moment to overshadow the choice of my whole life.'"

But, you will say, and Rousseau's theories? Which? The opposition of nature and society, and, that society had corrupted nature. Marriage is certainly, I fancy, a social institution, and yet marriage purifies Julie. She says herself that an unknown power re-establishes her affections "according to the law of duty *and* of nature." "Nature *and* duty" can only here be a social duty—does Rousseau realize this? Are nature and society, therefore, no longer at war? Can a social institution, therefore, be beneficent? Does not society, therefore, necessarily corrupt nature? Well, and after all, Rousseau contradicts himself; that is self-evident. But that is why this third part of the "Nouvelle Héloïse" is so fine a production. And it contains many another contradiction to Rousseau's habitual theories.

Julie loves her husband because she is his wife, and is determined to love him. Such, the Pauline of "Polyeucte." And so, for once, Rousseau and Corneille meet. Julie's love for Wolmar is, perhaps, nothing but affection and tenderness. But she expresses this eminently sensible thought: "To make a happy marriage, love is not necessary," and this thought of still greater wisdom, and which gives the death-blow to the "morality of sentiment," condemns the whole of Rousseau's own life, and the three-fourths of his production:

"Despite the firmness of my heart, *I will no longer be judge in my own cause,* nor give myself up, as woman, to the same *presumption* which caused my fall as a girl."

And how magnificently, in this third part, the sophistries and impure sentimentalism of the first volume—so dear to Jean-Jacques, when he wrote them—are swept away as by a strong and salubrious wind! Already, in Saint-Preux's first letters, and even in Julie's, one foresaw the theory of the fatalism of love, and even that of passion's sovereign right. "Have you not," said Saint-

Preux, "followed nature's purest law? How can you expect a thrilling soul to taste with moderation of the infinite good?" And again, "Know it at last, my Julie, an eternal decree of Heaven destined us one for the other —this is the first law which we must accept." And Julie, fallen, he once more speaks of virtue, and she also. But listen to Julie, once married:

"I shudder to think that we dared to speak of virtue. Do you understand what meant for us so sacred and so profaned a word? It was this wild love which burned within us, which disguised our transports under the name of its holy enthusiasms, *to make it yet dearer to us, and to deceive us longer.* : . . It is time that the *illusion should cease.*"

And again Julie says to Saint-Preux:

"With the feelings I entertained for you and what I now know, were I free and mistress of my fate, it is not you whom I should choose as husband, but M. de Wolmar."

And she says even this decisive word: "Were Heaven to take my husband from me, my firm resolution is never to accept another."

Yet (and that shows keen observation), Julie did not, at one bound, reach perfect wisdom. She was imprudent enough to say, "Be my soul's lover," a dangerous sentiment, which will find its echo in hundreds and thousands of novels during the nineteenth century. That was not all. When she allows herself to be married, having yet but a vacillating and divided conscience, she promises her father not to confess her past conduct to M. de Wolmar. Now, that she has found light and reflects, this secret weighs cruelly upon her. "For," says she, "unreserved sincerity forms part of the fidelity I owe my husband." She deems it right to consult Saint-Preux himself on the subject. The question is a highly interesting one. It is of the same order (in spite of differences in details) as the one agitated in "Monsieur Alphonse,"[1] in George Sand's "Jacques," in the "Lady of the Sea" of Ibsen, and even in the "Princesse de Cleves."[2]

Saint-Preux, for specious reasons, does not advise the disclosure. Julie answers; he again writes. The discussion is a very close and very fine one. Julie, wavering, consents to wait. But she bravely and definitely bids adieu to Saint-Preux: "It is time to perform our duty. This is my last letter to you; I beg you to write to me no more." Saint-Preux is on the point of killing himself. He refrains, but he starts on a voyage which lasts three years.

Julie is now twenty-eight. She has been married six years. Her secret grows heavier and heavier. She does not speak for fear of too cruelly afflicting her husband. But she has a child, and then courage comes to her. She confesses all to Wolmar. But the scene that we expected, unfortunately, remained in the writer's pen; we learn of it only through this astounding letter from "M. de Wolmar to Julie's lover":

"Though we do not know each other, I am commis-

[1] Alexander Dumas, fils. [2] Mme de LaFayette.

sioned to write to you. The wisest and most beloved of women has opened her heart to her happy husband [that is, I suppose that she confessed having received Saint-Preux in her room, as a young girl, and that she, later, had a miscarriage]. He [the happy husband] thinks you worthy of having been loved by her, and *opens his house to you.* Innocence and *peace* reign in it; here you will find friendship, hospitality, esteem, and truthfulness. Consult your heart, and, if you see nothing which need alarm you, come fearlessly. When you depart, you will leave a friend behind you.

"*Postscript by Julie.* Come, my friend, we await you eagerly. Do not give me the sorrow of a refusal."

And thus, after a hundred and fifty pages, luminous with something like purity, with reason and emotion, and, in one word, with human truth, we are plunged anew in most displeasing fantasy.

Why? Because Rousseau loves Saint-Preux, who is his own self, weak, passive, plaintive, uncertain, and passionate. How can he dispose of Saint-Preux? He cannot send him around the world; he has not the courage to make him die; he refuses to cure him of a passion which owes it to itself to be incurable. . . . But then? . . . What if he were to bring him back to Clarens, near Julie, near Wolmar? Why not? That would satisfy everybody. We are not among ordinary people. Jean-Jacques remembers the imperturbable Saint-Lambert. Did Saint-Lambert, after the first few days, feel ill at ease between

Mme d'Houdetot and himself, Jean-Jacques? Or Mme d'Houdetot between Jean-Jacques and Saint-Lambert? Or Jean-Jacques between Saint-Lambert and Mme d'Houdetot? And, in former times, was he ill at ease between Mme de Warens and Claude Anet? Or Claude Anet between him and Mme de Warens? Or Mme de Warens between him and Claude Anet? Are not all situations acceptable when one is virtuous and sincere? He forgets that neither he nor Claude Anet was the husband of the lady of the Charmettes. He forgets that, with regard to the other trio, he, Jean-Jacques, had never been Mme d'Houdetot's lover, and that Saint-Lambert, on that head, was quite reassured. Never mind. Why should not Wolmar be a superior Saint-Lambert—Saint-Lambert as he might have been?

And so it came to pass. He united, for their happiness, a happiness watered by his tears, all whom he loved: Julie, her husband, her lover—and, later, Claire d'Orbe, her confidante and accomplice. All these people lived very comfortably together, for to the pure all is pure, and among virtue's duties, Jean-Jacques deliberately omits the avoidance of temptation.

And, then, what happens is really extraordinary.

If M. de Wolmar was so little moved by Julie's confession, it was that he knew all about the affair—all—when he married her. As soon as he learns from her that she had had a lover, he says to her (as we have seen): "Let us invite him." Saint-Preux, therefore, returned. There was scarcely a shade of embarrassment at the first interview. But, soon Julie began to talk of the past with Saint-Preux, in the presence of her husband. And, as the former lover showed a little reserve: "Embrace her," exclaimed Wolmar, "and call her Julie. The more familiar you are with her, the better I shall think of you."

They all three lived in a state of perpetual emotion, of which here is an example (in a letter from Saint-Preux to Lord Edward). Saint-Preux, while conversing with her, says sadly to Julie: "Madame, you are a wife and a mother; those are joys which you have a right to know."

"Immediately," continues he, "M. de Wolmar, seizing my hand and pressing it, exclaimed, 'You have friends; those friends have children; how should paternal affection be unknown to you?' I looked at him; I looked at Julie; they looked at each other and then at me, with so touching an expression that, much moved, I exclaimed: 'They are as dear to me as to you!'"

And, later on, Wolmar asks Saint-Preux to be his children's tutor.

Another time, when they were together visiting a garden which the Wolmars were having made: "I have but one reproach to address to your Eden," said Saint-Preux, looking at Julie, "that is its superfluity. Why should you want new walks when, close to the house, you have such charming and such neglected shrubberies? [You remember the kiss given and returned in one of those shrubberies?] Then, M. de Wolmar interrupts: "Never has my wife, since her marriage, entered the shrubbery to which you allude. *I know the reason of this,* though she never told it to me. *You who are aware of it,* learn to respect the place in which you are; it has been cultivated by the hand of virtue." That Wolmar was certainly an original person!

Wolmar proved this on more than one occasion. One day he announced to them that he was about to absent himself for a week, and he desired them to remain together.

During his absence, while sailing on the lake, the two lovers are sorely tempted; but, naturally, they overcome the temptation. Outside of that incident, they spent their time bewailing Wolmar's incredulity; he was perfection itself, but he was an atheist. And this common fear for Wolmar's soul was another bond between Julie and her former lover, which might have proved dangerous had they, at that time, been merely human. . . .

Here, for the fourth time, Rousseau was rather embarrassed. What could he do with his trio? . . . Well, he will change it into a quartette; create a still more complicated moral situation, out of which he can extract more emotion and more touching speeches. The "vivacious" Claire, who had married a M. d'Orbe, had become a widow. She returned to Clarens. The four friends spent a whole day in effusions and transports.

However, and by way of a little change, Saint-Preux started for Rome, called thither by Lord Edward. Wolmar, seeing the despair of Saint-Preux on the point of leaving, gave him this delicate advice: ". . . See but a sister *in her who was your mistress.* . . . Think by day of what you are to do in Rome—you will think less *at night of what happened at Vevey.*"

But Saint-Preux soon returned. The lively Claire, by dint of being the confidante and accomplice of Julie's loves, was scorched by the flame. Julie discovered that Claire loved Saint-Preux. She advised marriage, for she herself felt that things could not continue thus. . . . "Claire resisted, not wishing for a heart worn out with passion for another." . . . Then, she sounds Saint-Preux. He declined, not feeling sure of himself: "The wound is healing, but the scar remains."

As you have noticed, during the second half of the novel (six hundred pages) all the personages, and that by their fault, are in a false position: Julie between her husband, her former lover, and her friend in love with that lover; Saint-Preux between his former mistress, her husband, and this latter's friend, now in love with Saint-Preux; Wolmar between his wife, the former lover of his wife, and the former accomplice of his wife; Claire, finally, between her friend, and the former lover of that friend, with whom she is in love. . . . And they all live, all four of them, near each other, in close communion.

Oh! I know that in the world of sentiment anything may happen, and that psychology is not an exact science. Still, while they wander, eat, converse, and grow sentimental day in, day out, unavoidably, the same precise and concrete images arise before their minds; each knows what images are in the minds of the three others. I do not speak of that excellent Wolmar, who goes to the very extreme limits of philosophical eccentricity, but there seems great danger that Saint-Preux, called back, might once more become Julie's lover, or that he might become Claire's—did all these people belong to common humanity. But they did not (and Rousseau intended in this third volume that this should be their particular trait); they differed broadly from it; in the midst of their sufferings they rejoiced at being exceptions, at being wildly romantic, and "they particularly desired, partly from pride, partly from a refinement of imagination, not to be like others" (Faguet).

In a word, they resembled their father, Jean-Jacques. Jean-Jacques like them, and for them, and for themselves, craved singular situations. . . . In the first place, because he himself had been accustomed to them, having often been in love with, and tolerated by, women who had lovers; then, because he was strangely exempt from physical jealousy; finally, because these abnormal and complicated situations gave rise to rare sentiments, which by their strangeness seemed to him sublime.

And so he pushed his heroes into a blind alley. . . . At that point he, decidedly, no longer knows what to do with them. Allow them to sin? But, then, what about the foregoing sublime sentiments? Allow them to grow old, and peaceful, and indifferent? Horror! "The situation is without any logical issue" (Faguet).

Julie then throws herself into the water to save her little boy. She contracts a disease which the author does not specify, but which is evidently pleurisy. On her sickbed she grows maudlin, before her husband, over her first love; by anticipation, she declaims the essential parts of the "Profession de foi du vicaire Savoyard," and dies.

That is how, I am convinced, this story was formed, and developed itself in Rousseau's imagination; was, so to speak, fed on Jean-Jacques himself, from day to day, as it were, and without any well-defined plan. I do not know whether I have succeeded in showing this.

I have analyzed the novel's plot—the "story." It would have been an interesting one but for the declamations of the first volume, which seem to us very much out of date. The action is a simple one; the situations and the facts spring from the sentiments. Wolmar could never have existed, but Claire is full of life; Saint-Preux is one of the first types of the romantic hero, weak, restless, full of desires and impotent, and Julie, though overmuch given to sermons, is charming, and offers an example, a pretty rare one in novels, of a passionate and unreasonable girl, slowly transformed by her functions of wife and mother. All this has often been said. Had the "Nouvelle Héloïse" been reduced to the sentimental story of Julie, of Saint-Preux, of Wolmar, and of Claire, the "Nouvelle Héloïse" would have consisted of four hundred pages, and would have been a far more perfect book, and more classical, in spite of its rather loose composition.

But the "Nouvelle Héloïse" has twelve hundred pages; the "Nouvelle Héloïse" is a huge book, eloquent and without system, where the author poured all that passed through his mind. Beside the "story" itself, there are discourses, descriptions, digressions of every kind: Saint-Preux' journey in the mountains of the Valais, the episode of Fanchon's wedding, the dissertation on French and Italian music, the discussion on dueling, Saint-Preux' letters on Parisian manners and customs, the discussion on suicide, the description of life as it was led in the Wolmar household, which is a veritable treatise on domestic economy (comprising twenty pages and two parts), the discussion on the art of gardening, the description of the vintage, considerations on the education of children, on the character of the Genevese, on prayer, on liberty, the profession of religious faith of Julie on her deathbed, etc., etc. . . . (I merely mention items really independent of the plot itself), and, finally, the narrative of the "Loves of Lord Edward," where we see a courtezan refuse to marry her lover, and thereby retrieve the past through her sacrifice, which is, therefore, another story of redemption, and like a sort of first sketch of all the "dames aux camélias" we have since seen.

All that is eloquent, harmonious, and all that is sincere and almost ingenuous; and in all that are many things which we scarcely notice, unless we are forewarned, but which, then, were new—a novel that was not Parisian; love, marriage, adultery taken seriously; a novel full of reflections (all the personages in it are argumentative), and full of landscapes (all the personages living in the most beautiful of countries), and full of lyrism (the personages, and above all the lover, who is generally passive, indulging in effusions on such themes as absence, desire, regret, memory, nature indifferent, or consoling, etc.).

And that is why, whatever preference we may have for the "Princesse de Clèves" or "Manon Lescaut,"[1] we must yet own that the "Nouvelle Héloïse" is of another order, that it renovates imaginative fiction, that it dignifies it, broadens it, diversifies it.

We can no longer understand the effect produced by "Julie." Compare it merely with the "Égarements du cœur et de l'esprit,"[2] or even with "Marianne."[3] The literature of the day, we must confess, had run rather dry. The vagrant, the dreamer, the solitary Rousseau turned on it new and abundant springs of fresh water.

Thanks to "Julie," the society of the day began to love nature and country life (which was excellent), and to cultivate feeling (which might be good), and, also, sentimentality disguised as virtue (which was dangerous). People were more impressed, I fear, by the sophistries of the first volume and the psychological paradoxes of the third than by the excellent and traditional morality to be found in the second volume. And it came to pass that the kind of novels till then in favor, the ingenuously ro-

[1] L'Abbé Prévost.

[2] "The errors of the heart and mind." Crébillon fils.

[3] Marivaux.

mantic novel, and the cynically licentious novel (easy to distinguish from each other) gave way to the novel, both serious and false. And thus, in the ages that followed, all novels where the inevitability and the right of passion were proclaimed, all novels of social and moral inequalities in marriage, all those where love triumphs, often against all reason, all prejudices of traditions of classes, and those where vice speaks the language of virtue, and those where touching courtezans abound, and those where the heroes make for themselves their own code of morals, superior to that of the common herd, taking sentiment for conscience, and committing doubtful actions with fine speeches and gestures, all these novels where reigns what I should call "illusion as to the morality of acts," the "Indianas," the "Lélias," the "Jacques,"[1] and their innumerable progeny . . . one can say that, directly or indirectly—and without, perhaps, that it could be imputed to Rousseau—they were born of the "Nouvelle Héloïse," prolific mother of romantic sophistries and proud dreams.

But, so as not to end on these rather somber words, in order to make you feel, after a century and a half, what new accent "Julie" brought, I shall read a fragment which I call "lyric," a page which is like a theme ready prepared for the verses of some poet of 1830—which, doubtless, would have been inferior to this prose. It is in the sixth part, a letter from Saint-Preux to Mme de Wolmar, at a moment when he is in love both with Julie and with Claire:

[1] Novels by George Sand.

"Woman! woman! dear and fatal object, whom nature adorned for our torture, who punishes him who resists you, who pursues him who fears you, whose hatred and whose love are equally dangerous, whom one can neither seek nor avoid with impunity! Beauty, charm, fascination, sympathy, inconceivable being or chimera, abyss of suffering and joy! Beauty more terrible to mortals than the element that gave thee birth, woe to him who yields to its deceptive charm! It produces the tempests that torment humanity. Oh, Julie! oh, Claire! how dearly do you sell to me that cruel friendship of which you dare to boast! I have lived in storms, and they were evoked by you. But, how different are the agitations which each one of you has excited in my heart! The waters of the Geneva Lake differ as widely from those of the vast ocean. One has short and tumultuous waves, the perpetual agitation of which moves on and sometimes submerges, without however taking one far. But on the sea, tranquil in appearance, one is uplifted, carried gently afar by a slow and almost imperceptible swell; one fancies that one is motionless, and one reaches the end of the world."

EMILE

CHAPTER VII

EMILE

We have seen that, probably in 1758, Rousseau, having finished the "Nouvelle Héloïse," began to write "Emile ou de l'éducation."

That he should have written it seems to us almost inevitable.

For the last sixty years or so educational matters had been much discussed. To recall only the principal books written on the subject we must mention the "Education des filles" by Fénelon; "Télémaque" (1699); the "Traité des études" of that excellent Rollin; the "Thoughts on education" by Locke (translated into French in 1728); the "Avis d'une mère à son fils" and the "Avis d'une mère à sa fille" by Mme de Lambert (1734). Philosophically inclined mothers, like Mme d'Epinay and Mme de Chenonceaux, continually consulted Rousseau on these questions.

In Mme d'Epinay's "Mémoires" there is an amusing chapter where this lady visits with Duclos, her son's tutor, gentle and indolent M. Linant, and where we see that the most reasonable of the innovations in "Emile" were already, as the saying goes, "in the air."

"'Monsieur,' said Duclos to the tutor, 'but little

Latin, very little Latin; and, especially, no Greek. . . . To what purpose your Greek? . . . It is not a question here of forming an Englishman, a Roman, an Egyptian, a Greek, a Spartan, . . . but a man *fit for almost anything.*' 'But, Monsieur,' objected poor Linant, 'that is not a customary education. . . . One must reform and make over a character, so to speak.' 'Who the devil is talking of that?' replied Duclos. '. . . Beware of it; a child's character should not be changed; besides, one could not do it if one would, and the greatest success you could achieve would be to make a hypocrite of him. . . . No, sir, no; you must make the best of the character nature gave him; that is all that is required of you,'" etc.

Another time, when Rousseau was still at the Hermitage, Mme d'Epinay had with him a conversation where we see that the idea of "Emile" was already germinating ("Mémoires" of Mme d'Epinay, vol. iii., letter to Grimm).

Add to this, in the "Nouvelle Héloïse" (part v. letter 3), concerning Julie's children, about forty pages, which are almost a first version of the first volume of "Emile" put into the mouths of M. and Mme de Wolmar—a systematic and truer version. However, such axioms as these are here to be found:

"All characters are in themselves good and sane, according to M. de Wolmar. Nature makes no mistakes;

all vices imputed to a nature are the effects of evil training. There is no criminal whose instincts, better directed, would not have produced great virtues," etc.

Rousseau himself had done some tutoring (at M. de Mably's at Lyons, during about a year). He was fond of teaching. Since his great reputation, he had become, in the eyes of all revolutionaries, the public professor of virtue, society's reformer. Now, society can be reformed by education. Rousseau was bound to write a treatise on education; he could not do otherwise. And he was necessarily bound to conceive education as the art of respecting nature in the child, of permitting its free development, content merely to protect it against the pernicious influence of social conventionality. He was forced to do this, by the fact of having written his first books.

And his own experience likewise led him to it. He had been himself developed in solitude, not, it is true, quite outside of society, but somewhat on its margin, and, in any case, outside of family influences, outside of schools. He had been taught, neither in his family, nor by masters, save for the two years spent with the pastor, Lambercier, and even there he played and wandered about more than he took to his books. From ten upwards he never read but what authors he fancied. His great teacher was life itself. His own foibles formed him, and taught him morality. And this training, without a family, without school, brought forth that marvel of wisdom, of virtue, of sentiment: himself, Jean-Jacques. Therefore, it is the training which he will give to his imaginary pupil. So to speak, we see Jean-Jacques at fifty, teach Jean-Jacques at ten, at fifteen, at twenty years of age; and that is beautiful; and all comes out just right; and Jean-Jacques will there taste that exquisite joy of being eternally on the stage, at all ages, and of never losing sight of himself.

Let us now analyze "Emile."

(I should not omit to say that toward the thirtieth page of book i. Jean-Jacques has the courage to speak of his own children.)

"He who cannot fulfill the duties of paternity has no right to be a father. (He had said the reverse, in 1751, in his letter to Mme de Francueil.) Neither poverty, nor work, nor human respect can dispense him from the duty of feeding his children, and of bringing them up himself. Reader, you can believe me. I forewarn anyone, that he cannot neglect this holy duty without being doomed to bitter tears over a fault for *which there is no consolation.*"

And, thereupon, according as one is well or ill-disposed toward him, one can say that it was a brazen thing for him to have written a treatise on education, after having deserted his five children—or that he wrote it by way of expiation.

Let us begin. The object of education is not to form a citizen, nor a man destined to such or such a profession —but a man. (I am not sure that it might not be simpler and safer to form, in the first place, the man of a certain country, religion, and profession, and whether the "man" in himself, would not, over and above, be formed; but let us proceed.)

"In the order of nature," says Rousseau, "men being all equal, their common vocation is the state of man; and whoever is trained to be such a man could not fail to accomplish the duties appertaining to that state. To live, is the trade I mean to teach my pupil. When he leaves my hands, I acknowledge that he will be neither magistrate, nor soldier, nor priest; he will be, first of all, a man; all that a man should be, he will be, if necessary, and as thoroughly as anyone else; whatever changes his fortunes undergo, he will find his own place. . . . He who, among us, best knows how to sustain the good and the evil of this life is, according to me, the best trained; hence, true education consists less in precepts than in practice."

But how should this object of education be realized? In the article on "Political Economy," written for the "Encyclopédie" (in 1745, I think), Rousseau said that the object of education is to form citizens, and he demanded education in common, education by the State. But it would seem that, since then, he had reflected. In a corrupt society, public education must necessarily be corrupt. Rousseau, therefore, described the bringing up of one child by one master. A rather futile conception, and one from which no absolute conclusions can be drawn—the author, on one hand, imagines an exceptional case; he conceives on the other hand, education to be evidently destined to large groups of real individuals, each differing from the other. Here, again, let us pass on and let us examine what may be an ideal education, according to Rousseau.

Certain conditions are necessary for it: First, for the pupil; second, for the master.

The pupil, Emile, imagined by Rousseau, was born in a temperate climate. He was strong and healthy; rich ("because we can then be sure of having freed one more man, whereas poverty alone will form a man"); noble because Emile will be freed from the prejudice of birth and that he will be "a victim snatched from that prejudice"); an orphan (Emile still had his father and mother; but he is an orphan in the sense that his parents abandon all their rights to the tutor).

His mother is bound to nurse him. In case of absolute ill-health, Rousseau gives advice as to the choice of a nurse, her food, etc. No swaddling clothes; plenty of cold water. The child should live in the country: "Men are not made to be huddled together in anthills, but scattered over the land which they should cultivate. . . . Towns are the whirlpools of humanity."

"So that a child should be properly brought up," said Jean-Jacques, in the passage of Mme d'Epinay's "Mémoires," which I recalled just now, "*it would be necessary to begin, by remodeling society.*" Evidently that would be impossible. Therefore, in order to prevent that in him society should corrupt nature, there is but one means: to remove him from society—and even from his parents, inevitably tainted with social prejudices—and to give him up entirely to the care of a professor, with whom he must spend his life.

This brings us to the conditions required for the teacher or tutor.

"A tutor!" exclaims Rousseau. "Oh, what a sublime soul! . . . In very deed to form a man, one should oneself be a father, and *more than a man.*"

The tutor should be young, to become at times "the companion of his pupil." *He should receive no salary.* He must be a friend of the parents, unmarried, and with plenty of leisure, who, by taste, takes charge of the child's education, and consecrates the better part of his life to that task.

As for me, I read these things with a little anxiety. One cannot here say, "This is doubtless an ideal system of education, which could be, in a certain measure, applicable to all children." One cannot say this, because this system presupposes—essentially, and to begin with—isolation and riches. It is, therefore, simply and purely a dream. But what kind of a dream? That of an education ultra-aristocratic. Should such conditions be required there could be, in all France, but a few hundred children who might receive such an education. Applicable only to a small minority, this education, *should it succeed,* would give a species of "super-man," of super-man sensitive and given to tears, according to Rousseau's conception, and thus, perhaps, might slowly reform society itself. Is that Rousseau's idea? I do not know. Nor did he. Besides, later on, one sees that these conditions, so solemnly and rigorously laid down (complete isolation, voluntary and perpetual tutorship), are not indispensable to the more sensible portions of his plan. But, what of that? He is a dreamer, and delights in his dream.

So, the child thus isolated, nature should be allowed to act upon him, he should merely be shielded from harmful influences.

But what is nature? We have often asked Rousseau this question. This time, he at last answers; it is, I think, *the only time in all his works.*

"But, perhaps," says he himself, "this word nature has too vague a sense; we must try to define it. . . . We are born sensitive, and, from our birth up, we are affected in diverse ways by environing objects. As soon as we are conscious, so to speak, of our own sensations, *we are disposed* to seek or to avoid the things which produce them, first, according to the harmony or discord between ourselves and those objects, and, finally, according to that judgment of happiness or perfection which reason gives us. These *dispositions* are extended and strengthened as we become more sensitive and more intelligent; but, influenced by our habits, they are more or less deteriorated by our opinions. *Before that deterioration, they are what I should call our nature.*"

I do not give this as a marvel of clearness and precision, but this is what may be deduced from it: "Nature is a disposition to seek for all that may be agreeable to us, what is good for us, what we consider as happiness and perfection, and a disposition to avoid the contrary."

But then, why, after having said (the first part of "Emile,"), "All is good that leaves the hands of the Author of all things," should Rousseau add, "All degenerates in the hands of man," that is, of man living in society? It is, however, self-evident that man is naturally *social;* that life in society explains itself (to take once more Rousseau's definition) by a "disposition to seek happiness," and that also, then, is natural.

It is (and Jean-Jacques twenty times repeated this distinction) the instinct of self-preservation, and the desire for happiness, in one word, the egotism natural to man which is necessarily inoffensive when man lives alone in a savage state. But this innocent egotism becomes baleful when men live together: for individual egotism clashes with that of others and is changed into self-love, vanity, pride, cupidity, hatred, envy, etc. And that is how nature is corrupted by society.

But, may we object, it is nevertheless true that society is in nature; that society is still nature. When theologians speak of the result of original sin, when moralists speak of the egotistical and animal instincts that are in us, and when some declare nature to be evil, and others deem it to be mixed, it is evident that they do not allude to prehistoric man, living (if he really ever did so live) in a state of solitude, of which we can know nothing, but to man living with his fellows, for there only can we study "nature." And there, we cannot really say that nature is good; we can but say that it is good or bad, according to individuals; and that, precisely, the object of education is, and always has been, to wrestle with it, to reform and to purify it.

But Rousseau, doubtless, would say, "I care not. I call natural what is good, and what is like me. I say that what is not good is not natural. Nature is good; society is not natural because it is not good; Emile must be brought up according to nature." To this there is no answer, since it is nothing but a play of words and a misuse of them, and that Rousseau calls things by what names he chooses.

Let us take up once more the study of Emile's education. We shall, perhaps, be at times somewhat surprised.

In order that the child may be developed "according to nature," the method adopted is simple: he must be taught nothing. Rousseau calls this "negative education."

He must, on the one hand, be left as free as possible; he must enjoy the happiness fit for his age. But, on the other hand, he must be subjected directly to object lessons, in order that he may learn, at his own expense, what should be sought after, and what avoided. Things are sometimes hostile. It is excellent that he should suffer from them, that he should accustom himself to simplify his life, to distinguish what depends upon him, and what does not, to accept the inevitable. Thus, to the child brought up according to nature, the first dumb lesson is a lesson of resignation.

"Oh, man," says Rousseau, "simplify thy existence within thyself and thou shalt not be miserable. Remain in that position which nature assigned to thee in the chain of beings, for nothing can take thee from it; do not struggle against the hard law of necessity, and do not exhaust, in resisting it, the forces which God did not bestow upon thee to extend or prolong thy life, but only to preserve it as much as He pleases. Thy liberty, thy power extend only as far as thy natural forces, and no further; all the rest is but slavery, illusion, delusion."

And, most eloquently, he shows that the powerful sovereigns themselves submit, without knowing it, to this law. And, by way of conclusion:

"The only man who accomplishes his own will is he who, in order to do so, is not obliged to use another man's arms in addition to his own. . . . A man truly free is he who wills but what he can accomplish. . . . This is my fundamental maxim. It must be applied to childhood."

And further:

"Keep the child merely in the dependence of things . . . never give him orders. . . . Let him only understand that he is weak, and that you are strong. No verbal lesson. No punishment, since he could not understand its meaning, having as yet no moral sense. 'You should never inflict on children a punishment, as punishment; you should always let it overtake them as a *natural consequence* of their evil act.'"

The teacher's intervention should take but two forms:

1. To protect the child against himself when he might wound or hurt himself. Then, the master should simply say "no," without giving any explanation.

2. In order to save time for the child (who has all of life to learn by himself, which might be a long process), the tutor should ingeniously place him in such circumstances that necessity will give him a lesson, and he may himself, perhaps, bring about those circumstances.

Rousseau gives several examples of this: In connivance with the gardener he elaborates a little drama to teach Emile that work is the foundation of property. Emile receives from time to time notes inviting him to a luncheon, to a sailing party, etc. He seeks out someone who might read them to him; all refuse; then the child makes up his mind to learn to read. Or else, Emile, who capriciously disturbs his master so as perpetually to take a walk, is allowed to go out alone; but at his first step in the village he hears to the right and to the left unkind remarks: "Neighbor, just look at the pretty little gentleman! Where is he going all alone? He will surely lose himself. Neighbor, don't you see that it is a little scapegrace who has been driven from his father's house," etc. The tutor himself prepared this comedy. . . . (What a fuss, great Heavens, when a box on the ear would have sufficed!)

Outside of such interventions, the tutor allows nature to take its course. No languages, no geography, no history. No books, no reading, up to ten years of age. Emile must learn nothing by heart, not even the fables of La Fontaine, because he is not capable of understanding them. But the training of his senses must be carefully attended to, unknown to him. On this subject there are excellent pages. He is led (without being forced to it) to live mostly out of doors, to take a great deal of exercise. By way of food, he is given vegetables and fruit—the vegetarian diet.

In truth, there is no mistake about it, this education, where the child is left so free, is a rough one. Unfortunately for Emile, there was once upon a time a convent town known as Sparta. The lessons of wisdom given by things are at times brutal. Emile is not forced to work, but if he breaks a pane of glass in his room it is not replaced; and so much the worse for him if he catches a heavy cold! Tenderness is singularly absent from this pedagogy. A little remnant of maternal weakness would do no harm. And one remembers that Rousseau never knew his mother, nor his children.

This man is full of surprises! Though nowhere has he exposed in so many words this foolish axiom, "the right to happiness," it is, however, certain that the aim in all his books was the happiness of man. Here, his aim is Emile's happiness. And we find, as we go along, that this happiness consists in as little suffering as possible. The art of being happy is the art of supporting and simplifying life. It is patience, resignation, even passivity; a sort of stoicism, or more exactly, of fakirism, which Rousseau always had in him: admirable philosophy for an invalid, for a solitary, self-concentrated man; but, at all events, a philosophy of ripe years, and a very sad one, and very full of disillusions, for a young child.

Rousseau thus leads his pupil up to the twelfth year. At that point he contemplates his work with admiration. Emile is healthy, strong, frank, loyal. He possesses good sense, pride, will. Rousseau sees him thus because he wishes to do so, and because he chose that "nature should be good" in Emile's case. Otherwise, this fine system might have turned out a scamp or an idiot.

For that which succeeded so well for Emile was disastrous for Victor and Victorine in "Bouvard et Pécuchet."[1] And yet Flaubert's two puppets know their Rousseau by heart. They often quote him.

"So that a punishment be effective, it must be the natural consequence of the fault. The child has broken a pane of glass—it must not be replaced; he must suffer from cold; if, without being hungry, he asks for food, give

[1] Flaubert's last work.

it to him: an indigestion will soon bring repentance. He is indolent, let him remain without work; *ennui* will soon force him back to it."

But Victor does not suffer from cold; his constitution can stand any strain, and idleness suits him admirably.

Then? . . .

In book iii., from twelve to fifteen, comes the education of the intelligence and reflection—still by the things themselves, by direct experience, without books—with the least possible effort on the pupil's part.

He is taught, especially, astronomy, geography, physical sciences, and chemistry; or, rather, things are so managed that circumstances and necessity teach them to him. During an excursion, the tutor pretends that they have lost their way, so that Emile may find it again; and, thus, a lesson in astronomy is insinuated. There is a grotesque and very complicated story of how the tutor entered into a plot with a sleight-of-hand man, so that he might impart some physical science, and also, at the same time, punish Emile's vanity. Thus, out of great respect for nature, things are taught him without teaching them, or by teaching them by a sort of subtle fraud.

"Robinson Crusoe" is given to the boy, and, as much as possible, he is made to put the story into practice. He is persuaded (and that is excellent) to learn a manual trade—an honest trade, of course—"not, therefore, that of embroiderer, or gilder, or tailor, or musician, or comedian, or writer," but that of carpenter.

We now come to book iv., where Emile's sensibility is awakened, and where his tutor prepares him to receive sympathetic and social ideas.

Emile is fifteen; a dangerous age. (Rousseau insists greatly on this delicate period of Emile's life. Perhaps we may see here reminiscences of his own adolescence.) Emile is still ignorant. That ignorance must be prolonged. . . . But, if that is impossible? . . . Rousseau hesitates. . . . Then he makes up his mind, and resolves to maintain Emile's innocence until the twentieth year.

How? Rousseau first thinks of divulging to Emile the consequences of vice. . . . But the best way of keeping Emile pure (and that is beautiful, and should not excite a smile), is to conquer sensuality by sensibility, to inspire affectionate feelings: gratitude, pity, love of the humble, love of humanity. Here we find eloquent and generous thoughts.

"It is the people that forms humanity—what is outside of the people is so insignificant that it need not count. . . . Even were he more unhappy than the poor, the rich man should not be pitied, for his woes are of his own making, and he could be happy if he would. But the sorrows of the poor man come to him from outside, from the cruelty of a fate which oppresses him. He cannot grow accustomed to the feeling of physical fatigue, of exhaustion, of hunger; neither good-will nor wisdom suffice to exempt him from the miseries inherent to his state.

. . . Respect your kind; remember that it is composed essentially of the people; that, were all kings, all philosophers taken away, things would remain as they are, and would not be worse managed. In a word, teach your pupil to love all men, and even those who despise humanity; let him place himself in no particular class, but let him be at home in all; speak to him of the human race with emotion, even with pity, never with contempt. A man should never degrade man."

Now, the time has come to make Emile acquainted with humanity, first, through history, and, especially, through Plutarch.

And the time has also come to make him know God. It is here that the tutor acquaints him with the "Profession de foi du vicaire Savoyard."

And here, whatever he may say, the tutor at last *teaches*. . . . Never would Emile, left to nature alone, have found so beautiful a demonstration of a personal God, of the immortality of the soul and of the future life.

Then, why not have taught this earlier—that, and a few other things useful to know? How much time would have been saved!

Rousseau answers:

"At fifteen Emile did not know of his soul's existence, and perhaps at eighteen it was not yet time that he should learn of it. At any rate, had these things been taught him earlier, he would not have understood them."

Who knows? He would have understood of them what he was capable of understanding. This same Rousseau writes in book ii. of the "Confessions":

"When I said that it was well not to speak to children of religion, if one desired them later to be religious, and that they were incapable of knowing God, even after our fashion, I spoke according to my observations, not according to my own experience; I knew that this was no proof for others. Find other Jean-Jacques of six, and seven, speak to them of God, and I assure you that you run no risk."

Yes, we know that Jean-Jacques was a child of genius. But was Emile, that dear little Emile, quite an idiot?

But let us leave the "Profession de foi du vicaire Savoyard," of which I shall treat separately, and let us follow Emile's development.

Emile became more and more ill at ease, during the crisis of the eighteenth year. How would it be possible to "restrain in him, until twenty, the ignorance of desire, and the purity of the senses"?

"Let him retire worn out, longing for sleep, and let him rise as soon as he wakes." Then, he must be kept out of towns, given plenty of hard manual labor, sent out hunting, talked to eloquently.

"Talked to eloquently?" That recalls Bouvard and Pécuchet doing their best to instill morality into Victor. Fénelon recommends an "innocent conversation from time to time." Impossible to find a single one. . . . Bouvard and Pécuchet give their pupils edifying little stories to read, so as to inspire love of virtue. These bored Victor to death. . . . etc. Perhaps, after all, in these matters and in most cases nothing is comparable to, nothing can replace, the categorical commands of a religious faith. But that is what "nature" does not give: quite the reverse.

Let us return to the narrative. If Emile continues to be restive, there remains but one resource: his tutor starts with him in search of a mate, and the search must last as long as possible.

In the same way that little dramas had been invented beforehand, in order to teach cleanliness to the child Emile, or to take away his wish to go out without his tutor, or to teach him at the same time physical science and modesty—in the same way the marriage of the happy young man was to be the result of a carefully premeditated plan of his master.

This is it: the tutor, for a long time past, has known the young girl who will suit his pupil, and to whom he destines her; he knows her family, and where she lives. But, to begin with, he describes her to Emile as an ideal being, the thought of whom will conquer real objects. He says negligently, "In order to give her a name, let us call her Sophie." And he starts with his pupil in search of some young girl who may resemble this Sophie of his dream.

Emile and his tutor, meanwhile, go to Paris. Emile

frequents the world and society. Brought up as he has been, society and the world present no dangers for him. He sees them as they are, despicable and ridiculous. He is more and more in love with simple country life. And here it is that we meet with the passage on the "white cottage with the green shutters," and the apostrophe to Paris:

"Farewell to thee, Paris, renowned city, city of noise, of smoke, and of mud, where women no longer believe in honor, nor men in virtue. Farewell, Paris. We seek for love, happiness, innocence; we can never be too far removed from thee!"

And not finding in Paris the faintest semblance of the ideal Sophie, they go to seek for her in the country.

And now, while waiting for Emile to find her, let us transport ourselves near the real Sophie, with her good parents, in her pretty rustic home.

Rousseau tells us what this young girl's education has been, and what should be the education of girls. It is the most conventional of educations, as different as possible from that of Emile.

"Nature" lets us clearly understand that it is not at all in favor of women's rights. Neither was Rousseau; not at all; not the least in the world. And one can marvel that his hobby of equality should not have given him the idea of equality between the two sexes. It seemed as though no crotchet could be wanting to his collection.

This one, however, got away from him. Rousseau was not feminist. He was even anti-feminist. Probably because he had greatly loved women. He thought, or felt, on that point like Michelet, like Sainte Beuve, like all who, greatly attracted by feminine nature, would have liked not to attenuate, but, on the contrary, to cultivate, and even to accentuate the differences between the two sexes.

Rousseau carried this sentiment so far (he had already expressed it in the "Lettre sur les spectacles" and elsewhere) that he declared himself entirely against applying to girls any of the methods recommended for the education of boys—as though, intellectually speaking, the two sexes had nothing in common, and as though what suited one could by no means suit the other.

Whereas the tutor granted Emile all possible liberty, and was of opinion that he should only be punished by consequences, and while he encouraged his pupil to think for himself and to put himself above the judgment of men, two severe muses, Restraint and the Respect of Public Opinion, should preside over the education of girls:

"Girls, very early, should feel restraint. . . . Dependence is the natural state of women, girls feel that they were created for obedience. . . . [They, at least, can be punished.] . . . From this habitual restraint comes a docility which women will need all their lives, since they are always to be subject either to a man, or to the judgments of men, and must never be allowed to put themselves above those judgments. It does not suffice that a woman should be faithful, but that she should be judged faithful by her husband, by her relatives, by the world. . . . The outward appearance of virtue is among the duties of women. . . . Woman, in doing right, only accomplishes half her duty, and what is thought of her is as important as what she really does. . . . All female education is subservient to men."

Moreover, a woman should please. She should dress well, possess accomplishments. . . . As to religion, daughters should practice their mother's religion; wives, that of their husbands. "Since *authority should regulate the religion of women*, it is not so necessary to explain to them the reasons for believing as to expose to them what is believed." As to intellectual culture, no abstract books, no science. "Their studies should always be practical. All their reflections, not absorbed strictly by their studies, should tend to the study of man or of those agreeable accomplishments which tend to the culture of taste," etc.

In book v. Rousseau often held forth like a superior Chrysale.[1] This proved a sort of awakening of his traditional and ancestral soul, as in the third part of "Julie." But I have an idea that he wished to annoy his fair friends. Oh, how retrospectively his fair friends exasperated him! Oh, how weary he was of those emanci-

[1] In Molière's "Femmes savantes."

pated female philosophers, those female atheists who thought they were free thinkers! He turns into ridicule, in a fine page, this so-called distinguished and respectable type of woman, who is false to modesty and feminine duty, but who possesses, it is said, the virtues of an honest man. He has no faith in those virtues: "When the great curb of their sex is thrown aside," says Rousseau, "what remains to restrain them? and what honor can they respect when they have made light of their own?" . . . And so much the worse for Mme d'Epinay, and for Mme d'Houdetot, and even for Mme de Luxembourg!

But, let us come to Sophie herself.

The description which he gives us of her is prolix, but agreeable. Here is a short extract from it:

". . . Sophie is not beautiful, but, when with her, men forget beautiful women, and beautiful women at her side are dissatisfied with themselves. At the first glance she scarcely seems even pretty, but the more she is seen, the more lovely she grows; she gains where others lose, and what she gains she never loses. . . . Without dazzling, she excites interest, she charms, and one can scarcely say why. . . . Sophie likes to be well dressed, and possesses good taste. . . . but she hates finery. . . . Sophie has natural talents. . . . Sophie is extremely clean and neat. This care of her person, however, does not degenerate into vain affectation, into effeminacy. . . . In her apartment nothing but fresh water is used; she knows no perfumes but those of flowers, and her husband will know none sweeter than her breath. Finally, the attention she gives to exterior things never causes her to forget that life and time should be spent in nobler cares; she ignores or disdains that excessive cleanliness of the body which defiles the soul; Sophie is more than clean; she is pure."

With all its prolixity, this moral and physical portrait of Sophie is delightful. It can be summoned up as a combination of *secondary* qualities, from which emanates a *superior* charm. . . . I never picture Sophie to myself except with a striped rose-colored skirt, and a great, great deal of fresh linen, and eyes that moisten easily.

Her mother was poor, but well born. Her father had been rich, but was half ruined; but he still possessed the pretty house with the green shutters, a fine garden, some fields and pastures. Both were good and honest. Sophie had been brought up according to the foregoing principles. As a child she had been scolded and punished because she was nothing but a girl. Her father discoursed to her after the most sensible and tender fashion. All this forms a charming and heartsome home picture, a pretty bit of middle-class novel—and in those days that was a novelty.

Certain indelicate touches spoil it a little. Sophie languishes. The author speaks too much of Sophie's "senses" and "desires," and even of her "inflammable temperament." And we know very well that young girls can have senses and desires, but we like to imagine these as unawakened, and it is displeasing to hear such a subject treated too openly.

Her family become anxious. Sophie is questioned. She has read Fénelon's novel and she is in love with Télémaque! And that is what is undermining her.

But, lo, here come Télémaque and Mentor, that is, Emile and his tutor; they have been surprised by a storm and drenched. They claim hospitality of Sophie's parents. All this was arranged beforehand by the tutor and the father. The travelers having been sufficiently dried, all sit down to table and talk. Sophie's father is led on to tell of his misfortunes, and of the consolations he had found in his wife:

"Emile, moved, ceases to eat so as better to listen. At last, whilst the most honest of men expatiates with the greatest pleasure on the attachment of the worthiest of wives, the young traveler, transported, presses the hand of the husband, which he had seized, and also takes that of the wife, bowing over it with rapture, and bathing it with his tears. . . ."

A picture in the style of Diderot and of Greuze. You know, and we have defined, when treating of the "Nouvelle Héloïse," this sort of sentimentality.

". . . Sophie, seeing him weep, is on the point of mingling her tears with his. . . . Her mother, noticing her emotion, and in order to spare her, sends her on an errand."

But listen attentively, we are on the verge of a dramatic crisis:

"A minute later the young girl comes back, but still so disturbed that her emotion is visible to all. The mother says gently: 'Sophie, calm yourself. . . .' At this name of Sophie [you remember that it was thus that he called his ideal] Emile was seen to start. Struck by a name so dear, he awakes as from a dream, and casts a fervid glance on her who bears it," etc.

You think, perhaps, that at this point the young man's tutor will leave him in peace. Oh, not at all! The tutor deems it proper on account of the "inflammability" of their natures that Emile should remain at a distance of two leagues from Sophie, and that they should not meet more than twice or thrice a week. Then one day he makes a long speech to Emile, a very fine one certainly, admirable, and of the purest stoicism, wherein he exhorts him to leave Sophie for two years, so as to secure their happiness by this trial. And he persuades Emile, and Emile persuades Sophie with torrents of tears.

Thus Emile travels "to study governments and manners." From his voyage he brings back a sketch of the "Contrat social"—and also this thought, among others, which is perhaps true, but not easy to demonstrate:

"France would be far more powerful were Paris destroyed."

At last Emile and Sophie are married. And you fancy that this time the tutor's task is over and that it behooves the young people themselves to "govern" their conjugal happiness? No; the eye of the tireless tutor penetrates into their private apartment. The natural immodesty of Jean-Jacques abounds in advice to young married people, all the more that he himself did not marry, and that he appears as little fit to undertake the education of husband and wife as that of children. But let us leave that! Or, rather, let us say that here again he dreams his life, that he gives himself the spectacle of what he could not do, and that he expatiates over the young loves of Emile and Sophie through a bitter sentiment of regret.

Therefore, taking them apart, he recommends them ever to be lovers in marriage. "Obtain everything from love," says he to Emile, "without exacting anything from a sense of duty, so that the slightest favors be to you, not what you can claim as your right, but a free gift." And he goes into such details that Emile is revolted, and Sophie, abashed, hides her face behind her fan. And some days later, guessing that his sermon has taken effect, he talks to Sophie with much noble indecency; so that the poor fellow—whom Rousseau had wished free, independent of men, never punished, never scolded, finally has his tutor by way of a mother-in-law; and what a mother-in-law! And one does not know whether the youth will ever shake his tutor off, or whether he will not, all through his life, be a pupil.

(Yet, with all that, I must acknowledge that the tutor's discourse contains admirable advice as to the time when the first effervescence of love shall have calmed down, and that it resembles certain chapters of Michelet in "l'Amour," and that Michelet borrowed largely, very largely, from the fifth book of "Emile." Michelet seems to me, in spite of the differences in their genius, to be the most faithful follower of Rousseau in the nineteenth century.)

Such is that celebrated book. . . . Oh, it contains excellent ideas! That mothers should nurse their children; that there should be plenty of cold water and outdoor exercise—all that is very good. Very good, also, to love childhood, to wish it gay and happy. It is quite right to proclaim that to make a man is not to construct a machine, but to develop a living being. Progressive studies, proportioned to the physical and moral development of the child; experimental education, by the view and contact of things; the superiority of education over instruction; the reaction against worldly education, and also against that found in books (to which our society of functionaries is now-a-days a prey); the plan of forming a man thoroughly equipped for life. . . . All that is praiseworthy and just.

Only, children nursed by their mothers, cold water, exercise, had already been advised by Tronchin; and for the rest it was to some extent everywhere, and, especially and more than merely in germ, in Rabelais, in Montaigne, in Locke. And it is very certain that Rousseau put his mark on these known precepts, thanks to his eloquence. But it remains proved that what is good is scarcely his, and what belonged only to him appears absurd and insolent.

What belongs to him is the anti-natural idea of a supposed education according to nature, which requires the depossession of parents and the complete sacrifice of the master's life to a single pupil, and, also, the idea of an education which, were it possible, would deprive each generation of the labor and thought of those who had gone before.

The utility of education, if not its very effect, is precisely to dispense children from doing the work of the fathers over again, and Rousseau would force them to recommence that labor. But, as after all he feels that this would take too long, he cheats. No education was ever so full of artifice as this which pretends to respect nature. The tutor is driven to dramatize life and things for his pupil. He does not teach him—no; he does not punish him; but, in reality, he mystifies him and enslaves him—as did Fénelon with the Duc de Bourgogne. Hence, if the pupil is *forced*, at the last, to think like his tutor, it was, perhaps, scarcely worth while to take so much trouble. All this education is one continual lie. Lies are the very soul of three-fourths of all Jean-Jacques' books.

Finally, this education, if its aim is not the entire subserviency of the pupil to the master, tends to the breaking up of all tradition. Now, tradition economizes time by transmitting from the parents to the children self-evident opinions. It thereby unites and harmonizes the effort of successive generations. Teach children their father's belief. Later, they can free themselves from this belief if they choose; but, if most of them hold to it, what strength humanity, of which they form a part, will find in this continuity! What would become of a nation if each child were to be left free to judge of life, and to construct for its own use a religion and a code of morals? Emile is a nice boy, a very nice boy, but what would his master say if Emile, at eighteen, sent him flying with his deism and his Savoyard vicar's profession of faith? What a rascal Emile might have become, had he not had a good disposition, or if he had not fallen into the hands of one who was really the most tyrannical of tutors? An anarchist, or his master's satellite: such would have been the destiny of a child brought up strictly according to Rousseau's theories.

Nothing, therefore, out of "Emile" could be put into practice, except that which had been preconized by Locke, Montaigne, Rabelais. But of the original part, that which really belongs to Rousseau, I repeat it, there is nothing which can be used.

Nothing? That is a mistake. The worst part has been adopted. There remains this absurdity: the respect for the child's liberty, the fear of infringing on his conscience; hence, no religious instruction; and why should

I not add, no moral instruction until he can choose for himself his religion or his philosophy, or free himself from all choice. That which to-day is called neutrality, and which is in fact the irreligion of the schools, is already in embryo in "Emile," and is certainly implied by Rousseau's system of education; and, unless I mistake, we are beginning to perceive its results—results which no one thinks of attenuating for adolescents—as Rousseau did for Emile—by the "Profession de foi du vicaire Savoyard," now looked upon as "clerical."

"Emile" had great success; less, however, than the "Nouvelle Héloïse." But "Emile," more serious, was considered as the author's masterpiece. Women saw in it, especially, the novel of Sophie, and maternal nursing, and at the opera fine ladies had their babies brought to the box, so as, at the back of it, to suckle them between the acts. As to the men, they saw in "Emile" whatever they chose, because everything is in it.

I must, however, let you know how it was interpreted by that excellent Musset-Pathey (the father of Alfred de Musset), who, in 1825, published an apologetic history of Rousseau. Nothing could be simpler. Rousseau, with the eyes of genius, foreseeing the Revolution, chose to bring up Emile, a young nobleman, so that he could manage for himself whatever happened. And that is why, among other things, he taught him the carpenter's trade. "Emile," therefore, is a treatise of education for scions of nobility in prevision of revolutionary times. Evidently, Musset-Pathey was thinking of the Duc d'Orléans (Louis-

Philippe), brought up by Mme de Genlis, according to some of Jean-Jacques' precepts. This is rather curious.

But the essential, original, and absurd idea of "Emile" is so unpractical, that Jean-Jacques, consulted by mothers, by priestly tutors, even by princes, did what he already had done with regard to the "Discours sur les sciences" and the "Discours sur l'inégalité"—he acknowledges his own exaggerations, or he softens them, or even he contradicts himself. To Mme de T. (April 6, 1771) he advises strongly that an unruly child should be put to school, and did not think that the young scamp should be left to nature. To the Abbé M. (February 28, 1770), he writes (and I hardly know whether the letter did not show latent irony, a thing which, in general, was quite foreign to his nature):

"If it be true that you have adopted the plan which I attempted to sketch in 'Emile,' *I admire your courage;* for you are too intelligent not to see that, in such a system, one must have all or nothing, and that it would be a hundred times better to take up the ordinary routine of education, and to produce a little courtier, than to follow this one in a half-hearted way, and turn out a failure. . . . You can hardly imagine how tremendous a task you have undertaken; for ten years, at least, you will no longer exist for yourself; you, with all your faculties, will be devoted to your pupil—vigilance, patience, firmness, those are the three virtues which *you must practice unflinchingly, if you would not lose every-*

thing; yes, absolutely everything; a single moment of impatience, of negligence, or forgetfulness, would take from you the fruit of ten years' work, without leaving anything behind, not even the possibility of regaining it by the work of ten more years. Doubtless, if anything deserves the name of heroic and great among men, it is an enterprise like yours," etc.

This is mere folly. Of whom is Rousseau making fun? If the education of a single boy implies so total an abnegation and the Hercules-like work of ten years, Abbé M. had better give it up. Is it possible more clearly to acknowledge that "Emile" is but the romance of education?

Finally, in a journal, we read concerning Rousseau's stay at Strasburg in 1765:

"M. Anga paid him a visit, and said to him: 'You see before you, Monsieur Rousseau, a man who has educated his son according to the principles he was happy enough to find in your "Emile."' 'So much the worse for you and for your son.'"

But Rousseau destroyed yet more entirely his "Emile" by another novel, of which he wrote but two chapters, entilted "Emile et Sophie, ou les deux solitaires."[1]

Emile and Sophie are married. They have a son. You would imagine that, formed by Jean-Jacques, they would forever be good and happy. But they go to Paris. They take up a life of pleasure. One day Sophie shuts her door on her husband. This lasts for several months.

[1] "Emile and Sophie, or the two hermits."

Questioned closely, she ends by saying, "Stop, Emile, and learn that I can no longer be yours. I have been unfaithful to you."

What! this charming Sophie, so well brought up. Yes, this is one of Rousseau's hobbies. Sophie must be tainted like Julie, so as to recover virtue like Julie—and like Jean-Jacques himself, of whom I have already said that his life was a moral evolution, a purification ending in madness.

Emile flies in despair. Then he reflects, he recalls his master's lessons of stoicism; he finds excuses for Sophie; he even admires that, in spite of her fault, she should have kept so much sincerity and virtue. He forgives her, but he will go away with his son.

Meanwhile, in order to weary his body and exhaust his sorrow, he works with a carpenter, some leagues from Paris. Sophie finds him there, dares not enter the workshop, but exclaims softly to the child who accompanies her: "No, he could never take your mother from you; come, we have no business here. . . ."

And, as she foresaw, Emile gives up the child and starts off alone on foot. Then. he becomes a sailor, and is taken by a pirate. A captive at Algiers, he distinguishes himself by his patience, his gentleness, his courage, and becomes slave to the Dey, who esteems him.

Here the novel breaks off, and we say to ourselves: what was the use of Emile's special education, since, once in Paris, he led the life of those about him? Rousseau would answer that it served to make him conquer himself, to be just and kind toward Sophie, to behave bravely at Algiers. But a man of heart would have done all this, even had he been brought up at the College of Navarre, and according to the old system.

But there are real beauties in this fragment of a novel. But adultery is here regarded very seriously, at a time when it was usually a subject of jokes (at least in the upper classes). But Emile, deceived, forgives his wife, almost in the very words and with the arguments of a husband according to Dumas, *fils;* but, already, Jean-Jacques had shown in the "Nouvelle Héloïse," a courtesan still more heroic than the "Dame aux camélias." But, several years before, in a footnote of his "Réponse à Bordes," he had declared that the treason of the husband was as complete as that of the wife, and that the husband and wife were bound to the same fidelity.. . . . For this man, who for his part wrote more foolish things than all the great classics put together, was also the man who opened most new paths to literature and to sentiment. . . . And that is very true.

THE "CONTRAT SOCIAL"—THE "PROFESSION DE FOI DU VICAIRE SAVOYARD"

CHAPTER VIII

THE "CONTRAT SOCIAL"—THE "PROFESSION DE FOI DU VICAIRE SAVOYARD"

To my mind the "Contrat social" is, with the first "Discours," Rousseau's most mediocre book, the most obscure, the most chaotic, with all its apparent solemnity. Later on, it became the most disastrous of all.

It is also the most difficult to place in his biography, the one he might so easily not have written! The "Contrat social" is not easy to explain, whereas the two "Discours," "Julie," "Emile," and some other works that followed, were the outcome of some impetuous or critical circumstance of Jean-Jacques' life.

The final version of the "Contrat social" must have been written immediately before or after "Emile." But the "Contrat" was a fragment of a previous work, "Les institutions politiques," begun by Rousseau in Venice (1744). The "Contrat" is, therefore, Rousseau's only work (with the "Rêveries") which was not conceived and written in a moment of passion.

I believe that Rousseau at Montmorency, toward 1760-1761, simply took up and revised his old Venice manuscripts, because he was jealous of Montesquieu's fame. (He turns him into ridicule in book ii. of the "Contrat social," without naming him). Then, he was still in the period of his admiration for Geneva. What he builds up in the "Contrat social" is an idealized Genevese government.

Idealized? How? Geneva had a moderate democratic government. Outside of the "habitants," that is, strangers established in the republic, and the "natives," or sons of "habitants" (two unimportant classes), there were the "citizens," sons of citizens and born in the city, and the "burghers," sons of burghers and citizens, but born in foreign parts, or strangers having obtained the privileges of burghers. These two classes, the "citizens" and the "burghers," together formed the body of electors—about fifteen hundred voters (one could not be elector before twenty-five). But the "citizens" alone could become members of the government (called the "Lesser Council").

Now, when Rousseau published the "Discours sur l'inégalité," he had dedicated it to the Republic of Geneva, and, especially, to the members of the Lesser Council. But it seems that they received this dedication coldly, and while the people of Geneva as a whole grew enthusiastic over Jean-Jacques, they, alone, showed some reserve. Jean-Jacques had not forgotten this, as we know; it is, therefore, very possible that, in preconizing pure democracy in his idealized picture of a small republic, he had meant to annoy the privileged members of the Council, whom he had unprofitably dubbed in his dedication "magnificent and sovereign Lords."

I think that so far, only, can one place, as I have said, the "Contrat social" in the personal and intimate life of Jean-Jacques—Jean-Jacques wished for a democracy of Geneva out of spite for the cool feeling of the Genevese government toward himself. This would not be impossible.

One the other hand, it was certainly not inevitable, but it was quite natural, that Rousseau, censor of morality in in his first books, teacher of love in "Julie," oracle of education in "Emile," should have felt the need of being finally a legislator, so as to complete his mission as benefactor to humanity. For all these avocations hold together. He himself said in "Emile" (and here we can see the "Contrat social" foreshadowed):

> "What should be done so that man in the civil state may remain as free as possible, not submitting to particular and arbitrary authorities, but only to the general will? Law must be substituted to man; the general will should be invested with real power, superior to the action of any particular will."

In one word, the man who wrote the "Contrat social" is the man who plays a part and also the man offended by the "magnificent lords" of Geneva; and it was the Genevese, son of a very small republic; and, yet more, it was the Protestant. The "sovereignty of the people" is a Protestant dogma, opposed by the clergymen of the seventeenth century to the despotism of Louis XIV. The minister Jurien had said in so many words: "The people is the only authority that need not have right on its side to validate its acts."

And, if it is the Protestant who wrote the "Contrat social," it could not at the same time be the apostle of nature; and it would seem, indeed, impossible to reconcile this book with the theory exposed in the two discourses. For government "according to nature"—natural government, no matter how understood—can evidently not be an absolute democracy, the retarded and artificial product of political metaphysics (and which could never have been put into practice in the small ancient republics, where there were "slaves"); the government according to "nature" should be the one most allied to the immemorial and natural institution of the family; it should be monarchy—and that, according to Rousseau himself who, in the "Discours sur l'inégalité," considers the patriarchal organization of the tribe the best and happiest.

And, now, here is the plan of the "Contrat social" freed from the digressions which encumber it. I shall first quote a part of the principles exposed by the author, and from which all the rest is deduced:

"Man is born free, and everywhere he is enslaved. ["Born free" seems to me void of sense; but let us proceed.] How did this change take place? I know not. What can make it legitimate? ["It," that is, the change of the man born free into a man no longer free; that is, in reality, government, social institutions.] I think that I can answer this question."

There was, at the origin of society, a compact, known

or understood. How should that compact be formulated? What should be its clauses, and how should it work?

The difficulty may be thus stated:

"Find a form of association which defends and protects by means of the common force the person and the goods of each member, and by which each, uniting for the weal of all, should yet obey only himself, and remain as free as he was before. Such is the fundamental problem of which the social contract gives the solution.

". . . The clauses of this contract, naturally, are all reduced to one, that is to say, the *total* separation of each member with all his rights from the whole of the community; for, in the first place, each giving himself up entirely, the condition is the same for all; and the condition being the same for all, no one has any interest in making it heavy for his neighbors. [Rousseau is sure of this.] Moreover, each, giving himself up to all, gives himself to no one; and, as there is no member over whom one does not give the same right which one gives him, one gains the equivalent of what one loses, and the greater power to keep what one has."

(Oh, the logic is excellent, and looks well on paper!)

". . . Instantly, instead of the particular person of each contracting party, this act of association produces a collective moral body, composed of as many members as the assembly has votes; which receives, thanks to this act, its unity, its common personality, its life, its will. . . ."

This collective body is called the *state* when it is passive, *sovereign* when it is active. . . . With regard to the members, they take collectively the name of *people*, they call themselves *citizens*, as participators of the sovereign authority, and *subjects*, as being subject to the laws of the *state*.

And this is how the system should work, so that men may be as happy, and, as it would seem, as free as possible.

The people, as sovereign, makes laws. The people obey these laws as subjects. The people apply the laws as prince or magistrate, by naming, in order to enforce them, not "representatives," but "commissioners."

It is the direct and continuous government of the people by the people.

And this is what the system implies:

1. Absolute equality of the citizens. In order that this quality may last, the citizen must not belong to another group beside that of the state, he must not submit to a private hierarchy. Therefore, no partial society, no association, no corporation. "Otherwise, one might say that there are not as many voters as men, but only as many as associations."

As to the inequality of fortunes. . . . Communism is latent in Rousseau. He says in the "Contrat" (book ix.):

"The state, with regard to its members, is master of their possessions by virtue of the social contract. . . . The owners are considered as *depositaries* of the public wealth."

And he had said in "Emile" (book v.):

"The sovereign [here it is the people] can legitimately take possession of what belongs to all, as was the case in Sparta in the days of Lycurgus."

And yet, in the "Nouvelle Héloïse," he wrote at the same time the poem and the treatise of domestic government, and that presupposes both considerable inequality in fortunes and a stern hierarchy, and the result was a natural grouping, economical and moral, which evidently formed a "partial society," interposed between the individual and the state. And this grouping seemed to Rousseau useful and delightful.

2. The system presupposes the sovereignty of the people. This sovereignty can go far.

"One agrees," says Rousseau, "that all that each man alienates, for the social compact, of his power, of his possessions, of his liberty, only constitutes that part the use of which is important to the community; *but* one must also agree that the sovereign [that is the people as sovereign] is judge as to that importance."

That is to say, that the people must decide what is

right to leave to each citizen in the way of liberty and fortune—and that makes one shudder.

(And yet, in this same "Contrat social," Rousseau refuses to recognize in the people forethought and clear-sightedness, and calls it a "*blind* multitude, that often does not know what it wants, because it rarely knows what is good for it.")

3. Thirdly and by way of corollary, the system implies the unlimited right of the sovereign people even in the matter of conscience. The people imposes its law, even in philosophical and theological subjects. Jean-Jacques retrogrades as far as Calvin. He re-establishes the union of the spiritual and the temporal, the separation of which, according to Auguste Comte, was the masterpiece of the Middle Ages.

"There is," says he, "a profession of faith purely civil, of which the sovereign [the sovereign people] has the right to fix the articles, not precisely as religious dogmas, but as sentiments of sociability, without which it is impossible to be either a good citizen or a faithful subject."

He indicates the dogmas of this civil religion: "The existence of a Divinity, omnipotent, intelligent, beneficent, and helpful, a future life, the happiness of the just, the punishment of the wicked, the sanctity of the social contract and of the laws." And, on this head, he concludes thus:

". . . Without being able to force anybody to believe in these dogmas, the people can banish from the state all who do not believe in them; it can banish them, not as impious, but as unsociable, as incapable of sincerely loving law, justice, of being willing, if necessary, to sacrifice life to duty. That if any man, after having publicly recognized these dogmas, *yet lives as though he did not believe in them* [a terribly inquisitorial and ambiguous formula], *let him be punished by death;* he has committed the greatest of crimes; he has lied to the law."

When one remembers that the "dogmas" in question, beside the existence of God and future life, comprise the *sanctity of the social contract and of the laws,* one seems to hear the clauses of the sentences which, thirty years later, were to send so many people—among them Malesherbes, André Chenier, and Lavoisier—to the guillotine on the ground of incivis, which gives gusto to the phrase in which Rousseau, immediately afterward, condemns intolerance.

(Let us note, by the way, that Rousseau's political sons would not to-day persecute atheists—on the contrary. Thus varies human folly.)

Therefore Rousseau decrees death for the relapsed atheist. And yet in the "Nouvelle Héloïse" the virtuous Wolmar is an atheist, and would, as such, be exiled from the ideal Geneva, and condemned to death if he returned to it. And Jean-Jacques admires Wolmar. Everywhere, except in the "Contrat," Jean-Jacques is not intolerant. He even preaches tolerance with emotional sincerity in the "Profession de foi du vicaire Savoyard." And, singularly enough, he who condemns in the "Contrat" those whose belief is not in accordance with his orthodoxy, will be condemned, both on account of the "Contrat" and on account of the "Profession de foi," by two other orthodoxies, that of the Paris Parliament and that of the Lesser Council of Geneva. So that he might well say to himself: "*Patere quam fecisti legem.*" But, most assuredly, he will say nothing of the kind.

Thus, the sovereign people that was to take from each citizen only that part of his liberty "the use of which might be important to the community," ends by taking all. And, as doubtless Rousseau foresees that there will be some ill-disposed persons who might try either to resist or to escape, he imagines over and above, in order to keep the peace, a quantity of magistracies imitated from ancient republics—the *dictatorship* naturally for great occasions, but also the *censorship* to watch over morals, denounce the wicked, and regulate what may remain of pleasure to the unfortunate citizens—and the *tribunate*, "preserver of laws and of the legislative power," and that will "serve at times to protect the sovereign against the government" (that is to say, the people against its delegates), as the tribunes in Rome had at times to protect the government against the people, as did the Council of the Ten in Venice; and at times to maintain the equilibrium on both sides, as did the Ephores at Sparta. (Do you not already see rising before you, all the machinery of government during the Terror?) These are so many tyrannies added, and soon substituted—and more cruel still—to that of the state.

What is clear, after that, is that not a particle of liberty could remain to the citizens, unless it be to the clients of the governing magistracies.

As to equality, there remains no trace of it in the pure democracy invented by Jean-Jacques. And yet here, as in his two "Discours," equality seems to be his supreme ideal. Why? I do not know. Love of abstract symmetry. Unless one supposes that there was in his heart more envy, more rancor on the subject of his youth than transpired in his books; for it must be said that never was that sentiment of envy avowed. Why, then, this superstition of equality?

Equality is not a right (though the Revolution made of it the first of the "rights of man"); and it is not of nature's making, O Jean-Jacques, priest of nature! (All that one can say, perhaps, is that in *certain cases* the desire for equality coincides with the desire for justice.)

It is not a right. "Can you imagine that a man coming into the world could say, 'It is my right that no man shall be superior to me, that no one should have more power than I have! . . ." (Faguet.) That has no sense. What is true is this: It is the duty of man not to aggravate the natural and inevitable inequalities among men. The word *right* has no sense except in correlation with the word *duty*.

Neither is equality a fact in nature. Rousseau did not find it even among primitive men, that is self-evident. Unless one should simply say, "All men are born weeping, all die in anguish and suffering, all are subject to the same natural necessities," etc. But even from that, if there are conclusions to be drawn by the moralist and the Christian, there is nothing to be drawn from it for the state.

I must express my whole thought: Why should we regret that it be so? Or why feel irritated over what is inevitable? And, finally, why should equality seem delicious and desirable to Rousseau, and inequality, odious? Real equality between men could only exist if they were absolutely similar. And that, we cannot even imagine. Natural inequality, except in extreme cases, is not necessarily intolerable. We are unequal, but we manage to live, and to live without suffering from it. We are unequal, but we are especially *different*. La Bruyère's passage ("De l'homme," sec. 1131) has never ceased to be true since the Revolution. "Usually among men, there are innumerable combinations of power, of favor, of genius, of riches, of dignities, of nobility, of force, of industry, of capacity, of virtue, of vice, of weakness, of stupidity, of poverty, of impotence, of the plebeian state, of baseness. That these things, combined together in a thousand different ways and compensated one by the other in different persons, thus form divers states and different conditions," etc., has not ceased to be true since the Revolution. Louis Veuillot wrote: "If I could re-establish a class of nobles, I should do so at once, and I would not belong to it." Neither would I.

The whole duty of society, I have said, is, as much as possible—that is to say, as much as the public interest will allow—to be careful not to add to the inequality which comes from nature a surplus of inequality due to law; as much as possible to treat all its members with impartiality.

Now, this is possible in civil life. Equality before the law, though it is often a snare, seems due to us. That was the only equality claimed by Voltaire. We have it. Beyond, all is mere illusion. Political equality (universal suffrage) creates worse inequalities. Economical equality, or collectivism, would be the reign of functionaries, therefore a hierarchy, and would lead to inequality.

The "Contrat social" clearly demonstrates the first point (that political equality produces the worst sort of inequality).

Before the first societies, at the time of wandering savages, inequality existed the moment they met, and (in spite of Rousseau) the most brutal of inequalities is that of physical strength and dexterity.

One can certainly suppose that at the dawn of society there was a sort of tacit contract; but through this contract, the contributions being unequal, the contracting parties must have remained likewise unequal. Where the strong and the wily take command and have authority, and the others possess only a little security. (Besides, on these very obscure origins, I know of nothing more reasonable than Buffon's hypothesis in the seventh "Epoque de la nature.")

But Rousseau would have it that a contract where the strong should benevolently consider themselves as the equals of the weak, and should claim no privilege, may have been entered upon or understood. Or (let us put things at best) that a society might have been organized as if such a compact had been agreed upon. So be it.

All citizens, equal among thmselves, vote laws (and, besides, elect those who apply them). It is the law of direct government applied through universal suffrage. (It is astonishing that Rousseau should not have given it that name or another similar to it). But it is evident that votes would not be unanimous. Universal suffrage means the power of half the citizens *plus* one, and the other half, all but one, must, therefore, submit to laws which it has not chosen. And thus (I tell you things which are well known, but I am bound to repeat them here) universal suffrage—under the parliamentary rule, but still more under the direct government of the people —must necessarily end in the tyranny of a party. (And at the same time, most generally, in the enslaving, or rather the submersion, of the intelligent by the incapable, who are more numerous.) And we should like to know how, then, the voters of the minority can remain the equals of the voters of the majority, who are all powerful against the victims of the suffrage.

Rousseau recognized this objection. He thus formulates it:

"Outside of the primitive contract [where unanimity

was necessary] the voice of the majority controls all others; it is a result of the contract itself. But one may ask how a man can be free and yet be forced to accept decisions which are not his. How are the opposing parties to submit to laws made against their will?"

And here is his answer:

"I answer that the question is not well formulated. A citizen consents to all laws, even to those made in spite of him, even to those that punish him when he violates them. The constant will of all the members of the state is the general will; it is through it that they are citizens, and free. When a law is proposed in the assembly of the people, that which is asked of them is not exactly whether they approve the proposition, but if it is in conformity with the general will which is theirs—each man in giving his suffrage gives his opinion on the subject—and the declaration of the general will is deduced from the result of the vote. Therefore, if an opinion contrary to mine is adopted, that only proves that I had made a mistake, and that what I considered the general will was not what I supposed. If my own particular opinion had triumphed, I should have acted against my will; then, indeed, I should not have been free" (book iv. 2). (It is the "divine right" of the majority.)

To tell the truth, this page is meaningless. What, then, is the general will? From the preceding chapter it would seem to mean that will which is in harmony with the general interest, and which every citizen always and necessarily must possess. So be it. But who is to decide what is in harmony, *on such or such a point*, with the general will, thus understood? It must evidently be the majority; and as the majority is not infallible, it must, therefore, merely signify what is in conformity, on that point, not with the general will, but with the will of the majority, and nothing more, and the minority will be none the less cheated.

Besides, Rousseau, after his enigmatical reasoning, is good enough to add:

> "This, it is true, presupposes that all the elements of the general will [that is, according to him, perspicacity, justice, and disinterestedness] are still with the majority. *When they cease to be with it, whatever part one takes, there will be no more liberty.*"

But how can one maintain in the majority "all the elements of the general will"? In other words, how can one force the majority to be always "clear-sighted, just, and disinterested"? Rousseau does not answer, because there is no answer possible.

In reality the system dreamed by Rousseau is so horrible that he himself, with his character and his pride, could never have lived under it a single day. Why, then, did he dream of it? How could this solitary man, this anarchist by temperament, propose to us this exaggerated cult of the state?

I have already explained this to you—it was in order

to contradict Montesquieu, to annoy the Lesser Council, and, also, for the same reasons which cause, in our days, anarchists to appear on good terms with the collectivists. They, doubtless, harbor this secret thought, that they will find their advantage in a totally leveled society, where no force, no traditional group, can prevent their individual progress.[1] Thus, "Rousseau's socialism is, perhaps, but the means of his individualism" (Brunetière). Besides, Rousseau is not making laws for himself, but for others, which puts him quite at his ease.

And, then, one more contradiction in his case matters but little. The "Contrat social" is remarkable for its incoherency and obscurity. At times, the "Contrat," to Rousseau, is a mere supposition; then again he seems to believe in its historical reality. One never knows whether he is Aristotle or Lycurgus. It is a confused mixture of theory and pretended observation. He proposes to the citizens, as soon as the social compact is concluded, to choose a legislator after the manner of Lycurgus or Solon; he, Rousseau himself, is that legislator; but if the nation is incompetent to make its constitution, how should it then be so marvelously competent to make its laws? After having railed at Montesquieu about the division of powers (legislative, executive, judicial), he himself accepts this division by separating the powers delegated to the nation's commissioners, etc., etc.

[1] "Let us notice, however, that the syndical movement, so obscure as yet, seems to turn against absolute democracy. Certain syndicalists treat Rousseau as a "theorician of democratic servitude."

I confess that I perceive in the "Contrat social" some traces of mental derangement. There are certain things which Rousseau put in it at random—things quite in contradiction with the spirit of the greater part of the work, simply because they happened to cross his mind, or because they arose out of an old remnant of atavism. I have already shown in him the Calvinistic confusion of morals with politics. We must add to it a perfectly odious passage,—of which the origin might perhaps be found in some Protestant writer,—a passage where is seen all the anti-popery of his first education (perhaps he desired to flatter his co-religionists of Geneva), where he denies to "Roman Christians" the possibility of being good citizens because the head of their religion does not reside in their country; where, after having implicitly banished atheists from his republic, he likewise implictly banishes from it all Catholics. This is a homicidal passage, a generator and adviser of persecution; a page written by one doomed to be persecuted, and by whom? By Protestants.

Such is the "Contrat social." Undertaken to "render men happy and free," it turns out to be one of the most complete instruments of oppression ever forged by a maniac.

And now, you will see Rousseau himself ruin his Utopia, and that while he is constructing it, and also after it is built.

In his book itself, he confesses that, at the present

moment, men in general have been too thoroughly corrupted by society to be worthy of the "Contrat social." It would be fit, at most, for very small cities: Geneva, Berne. In reality, it is entirely fit only for nations, at the same time, very small and very young, still able to accept a legislator according to antiquity: Corsica, for example. Rousseau says in so many words:

"There is still in Europe a people capable of legislation—that of the Island of Corsica. The valor and fortitude with which this brave nation has been able to recover and defend its liberty [with Paoli] deserves that some wise man should teach it to preserve it. I have a presentiment that, some day, that little island will astonish Europe."

(This came to pass, but not exactly in the way Jean-Jacques had foreseen.)

Thus it is an understood thing that the government of the "Contrat social" is intended only for very small states. And is even that small size a sufficient condition? Rousseau does not think so.

He writes:

"How many things difficult to bring together does not such a government presuppose! First, a very small state, where the citizens can conveniently be assembled and where each can easily know the others; secondly, a perfect simplicity of manners, which prevents vast numbers of interests and stormy discussions; then a great deal of equality as to rank and fortune, without which equality could not subsist in the rights and authority of each; finally, no luxury, or as little as possible, for luxury comes from riches, or makes them necessary; it corrupts both rich and poor, on one side by possession, on the other by envy . . . it takes all its citizens from the state to enslave one to the other, and all to public opinion. . . .

". . . Let us add that no government *is so much subjected to civil war and intestinal agitations as a democratic or popular government*. . . .

". . . Were there a nation of gods, it would be governed democratically. So perfect a government *is not fit for men*."

Therefore, it is not fit even for Corsicans. Then, for whom is it fit? And why was the "Contrat social" written? Here, as with "Julie," as with "Emile," Rousseau's friends say (only they say it better): "Yes, this seems idiotic, but it is very noble: Rousseau presents to us an ideal to which it would be admirable to draw near." Why? Ideals, most undesirable, may exist. Certain ideals present such a conception of reality, or imply such suspicious sentiments in those who conceive or preach them, that it might be dangerous even to aspire to an ideal of so ambiguous a kind. "Ideal, ideal," that is easily said, and it is by no means synonymous with goodness, generosity or usefulness.

And here is the truth—Rousseau, in the "Contrat" itself acknowledges that the government of the "Contrat" is absolutely impracticable. And he will acknowledge it more fully still, a little later, in his letters.

We are accustomed to these retractions. We have seen him attenuate or even deny in his correspondence the too aggressive or too unreasonable paradoxes of his books. Furthermore, he must have been all the better disposed to disown the "Contrat," that, after all and whatever he may have done to bind it to them, the "Contrat" is pretty violently at variance with his other works.[1] (In these he had been in the habit of granting as little as possible to the social institution; in that he delivers up man entirely to the social institution.) Then, several years had passed. Those Genevese, for whom he wrote the book, had odiously persecuted him. This is the moment when he writes to the Corsican, Butta-Foco:

"I instinctively love your clergy (the Catholic clergy), as much as I hate ours. I have many friends among French priests, and have always lived in peace with them."

To d'Ivernois, he writes (January 13, 1767):

"In our intercourse, you may have seen that I was no visionary, and in the 'Contrat social' I never approved a democratic government."

[1] It must not be forgotten that the first draft of the "Contrat social" is anterior to Rousseau's first "Discours" and his theory on the goodness of nature.

(And he was able to say this and even to believe it, the book being full of contradictions.)

He writes to the Marquis de Mirabeau (July 26, 1767):

"Here is, in my former ideas, the great political problem, which I compare to that of the squaring of the circle in geometry: find a form of government which will put law above man."

(And it is certainly the squaring of the circle, since laws will ever be made by men and applied by men.)

"If this form is to be found," adds he, "let us seek for it. . . . If, unfortunately, it is impossible to find, and, *ingenuously, I confess that I believe it to be so, we must, according to me, then pass to the other extreme, and suddenly place man as far above laws as possible; consequently establish arbitrary despotism, and the most arbitrary possible.*"

(It is, perhaps, also at that moment that Rousseau had been greatly beholden to the King of Prussia.)

"I should like," pursues he, "*that the despot might be God.* In a word, *I see no possible medium between the most austere democracy and the most perfect Hobbism; for the conflict between men and law, which throws the state into perpetual intestinal warfare, is the worst of all political states.*"

Then, as though horrified at having written such things:

"But Caligula, Nero, Tiberius! . . . My God, I throw myself face downward and moan at being a man."

That he should throw himself on the ground when he thinks of distant Nero, that is very well. But it would tend to prove that he no longer cares for the "Contrat."

Indeed, he cares so little for it, that six months later (January-February, 1768), in long letters to his compatriot, d'Ivernois, speaking of the troubles in Geneva, and the reform of the constitution,—he tries to find, as might have done Montesquieu himself, combinations and the balance of attributions between the different political bodies (Lesser Council, Higher Council, General Council or electors); and that, finally, despairing of concord, he sends to his Geneva friends this exhortation, which might have come from an extravagant *Conciones*.

". . . Yes, gentlemen, there is but one resolution for you to take, and it is, if I dare say so, the only one worthy of you. It is, instead of staining your hands with the blood of your fellow-citizens, to give up to them those walls which should have been the refuge of liberty and *which are destined to be nothing but a den of tyrants;* it is to leave the city, all together, in broad daylight, your wives and children in your midst, and, since you are doomed to irons, to wear those of some great prince, and not the *insupportable and odious yoke of your equals.*"

These last words are very beautiful. They resume all the absurdity of the "Contrat social" and of democracy itself.

Hence, there are three stages: first, Jean-Jacques, in his book itself, declares the "Contrat" to be applicable only to small cities; second, he declares it to be inapplicable to simple mortals; third, five or six years later he totally disowns it.

Now this form of government which the author described as being fit only for the use of a city containing twenty thousand souls and fifteen hundred electors (and that, later, he had acknowledged to be impracticable even in so small a city, and finally disowned with a sort of fury), the Revolution thirty years later will adopt like a gospel, seeking to impose it upon a people ten centuries old and with a population of twenty-five millions. And that venture will be called the Reign of Terror.

It was not Rousseau's fault, you will say.

Let us understand each other. I do not say that Rousseau's writings brought on the Revolution (for which there were deep-rooted economical causes): above all, I do not say that they alone were responsible for it. But it so happened that, more than any other writer, Rousseau furnished a state of mind, a sentiment, a phraseology and formulas, to the most systematically violent men of the Terror, and even to the most ignorant of the revolutionary rabble.

All the more that, outside of the essential error on which it was built, the "Contrat social" in its details is full of counter-truths. In it one reads that "the public voice scarcely ever brings to the first ranks men who are not enlightened and who do not honor these ranks." One reads that "the people make fewer mistakes in its choice than a prince";—"that a man of real merit is almost as rare in a ministry [of a king] as a fool at the head of a republican government." About kings, one reads: "that all things concur to deprive a man raised up to command of justice and reason." One reads that "republics attain their ends by straighter and easier roads than a monarchy." The feudal government is here called "the iniquitous and absurd government where the human species is degraded and where the name of man is a dishonor," etc., etc. . . . All the most stupid and murderous prejudices of the Revolution came from the "Contrat social."

"I heard," wrote Mallet de Pan, "I heard, in 1788, Marat, in public squares, read and comment the 'Contrat social,' to the applause of an enthusiastic audience."

And five years later, France tasted the benefits of the "Contrat social" doctrines, and of universal equality, and of the people's sovereignty, and of the absolute rights of the state, and of the exceptional magistracy such as the Committee of Public Safety and the revolutionary tribunal. From chapter 8 of book iv., came the anti-Catholic prejudice, and the civil constitution of the clergy, and religious persecution. And the "Contrat social" took the shape of law in the inapplicable constitution of 1793.

All that because, thirty years before, a half-demented man took it into his head to imagine for a city of twenty thousand inhabitants a legislation which was "fit only for gods,"—and to which, five years later, he declared, "the most arbitrary despotism" to be preferable.

Never, I believe, thanks to human credulity and stupidity, has a writer done more harm to man than this writer, who, it seems, did not exactly know what he was saying; he would, besides, have fled from his city had it been what he dreamed. Really, there are times when one it tempted to say that this wretched man was a criminal.

And it is because this idea was so painful that I have first collected all that seemed to me most odious in his works, in order to clear the way for the study of the "Profession de foi du vicaire Savoyard." After that we shall feel but pity for Jean-Jacques, and sometimes admiration, for, and I say this seriously, his soul grew purer as his ills and his madness augmented.

So, let us go back a little. When Emile's tutor deems it advisable to teach him natural religion, he makes the supposition that he, himself, in danger of losing his soul, formerly met a good priest, a country curate, a "vicaire Savoyard," whose instructions brought him back to the right path. Rousseau finds it indispensable that this good priest should have known human weakness: for Rousseau cannot fancy a sympathetic personage unless, like himself, he had been besmudged. But, nevertheless, this vicar is overflowing with virtue and charity, and I should have said that he rather made one think of Jocelyn,[1] if Jocelyn had not remained pure, and if Jocelyn did not keep, with regard to Catholic dogma, a kind of verbal orthodoxy.

Now this priest one morning takes his young friend into the country, and in presence of natural beauties, the view of which strengthens his discourse and lends it a magnificent testimony, he exposes to his disciple the purest and the most touching spiritual doctrine.

It will be well to sum up his very simple arguments.

It is self-evident that a power governs the universe. And if matter set in motion proves to us a superior will, this matter, moving according to certain laws, proves to us a supreme intelligence. So much for the universe.

And now for man: Man is *free* in his acts, and, as such, is animated by an immaterial substance.

Now, if the soul is immaterial, it can survive the body; and, if it survives it, Providence is justified as to the existence of evil in the world (without taking into account that moral ills are the work of man and physical suffering is reduced to almost nothing for natural man). A proof of the immortality of the soul, of a future life and of a future sanction, is the earthly triumph of the wicked.

And creation, must one believe in it? The vicar believes at least in the formation and ordaining of the world by God. And God, what do we know of Him? We can, at least, perceive His attributes—intelligence, power, justice, goodness.

[1] Poem by Lamartine.

The rule which we must accept, in order to accomplish our destiny on earth, according to Him who placed us here, remains to be found. In this, our light is conscience.

Here is placed the invocation:

"Conscience! conscience! divine instinct, immortal and celestial voice, *sure guide* of an ignorant and finite, yet intelligent and free being, *infallible judge* of good and evil, that renders man like unto God! It is thou that givest him the excellence of his nature and the morality of his actions; without thee, I feel nothing within me which puts me above the beasts, unless it be the sorry privilege of wandering from error to error with the aid of an unruly intelligence and of an unprincipled reasoning."

Conscience a "sure guide"? Conscience an "infallible judge"? Infallible always, and never deceived by the "unruly intelligence"? Alas! what sort of a guide, what sort of a judge, was Rousseau's conscience, when, at the desertion of his third child, "after a serious examination of his *conscience* ("Confessions," viii.,) he wrote:

"If I made a mistake as to results, nothing is more astounding than the *security of the soul* with which I accomplished it."

And a little further:

"This arrangement [the depositing of the children at

the Foundling-hospital] seemed to me so good, so sensible, so *lawful!* . . ."

Oh! how right was Julie when, regenerated and pious, she wrote: "I will no longer be judge in my own case!" Conscience, unaided by a fixed rule, a tradition, a dogmatic religion, or simply by the Decalogue, is so apt, in certain cases, to merge into pride or secret interest! Rousseau's faith in conscience—that is, in his conscience—is nothing more nor less than "individualism in morals," which is a contradictory term. There is no such thing as a general conscience: there is my conscience, your conscience, Rousseau's conscience, which had many a time been very uncertain and very murky. . . .

But I am wrong to interrupt Jean-Jacques, who is here at his best. The vicar continues; beautiful pages follow, full of stoicism, on this idea that to conquer our passions out of love of order is to obey nature. Then comes a dissertation on prayer; he would not have it prolix:

"The only thing I ask of God is that He should redress my error if I go astray."

And he comes to revelation and miracles.

This last part contains the passages for which "Emile" was condemned (I have said under what particular circumstances). Rousseau, however, shows here great prudence. In a few words he disposes of all that is supernatural—miracles, revelation—without any positive negation, and, especially, because the demonstration is impossible. He says with regard to revelation:

"I neither accept nor reject it—I only reject the obligation to understand it."

He says of miracles that—without taking into account that there is no possibility of verifying them—they are useless from the fact that, in turn, the truth of a doctrine is proved by miracles, and the truth of miracles by doctrine. He says of the Gospel:

"The holiness of the Gospel is an argument which appeals to my heart."

And you remember the famous passage which ends with these words, of which I cannot say whether they express serious faith or whether they are but a fashion of talk and a rhetorical effect:

"Yes, if the life and death of Socrates were those of a sage, the life and death of Jesus were those of a God."

He is, moreover, careful to say on every delicate subject:

"I only make up my mind, trembling, and I submit to you my doubts, rather than my conviction."

He professes that in all religions there is the same solid nucleus: faith in a personal God, in the soul, in future life, and that for the rest each man should follow his country's belief. Therefore, let us be tolerant. And I must quote the real conclusion of the vicar:

". . . Such is the involuntary skepticism in which I have remained; but that skepticism has nothing painful in it, because it does not extend to the essential points of practice, and because I am firm as to the principles of all my duties. I serve God in the simplicity of my heart. I seek to know what is important with regard to my conduct. As to dogmas which influence neither actions nor morality [but are there such? . . .], and about which so many people trouble themselves, I remain in peace. . . . I believe that all religions wherein one serves God, are good. *The essential worship is that of the heart.*"

This profession of faith by the Savoyard vicar remains, I think, the most beautiful spiritual *Credo* which was ever written. I fear that this doctrine may seem a little superficial to the new generations of thinkers. Since then, other metaphysics have seemed stronger and more learned, and have been more in favor. What young professor of philosophy would deign to declare himself simply a spiritualist and a deist? . . . It is because one always thinks of the official, insincere, motionless, dead spiritualism of Victor Cousin, and of the old text books of philosophy. And yet. . . . The spiritual arguments are fully worth those of metaphysics which are looked upon as of a higher nature, for in such matters there can be no thought of a real demonstration. "The metaphysical proofs of God," said Pascal, "are so far removed from the intelligence of man, and so involved, that they strike one but little; and, while they might serve a few, they would serve these but during the moment when they see this demonstration; an hour later they would fear lest they had been deceived." But the "proofs of God" retained by Rousseau, if they are certainly not unanswerable, are the simplest, the most accessible to an ordinary intelligence, and, so to speak, the most easily "carried." They are the most simple among the traditional proofs of Plato, of Descartes, of Malebranche, of Bossuet, of Fénelon. . . . Remember that before spiritualism had become the philosophy of the baccalaureate (I mean the baccalaureate of my youth), it had been the philosophy of "Phædon," of the "Banquet," and of "Scipio's dream." And, again, remember that spiritualism, if it is not the most subtle, is the most generous explanation of the universe,—that which gives to the world its most beautiful meaning, that which contains most love, and which renders the most magnificent tribute to the First Cause.

And it is thus that Rousseau understands it. His deism is not, like that of Voltaire, a political deism, a police officer's deism. Voltaire's deism leaves Voltaire perfectly free. With Rousseau's there are obligations. For him it really is an emotional and active religion, which reacts on life and deeds. The deism of Jean-Jacques is for him so entirely a religion that he clearly opposes it to irreligion, that is to say, to the atheism and materialism of the "philosophers" (who will never forgive him for it). And the religious sentiment of Rousseau, his persuasion of the absolute necessity of belief in God and of the love of God, has so firm a hold upon him that he does not fear, in a "Note," to prefer fanaticism to irreligion. One should always read Rousseau's "Notes," for they often are more full of meaning and bolder than his text. In this one, which is magnificent, he unflinchingly and energetically runs full tilt against the philosophers' party, and dares to say things like the following, to which, now-a-days, we could give an application:

"One of the most usual of the sophisms in use with the philosophers is to oppose a nation of veritable philosophers to one of bad Christians, as though it were easier to form a nation of true philosophers than one of true Christians. Religious fanaticism, though sanguinary and cruel, is yet a great and strong passion, which elevates the heart of man, which causes him to despise death, which gives him prodigious energy, and which, better directed, might produce the most sublime virtues; whereas irreligion and, in general, a reasoning and philosophical spirit, attach one to life, effeminate, debase souls, concentrate all passions into the meanness of private interest, the subjection to *self*, and thus undermine, little by little, the foundations of all society. . . .

"Fanaticism, though more disastrous in its immediate

effects than what is to-day called the philosophical spirit, is far less so in its consequences. Besides, it is easy to display fine maxims in books; but the question is whether they hold to the doctrine. . . . It remains to be seen whether philosophy, prosperous and enthroned, could master vanity, interest, ambition, the petty passions of man, or whether it could put into practice that gentle humanity which it exalts, pen in hand.

"Through its principles, philosophy could do no good that religion could not do even better, and religion accomplishes much good of which philosophy would be incapable. . . .

"Our modern governments unquestionably owe to Christianity their most solid authority, and their less frequent revolutions; it has rendered them less sanguinary; this can be proved by facts, by comparing them with the ancient governments."

It is Rousseau, it is not Joseph de Maistre, who wrote this. All these sentences must have caused the Encyclopedists to howl. Henceforth, Rousseau, in their eyes, was nothing but a dangerous fanatic.

Rousseau, however, on this point had not changed. Already, toward 1755, I think, at a supper given by Mlle Quinault, described by Mme d'Epinay, who was of the party, Jean-Jacques, full of indignation at the impious conversation, exclaimed:

"If it is cowardly to allow an absent friend to be

maligned, it is a crime to allow one's God, who is present, to be attacked; and I, gentlemen, believe in God. . . . I leave the house if you say another word." And he added: "I cannot endure this madness of destruction without building up. . . . Besides, the idea of God is necessary to happiness, and I wish you to be happy."

It is remarkable that in this "Note" of the "Profession de foi," Rousseau does not speak of "deism"; he no longer says "natural religion," he says "religion" or "Christianity." In the "Profession de foi," he is perhaps as near Catholicism as to Protestantism, for he takes all that is common to the two religions, and his attitude is rather Catholic than Protestant. It is furthermore noticeable that, in order to teach Emile true religion, he should have chosen, not a Protestant minister (which would have been natural, since he had returned to the religion of his fathers), but a Roman Catholic priest, formed of the remembrance of two Roman Catholic priests, Abbé Gaime and Abbé Gatier.

It must, however, be acknowledged that this Christianity of Rousseau is a rather enervated Christianity. It is Christianity without what constitutes its solid basis —the dogma of orginal sin with all its theological consequences.

Jean-Jacques, at twenty-two, fed on Port Royal books, had been almost a Jansenist. What was bound to attract him was that the Jansenist was the man who entertained the most tragical, the most passionate communication with the Unknown. Jean-Jacques in those days was horribly afraid of hell. One day he threw a stone against a tree saying: "If I hit, sign of salvation; if I miss, sign of damnation." But his terrors were allayed, thanks to the influence of the two good Jesuit fathers and of Mme de Warens. The latter enjoyed the most confiding religion. She was a "quietist" (love God and do what you will). Mme Guyon still had some followers in Switzerland, with whom Mme de Warens was acquainted. And that is, perhaps, why there is a sort of quietism in Rousseau's latitudinarian and sentimental Christianity—and a little, also (as to the accent), of Fénelon's tenderness, and of that of the former bishop of Geneva and provost of the Annecy Church, François de Sales.

This emotional and religious spiritualism, this half-Christianity of Rousseau, is to be that of Bernardin de Saint-Pierre; with the exception of some shading, it is to be that of Chateaubriand; that of Lamartine, whose "Jocelyn" will owe much to the vicar of Savoy; it is to be that of George Sand, even of Michelet, when he was young, and of Victor Hugo.

Spirituality, taken thus, is so entirely a religion capable of influencing life, that, up to the middle of the nineteen century, and even to the first part of the Second Empire, we had in the French "bourgeoisie," and even among peasants, (I have known such) grandfathers and fathers—many of them—whose souls were fed on that religion; they were a little on the border, but not quite outside of the Catholicism of their wives and daughters.

It is a pity it should not have persisted (on account, perhaps, of its lack of dogmatical consistency), for, without being all-sufficient, it yet served some purpose, and was still, so to speak, reflected Christianity.

And, no doubt, it was Robespierre's spirituality, and that of Saint-Just, and of the theophilanthropists; but, all the same, in remembrance of so many grandfathers, grand-uncles, or ancestors, who, under the First Empire, under the Restoration, under Louis-Philippe, were a little better than they might otherwise have been, thanks to this spirituality—in all that remains to be said of Rousseau's sad life, I shall listen but to pity.

THE "LETTRE À L'ARCHEVÊQUE DE PARIS" —THE "LETTRES DE LA MONTAGNE"— LAST YEARS OF ROUSSEAU—THE DIALOGUES

CHAPTER IX

THE "LETTRE À L'ARCHEVÊQUE DE PARIS"—THE "LETTRES DE LA MONTAGNE"—LAST YEARS OF ROUSSEAU—THE DIALOGUES

I HAVE not disguised my real admiration for the "Profession de foi du vicaire Savoyard." Yet these generous pages caused Rousseau's final misfortunes. It is often so in this world.

You remember under what circumstances, despite the protection of Mme de Luxembourg and the Prince de Conti, despite the protection of M. de Malesherbes, "Emile" was condemned by the Paris Parliament, and Rousseau threatened with imprisonment.

No one, however, cared to be burdened with him. He was allowed plenty of time to leave, and on his way he met the men sent to arrest him, and was saluted by them.

Rousseau submitted to the inevitable with that passivity, or rather, we should say, with that resignation peculiar to him, and which he had so eloquently preached to Emile. He at once thought of moving to Switzerland. In his traveling coach he read the Bible, and scribbled a prose poem on the "Levite of Ephraim." He was not much disturbed. He loved his native land, and fancied that, in return, he was loved by his compatriots. His genius reflected credit on Geneva. When he wrote the "Contrat social" Geneva was ever before him. And how should the Genevese ministers object to "Emile," for had not d'Alembert (in his article on Geneva in the "Encyclodepia") accused them of "socialism," that is, really, of rationalism?

Yes, in Switzerland he might be happy.

"On entering the territory of Berne," says he, "I made the coachman stop; I alighted, I prostrated myself, I embraced, I kissed the earth, and called out in my transport: 'Heaven, protector of virtue, I praise thee, I have reached a land of liberty!'"

He was full of illusions. This was, for the unfortunate man, the beginning of real persecutions, of three years of lamentable wanderings; he was to be hunted from place to place, and his own church was to be much more cruel to him than ever had been the Church of France.

Why? You will find the reasons set forth very clearly in M. Edouard Rod's excellent book, "L'affaire Jean-Jacques Rousseau."

So he reached Iverdun (territory of Berne), where he was received by his old friend Roguin. At once he learned that "Emile" had been condemned and burned at Geneva (on account of the pages on miracles and revelation), and he himself threatened with prison by his dear Genevese (June 18-19, 1762). However, Roguin's nephew offered him a small cottage, which he accepted. He could think himself settled; but three weeks later the Berne Senate exiled him from Iverdun.

Then he crossed the mountain and went to Motiers-Travers, in the county of Neuchâtel. Roguin's niece, Mme Boy de la Tour, offered him a house of hers at Motiers. (For it was Rousseau's fate always to be some-one's guest.)

The county of Neuchâtel belonged to the King of Prussia (Frederick II.). Rousseau placed himself under his Majesty's protection by letters wherein (this one feels) he enjoyed showing the whole world how a free man can address a monarch with becoming civic and Lacedemonian pride. But, already, in his heart, he had repudiated the "Contrat social."

Thérèse joined him. He became acquainted with Lord Keit, Marshal of Scotland (Lord Marshal), Governor of Neuchâtel for the King of Prussia—an excellent man, who treated Rousseau most kindly, and by whom he was tenderly loved. Jean-Jacques began to breathe freely. Once more he believed himself to be safe. He took long walks, busying himself with botany; he took pleasure in making braid, which he offered to the young daughters of his friends, on condition that when they married and had children they should themselves nurse their babies.

It was at this time that he adopted the Armenian dress.

"This was not a new idea. . . I had thought of it often at Montmorency, when my infirmities forced me to remain in my room; a long garment seemed most fit for me. The opportunity offered by an Armenian tailor, who often visited a relative at Montmorency, tempted me to try this new garb, in spite of gossip, about which I cared little. . . . I, therefore, had an Armenian outfit made; but the persecution I then endured induced me to put off wearing it until quieter days, and it was only some months later, when I again fell ill, that I ventured to put on the new dress, at Motiers, especially after having consulted the clergyman of the place, who assured me that I could wear it in church without exciting any scandal. I, therefore, adopted the jacket, the caftan, the furred cap, the sash; and, after having worn this accouterment at divine service, I did not see why I should not wear it at my Lord Marshal's. His Excellency, seeing me thus dressed, merely said, 'Salamalcki,' after which it was an understood thing and I wore no other dress."

In reality his infirmities scarcely called for so eccentric a costume. Some loose, long cloak would have sufficed. Evidently, the latent madness was gaining on him. Goethe, he who was never menaced by madness, writes in "Wilhelm Meister" (book v. chap. xvi.), in speaking of the old harp player: "If I succeed," says Wilhelm, "in making him give up his beard and his long robe, I shall have gained much; for nothing inclines us more to madness than to singularize ourselves, and nothing maintains common sense more than to live in a crowd like everybody else."

It was, I believe, about the same time that Rousseau

acquired the peculiar habit of substituting for the personal pronoun "I" or "me," his name, and especially his Christian name, of speaking of himself in the third person, saying: "Jean-Jacques cannot . . ." "It would not do for Jean-Jacques . . ." "What would be said of Jean-Jacques . . ." You can be sure of it, this is another sign of brain trouble.

To resume: The Motiers clergyman, Montmollin, began by showing himself a warm advocate of Jean-Jacques, and, at Rousseau's request, admitted him to communion. Jean-Jacques says on this occasion:

". . . It seemed to me sad ever to live alone on earth, especially in adversity. In the midst of proscription and persecution I found great sweetness in being able to say: 'At last, I am among my brethren; and I received the sacrament with heartfelt emotion and tears of tenderness, which, perhaps, were the best preparation for it, and the most agreeable to God.'"

(About the same time Voltaire at Ferney accomplished his Easter devotions, and caused the fact to be verified by a notary public. One might compare the sincere and pious communion of poor exiled Rousseau, and the sacrilegious and farcical—as well as prudent and conservative—communion of the rich Lord of Ferney. . . . It is true that not much can be proved by this parallel, except that the more religious of these two men was precisely he who proved the more fatal to us.)

Almost on the very day when Jean-Jacques so devoutly received the sacrament, Christophe de Beaumont, Archbishop of Paris, signed a *Mandement portant condamnation de l'Emile*[1] (August 20, 1762). The Archbishop was performing his duty. In that book he pointed out twenty propositions contrary to the Catholic orthodoxy. The order began (or nearly so) by a really somewhat brilliant portrait of Rousseau—and even fair, especially if one remembers that the critic was an archbishop. We must quote this part of it:

"From the midst of error sprang a man full of the language of philosophy, though he was no true philosopher; his mind was endowed with great knowledge which did not enlighten it, and which spread darkness in the minds of others; his character was a prey to paradox, both of opinion and conduct; he allied simplicity of manners with ostentation of thought, the zeal of antique maxims with a mania for introducing novelties, the obscurity of retreat with the desire to be known of all; he has been heard to rail against the sciences he cultivated, praise the excellence of the Gospel, whose doctrines he destroyed, describe the beauty of virtues which he smothered in the souls of his readers. . . . In a work on the equality of conditions, he degraded man to the rank of beasts; in another and more recent production, he introduced the poison of voluptuousness, while seeming to prohibit it; in this one he takes possession of the

[1] "Order condemning Emile."

first age of man, the better to establish the sway of irreligion."

The remainder of the order was what it could and necessarily must be, with, perhaps, some useless accusations of insincerity.

Jean-Jacques answered by the letter, theatrically entitled, "Jean-Jacques Rousseau, citoyen de Genève, à Christophe de Beaumont, Archevêque de Paris, Duc de Saint-Cloud, Pair de France, Commandeur de l'ordre du Saint-Esprit, Proviseur de Sorbonne,"[1] etc. This letter is not the most original of his works, but it is, perhaps, the most perfect of them all. Naturally, the Archbishop and the Protestant latitudinarian could not agree, since Rousseau denies or contests that which the prelate takes for granted—revelation and miracles. One may say that the two adversaries wield arms that do not clash. On the other hand, the letter to Christophe de Beaumont shows in the main nothing new—it only repeats, in an extenuated and persuasive form, some of the theories of "Emile" and the "Contrat." But on the whole the letter is a masterpiece of polemics, a marvel of clever, vigorous, emotional, eloquent discussion. The "citizen of Geneva" first affects deep respect for the prelate; he exaggerates his own attitude of a man obscure and insignificant, of mod-

[1] "Jean-Jacques Rousseau, citizen of Geneva, to Christophe de Beaumont, Archbishop of Paris, Duke of Saint-Cloud, Peer of France, Commander of the Order of the Holy Ghost, Head Master of the Sorbonne," etc. . . .

est citizen—but who carries truth within him—before one of earth's great potentates. Then, little by little, rises the plaint of one oppressed; finally his anger bursts forth. All this is admirably conducted. He ends thus:

"How easy is it for you men who are firmly established in your dignities to lay down the law! . . . You proudly crush the weak, for you are answerable to none for your iniquities. . . . On the slightest provocation of interest or of state, you sweep us before you like dust. Some give out decrees and condemn to the stake, others calumniate and dishonor, without right, without reason, without contempt, without anger even, simply because it is convenient, and that poor wretches are in the way.

"Monseigneur, you have publicly insulted me [is not this already the tone and manner of some harangue in a drama by Hugo, where a low-born hero gives "a piece of his mind" to a prince?]. Monseigneur, you have publicly insulted me; I come to prove that you have calumniated me. If you were a private person like myself, I could force you to appear before some equitable tribunal, where we might stand, I with my book, you with your order, and there you would certainly be declared guilty and condemned to give me reparation as public as was the offense. But you hold a rank which dispenses you from all justice, and I am nothing. Nevertheless, you who preach the Gospel, you, prelate, delegated to teach men their duty, you know what yours should be in such a case. As for me,

I have performed mine; I have nothing more to say to you, and I hold my peace.

"Deign to accept, Monseigneur, my profound respect.

"Motiers, November 18, 1762."

I have said that, in reality, the "Lettre à M. de Beaumont" offered nothing new. I make exception for an interesting page. Even while he defends natural religion against the prelate, Rousseau separates himself from the "philosophers." One of their manias was to treat all founders of religions as knaves, impostors, charlatans, sacred jugglers. Jean-Jacques, who has the intuition of religious matters, judges otherwise:

"One should, as a general thing, honor all founders of different modes of worship. . . . They were men of great genius and of great virtue—that is always praiseworthy. They called themselves the elect of God; that may or may not have been; it is what the majority cannot always know, proofs not being at hand. But, even should this not be, they should not lightly be called impostors. Who knows how far perpetual meditations on the Divinity, how far enthusiasm for virtue, might not, in their sublime souls, trouble the low didactic system of vulgar ideas? At too great a height the head grows dizzy, and one does not see things as they are. . . ."

Here, Rousseau is infinitely more intelligent than Voltaire.

I fancy that, after his magnificent answer to the Archbishop of Paris, Rousseau expected to recover the good graces of those among his Geneva fellow-citizens who were hostile to him. There had been (see Rod's fine book on the subject), in the decree of the Lesser Council against Rousseau, an irregularity of jurisprudence. Jean-Jacques was persuaded that all the burghers would protest against this infraction of the law. And, in fact, he had, in Geneva, friends, the leaders of what might be called the democratic party, who even greatly wearied him with letters and visits. (Two of them carried their indiscretion to the point of falling ill at his house, where they were cared for). But nothing came of it but words. After having waited more than a year "that someone should protest against an illegal procedure," Rousseau made up his mind, gave up "an ungrateful country," and, by a letter to the First Syndic, abdicated his citizenship.

At that time he must have been most unhappy. We see it in his correspondence (which should always be consulted in connection with the "Confessions"). Alone, exiled, fancying himself abandoned by all, suffering more than ever from his malady, he wrote to Duclos (the only one of the "philosophers" with whom he had never quarreled) that he had decided upon suicide:

". . . My physical state has grown so much worse . . . that my sufferings, unrelenting and hopeless, place me in the exceptional case mentioned by Lord Edward answering Saint-Preux."

(This letter of Lord Edward is the twenty-second of the third part in the "Nouvelle Héloïse.")

And, at the same time, Rousseau wrote to M. Martinet, owner of the Motiers Château, to give him his testament, and to recommend Thérèse to his care; he had already done so to Duclos.

"Farewell; I am on my way to the land of just souls —I trust to find there few bishops and churchmen, but many men like you and me."

We must note this thought of suicide. Later, in the "Dauphiny," when he wrote to Thérèse to propose separation, he promises not to destroy himself. Which tends to prove that he sometimes harbored the thought of it.

However, he did not kill himself. He recovered, only to suffer again. Winter is a hard season at Motiers. During six months, he was unable to go out of the house. While making his braid, or sawing wood by way of exercise, he meditated on the universal injustice of which he was the victim, on his misfortune to which, thought he, none was ever comparable. Thérèse grew less gentle, for she was unhappy in this strange land—a Protestant land, whereas she was a Catholic—and a gossip.

At Geneva the agitation continued. Rousseau's adherents presented "protestations" to the Council, and the Council turned a deaf ear. In order to defend the Council, the procurator general, Tronchin, wrote on Rousseau's case, and against Rousseau, the "Lettres de la campagne."[1] Rousseau, beside himself this time, answered by the "Lettres de la montagne"[2] (nine letters in two parts, about three hundred pages).

In the second part he examines the constitution of Geneva, and the mechanism of the "right of representation," and demonstrates the illegality of the suit against him.

The first part, even now, is interesting; it is sometimes very fine. No doubt, in most of these pages, he merely confirms the ideas of the "Vicaire Savoyard," and his right to express them freely, even in Geneva. But there are also in them things which Rousseau had not yet said.

First, the passage where he refers the Reformation to its true origin, which is personal free interpretation, and draws from it, long beforehand, the conclusions of "liberal Protestantism" (which is really no longer a confessional creed). Rousseau, however, makes a reservation on two points:

"Provided that *one respects the whole of the Bible*, and that *one agrees as to the principal points*, one lives according to the evangelical reformation."

One does not understand very well why free examination should stop at the sanctity of the Bible, and at certain points of its interpretation. One of the characteristics of a religion founded on free interpretation seems to be self-destruction, and that is what, doubtless,

[1] "Letters from the country."
[2] "Letters from the mountain."

would have happened to the Reformation had not, in reality, most Protestants been men, like all others, influenced by a practical sense, by habits and traditions, scarcely capable of criticism, and in whom the liberty of interpretation is a principle and a claim much more than a reality. But, barring this, Rousseau's deductions are irreproachable:

"Each man remains sole judge within himself [judge of the doctrine and interpretation], and in that recognizes no other authority but his own. Good instruction should less fix the choice that we ought to make, than put us in such a state of mind as to enable us to choose. Such is the veritable spirit of the Reformation, such its real foundation. Individual reason decides . . . and freedom is so entirely the essence of reason, that, even were it desirous to be enslaved by authority, it could not succeed in being thus enslaved. Attack this principle and evangelism would crumble away in a moment. *Prove to me to-day, that in matters of faith I am bound to submit to any man's decisions, and to-morrow I become a Catholic*, and every logical and sincere man would do the same."

And, further, against those clergymen who, before Rousseau's case, affected extreme liberty of thought, and even passed for Socinians:

"Your ministers are indeed singular people: *one does not know what they believe and what they do not believe; their only way of affirming their faith is to attack that of others. . . .*"

And he goes further. He puts into the mouths of Catholics what answer they might have made to the first reformers, he entangles these in their own contradictions by arguments which Bossuet might have accepted, and with an accent into which Bossuet would only have put more charity and gentleness. Rousseau simply calls to the bar the Reformation itself, and its principle. What a singular man! The whole of this second "Lettre de la montagne" seems to me a masterpiece, and a most unexpected masterpiece. Thus it was Rousseau's destiny to be an iconoclast, even of Protestantism, and in remaining true to what is the very essence of the Reformation, and showing what, should it remain true to its essence, it would advise one to be: a rabid individualist.

I cannot conceal that this blow given by Rousseau to those of his religion, greatly pleases me. It is certain that, for his soul, it brought about consequences which we shall presently examine.

But I cannot abandon this first part of the "Lettre de la montagne" without reading to you a page on Jesus, which proves that, not only Chateaubriand, Senancour, George Sand, Michelet, Dumas *fils* read Rousseau carefully, and were influenced by him, but likewise Ernest Renan.

"I cannot help saying," writes Rousseau, in this third letter, "that one of the traits that most charms me in the character of Jesus was not only the gentleness of his mode of life, his simplicity, but *his ease, his grace, and even his elegance.* He did not shun pleasures nor festivities. He went to weddings, he saw women, he played with children, he was fond of perfumes, he dined with financiers. His disciples did not fast, his austerity was not inhuman. He was as indulgent as he was just, gentle with the weak, terrible to the wicked. His morality had in it *something fascinating, caressing, sweet;* he was tender-hearted, *he was a man of good education.* Had he not been the wisest of men, he would still have been the most lovable."

Could you not imagine you were reading a page of the "Vie de Jesus"? [1]

Naturally, the "Lettres de la montagne" exasperated the fury of Rousseau's enemies. The book was burned at Neuchâtel, Berne, the Hague, and Paris. Repeated deaths added to his melancholy. He lost the Maréchal de Luxembourg, "that good lord, the only true friend he had in France," who had continued to write affectionately to him ever since his exile, and to whom Jean-Jacques had sent long letters on the manners of the Neuchâtel country, and on the beauties of the Val Travers. About the same time Mme de Warens died, "weighed down with years, infirmities, and misery." Rousseau, who never spoke of her but with tenderness and respect, places her in heaven, which is well; but near Fénelon, which seems to me exaggerated.

"Go, gentle and generous soul, close to Fénelon, Bernex [the former bishop of Annecy], Catinat, you who, in a more humble state, like them opened your heart to

[1] Ernest Renan.

charity; taste the fruit of that charity, and prepare for your pupil the place he trusts to occupy near you."

This was not all. Rousseau's best friend (with the Maréchal de Luxembourg), and his most powerful patron, the Lord Marshal, called back to England, left Neuchâtel. Against poor Jean-Jacques, ill, sad, disabled, persecution continued and grew more violent, aggravated, at one moment, by an atrocious pamphlet by Voltaire (the "Sentiment des citoyens" . . .). The minister Montmollin abandoned Rousseau, then excited the people against him. The poor man whose carnival costume made him a prey of ragamuffins, was insulted in the streets. During the night of the 6th-7th of September, 1765, stones were thrown against his windows and the glass broken. He left Neuchâtel and went to the island of Saint-Pierre in the lake of Bienne. This pleasant island, three miles in circumference, belonged to the hospital of Berne and was only inhabited by the "receiver" of the hospital and his family—excellent people.

Rousseau spent six delightful weeks in this island; he botanized, rowed, and especially meditated. . . . Verily, he ought to have been left there for the remainder of his days. Whom did he trouble? But a decree of the Berne Senate expelled him, October 17. Beside himself, he wrote to the Senate, begging that he might be placed in a good prison for the rest of his life. . . . Then he went to Bienne, where zealous friends assured him that he would be in peace.

He was again expelled from Bienne. Ah! the Protestant clergy, that now claims and honors him, did not then show itself very tender.

The poor man did not know what to do. He thought of taking refuge in Scotland near the Lord Marshal, in Venice, in Zurich, in Silesia, in Berlin, in Savoy, in Jersey, in Italy, in Austria, in Amsterdam, in Corsica. Finally, and before taking any decision, he went to Strasburg, where he was warmly received and where "society" comforted him a little.

So many misfortunes ended by making him illustrious,—hastened on his madness,—and purified him.

I am well aware that Choiseul was justified in considering him a dangerous writer. But if, instead of exiling him, Choiseul had offered him (before "Emile") honors and some good sinecure . . . who knows what would have happened? . . . Rousseau's ambition had long been to become an "official" personage. Though he often spoke of his "incapacity to endure any yoke," he often, on the other hand, expressed the desire to establish himself honorably in a solid situation—(as when he was reinstated among the Genevese burghers). Besides, incapable of defending his material interests, he had great need of protection, of feeling some peace and security, of escaping from the fear of the morrow. Yes, Choiseul might have found other means of rendering him harmless, besides that of ordering his arrest.

And, moreover, he did not thus render him harmless; on the contrary. As soon as Rousseau was persecuted by the French government, and still more cruelly by the Swiss churches, his glory became unique and his reputation European. And it was very different from Voltaire's glory: it was the renown of a benefactor of men, of a sage, of a legislator after the manner of the Ancients. Already he was beginning to be worshiped. The hermit of Motiers was perpetually disturbed by illustrious visitors. He could hardly answer all the letters he received. Corsica asked him for a Constitution. Princes, great ladies, great lords, magistrates, priests, young men, consulted him on education, on religion, on cases of conscience. And his advice was excellent, not only eloquent—or penetrating—but full of common sense and nearly all in a spirit of order and conservatism. For he was generally wise for others.

But this situation of European oracle excited his pride,—while his too real misfortunes, and the perpetual anxiety in which he lived, developed in him the monomania of persecution.

Yet even out of his misfortunes he drew some enjoyment,—so out of all proportion and so exceptional did they seem to him. Like Chateaubriand (and this is not the first time that I have been led to compare the two men) Rousseau considered everything that happened to him as extraordinary, spent his time wondering at his fate, and consoled himself for its cruelty by considering how unusual it was. Of this, I shall give but one small example. At the time when he was being hooted at Motiers, Rousseau, through the Lord Marshal, obtained a place of

Councillor of State at Neuchâtel for Colonel Pury, son-in-law of Dupeyrou:

"Thus," says he, "while fate, ever putting me too high or too low, was buffeting me from one extremity to the other, and while the rabble was covering me with mud, I was making a Councillor of State."

(Remember how many sentences of this kind are to be found in the "Mémoires d'outre-tombe"!)

And yet, with all his pride, with these beginnings of madness, it cannot be denied that Rousseau was growing to be a better man. His misfortunes did not detach him from self, but they freed him from many contingent and passing things. He showed that resignation which he so well described in "Emile." In the intervals of his fits of pride or folly, he was patient and gentle. It is remarkable that he was faithful to all the friendships he formed or confirmed in those days (the Lord Marshal, Dupeyrou, Moultou, even that bore, d'Ivernois). He remained attached to them until his death, and he almost exempted them from his mania of suspicion.

Finally, Rousseau's religious soul became more purely religious. Had the Genevese clergymen shown themselves indulgent to him, his spiritualism would easily have accepted the confessional form of the Genevese church. But, enlightened as well as irritated by Protestant intolerance, he freed himself from every vestige of Protestantism, and, I will not say tended toward Catholicism, in the belief of which, after all, he had spent twenty-six years of his life, and which he practiced in all sincerity during about ten; but I should say that he tended toward a kind of *Catholicity.* I mean, thereby, that his God was the common God of all religions, and also that his God was not the God-policeman of Voltaire, nor the geometrical God of those among the Encyclopedists who were not quite atheists, but a God "who touches the heart," and also a God-Providence (such a one as he alludes to almost as often as Bossuet); something more, in very truth, than the God of the deist-rationalists.

And, besides, it would doubtless be somewhat excessive to say that he tended *in his heart* toward Catholicism; but yet, judging the ministers of the free religion, cruel and stupid, for they persecuted him both through wickedness and through ignorance of the Reformation's real principle; on the other hand, considering and discovering, perhaps, the infirmity of most men's minds, and even, at times, feeling his own brain tottering, he was not without some degree of sympathy for the spirit of submission and non-examination of Catholics, who, at least never hunted him down.

Many passages of his letters indicate the state of mind to which I allude.

I shall quote a few at random:

To Mme de B——, December, 1763:

"Yours is a religion which requires no examination; follow it in all simplicity of heart."

To M. M——, curate of Ambérier in Bugey, to whom he recommends Thérèse:

". . . How are you, sir? I am full of you and of your kindness, and I should like to find myself, some day, in your vicinity and to embrace so worthy an officer of morality. You know that it was thus that the Abbé Saint-Pierre called his fellow churchmen."

To M. Marcel, dancing master at the court of Saxe-Gotha:

"I never aspired to be a philosopher, I never called myself by that name, I never was, am not, and never will be such."

To a priest who had conceived doubts on several points of Catholic dogma and thought of abandoning his vocation:

"Why . . . for a matter of pure speculation, wherein no one can distinguish what is true and what is false, and which is important neither to God nor to man, should we impute it as crime to defer to the prejudices of our brethren and to say 'yes' *where no one has a right to say 'no'?*"

To M. Séguier de Saint-Brisson, a young man of an unquiet spirit, who had quarreled with his mother on religious questions (July 22, 1764):

"You think of freeing yourself entirely from the yoke

of that religion in which you were born? I declare to you that, had I been born a Catholic, I should have remained a Catholic, knowing full well that your church puts a very salutary curb on the vagaries of human reason, which, when it undertakes to fathom the abyss of things, finds neither bottom nor shores. . . ."

And also to Abbé de X——, another fluctuating priest, (November 11, 1764):

". . . In reality, what is at stake in this affair? The sincere desire to believe, the submission of the heart rather than of reason; for after all, reason does not depend on us, but only will, and it is only through will that one can be either submissive to the church or in rebellion against it. . . . I should begin by choosing as confessor a good priest, a sensible and wise man, such as one can find anywhere, if one wishes . . . I should say to him: 'I feel that the docility required by the church is a desirable state, for one who wishes to live in peace with himself; I love that state, I wish to live in it. . . . I do not believe, but I wish to believe, and I wish it with all my heart. Submissive to faith in spite of my lights, what argument need I fear? I am more faithful than if I were convinced.' "

I do not very well know, not being a priest, whether this is irreproachable orthodoxy; I do not say either that the troubled priests who consulted Rousseau were very good priests. . . . But the fact remains that he advised them to make an effort to believe and to submit. Putting things at the worst, the Catholicism of Rousseau's last days was, for example, as good as that of Lamartine.

To the Chevalier d'Éon (Wootton, March 31, 1766):

"If my principle [that of free interpretation] seems to me the truer, yours [authority] seems to me the more convenient; and one of your great advantages is that your clergy holds to it, whereas ours [the Protestant clergy], composed of little meddlers whose heads have been turned by arrogance, knows neither what it wishes nor what it says, and takes away infallibility from the church to usurp it for each one in particular."

To M. Roostan (Wootton, September 7, 1766):

". . . The Catholic clergy, the only one that had any complaint to make of me, *never did me nor wished me any harm*, and the Protestant clergy, that had every reason to be pleased with me, only did and wished me harm because it is as stupid as it is obsequious to power."

To Moultou, troubled also, though a minister, he writes a very beautiful letter of comfort and of exhortation to believe at least in God (Monquin, February 14, 1769). And I especially recommend to you the letter to M. de M——, (another unquiet spirit, troubled with doubts), which is a moving commentary on the "Profession de foi du vicaire Savoyard." (Bourgoin, January 15, 1769), from which I detach these words:

". . . In my childhood I believed by authority, in my youth, through sentiment; *now I believe because I have always believed.* Whereas my fading memory can no longer grasp my reasonings, whereas my weakened judgment no longer permits me to recommence them, the opinions which result from them remain unaltered. . . . I keep them in all confidence and conscience."

And further, on the fact that, in such researches, reason reaches a point beyond which it cannot go:

"Then, seized with awe, man stops and does not touch the veil, content to know that under it is the omnipotent Being."

And on the gentleness of Jesus:

". . . Gentleness more of the angel and of the God than of man, which never abandoned Him, even on the cross, and causes him who knows how to read this story, as it should be read, to weep torrents of tears."

Let us not exaggerate. It is certain that Rousseau, since the Charmettes, had ceased to be a Catholic in the real sense of the word—that is, to believe in the dogmas and hierarchy of Catholicism. It is certain that after 1754 the anti-popery prejudices of his childhood came back to him, especially in the "Contrat social." But it is likewise certain that from the time when the Protestants had persecuted him he had ceased to be anti-Catholic. A part of the clergy of France felt for him a secret sympathy, first from hatred of the Encyclopedists, then because Rousseau had never indulged in impiety.

On the divinity of Christ, there exists no formal negation of his. In a fragment ("Morceau allégorique sur la Révélation")[1] which probably dates from the last years of his life, and which is written in the taste and the style of the "Paroles d'un croyant,"[2] he shows us Socrates going into the temple of idols—then Jesus enters; at the moment of His entrance:

"A voice was heard in the air, distinctly uttering these words: 'This is the Son of man; the *Heavens are hushed before Him;* earth, listen to His voice.' Jesus ascended the altar of the principal idol and without effort overthrew it, and, stepping on the pedestal, with perfect calm he seemed rather to *take His place* than to usurp that of another."

Then He speaks, and:

"One felt that the language of truth came easily to Him, *as though He Himself possessed within Himself the source of truth.*"

Even on mass, the "Vicaire Savoyard," who continued to officiate, expressed himself thus in the "Profession de foi":

". . . When the moment of the consecration approaches, I collect my thoughts so as to accomplish it with

1 "Allegorical fragment on revelation."
2 "Words of a believer" (Lamennais).

all the dispositions required by the Church and by the greatness of the sacrament; I endeavor to annihilate my reason before the supreme intelligence; I say to myself: Who art thou that thou shouldst measure infinite power? I pronounce with reverence the sacramental words, and, with all the faith that is in me, give them effect. Whatever may be this inconceivable mystery, I do not think that on the day of Judgment I shall be punished for ever having profaned it in my heart."

All that is not absolute faith, and therefore it is not faith at all. But neither is it negation. It is of a man who remembers having believed. Many French priests were grateful to Rousseau for never having uttered a blasphemous word.

Let us return to the Rousseau of 1762-1766.

He never showed more touching eloquence than in his professions of faith at that time; never did he give wiser advice to unquiet souls; never was he greater as writer. . . . And yet he was already mad.

He was mad on one point. He suspected everybody, even and especially, his old friends, of hating him, of spying upon him, of betraying him, of persecuting him, of forming a vast plot to render him odious and to dishonor him. Already, at the Hermitage, he had shown signs of this mental malady. But at this time it had taken possession of him, and almost unremittingly; and the last twelve years of his life were the story of a poor creature pursued and hunted by a pack of imaginary hounds.

We left him at Strasburg, seeking where he might find a refuge. He seemed about to choose Berlin. Then suddenly, pressed to do so by the Comtesse de Boufflers, he went to Paris with a passport. He stayed with the Prince de Conti in the Temple, which had a right of sanctuary, and where all Paris went to see him, greatly to his fatigue. And, January 4, 1766, he allowed David Hume to carry him off to England.

Hume had the reputation of being a very honest man, and certainly he was full of sympathy for Rousseau and wished to be of use to him. As soon as they arrived in London Hume wrote to Mme de Boufflers:

"*My ward* has reached here in good health; he is very amiable, always polite, sometimes gay, generally sociable."

And to the Marquise de Barbentane:

". . . He is gentle, modest, affectionate, disinterested, gifted with exquisite sensitiveness. . . . His manners are remarkably simple, and in every-day life he is *a veritable child.* This quality, together with his great sensitiveness, enables those who live with him to govern him with the greatest ease."

Surely, these are the words of a friend. But they let one, nevertheless, understand that in Hume's eyes Rousseau was a strange and weak being. He is judged with kindliness, but with a smile. Hume belonged to the circle of Mme du Deffand and of Horace Walpole, to that of

Mme Geoffrin and of d'Alembert. He was fond of Jean-Jacques, yes, certainly; but that had not prevented him, one day, at Mme Geoffrin's, from taking part in a joke of Walpole's at Rousseau's expense: a pretended letter from the King of Prussia, wherein Jean-Jacques was teased on his mania of suspicion and his "need" of believing himself to be persecuted. As after all he had really been persecuted, the joke was a cruel one, and of that Hume took no heed. In a word, he was friendly to Rousseau, yes; but with some compassion or protection in his friendship, and, at times, a little irony. Now, when Rousseau discovered such feelings in one of his friends, it simply drove him raving mad.

And that is why, carried off to London by Hume, then sent by him to an estate belonging to his friend Davenport (at Wootton, sixty miles from London), where Rousseau paid but a modest rent—that is why, a few months later, Rousseau broke abruptly with Hume, accused him of having conspired against his honor together with d'Alembert and Dr. Tronchin, and declared Hume to be the falsest and most wicked of men.

His grievances? They throw a sad light on his case. Rousseau recapitulates them in a long letter to Hume himself, July 10, 1766. Of what does he accuse him? Of this: Hume did not admit Thérèse to his table. Scarcely had he reached London than the newspapers, until then favorable to him, became hostile; that, evidently, at Hume's instigation. Hume affected to husband Rousseau's money, to treat him like a poor man. Hume, having ordered a portrait of him, caused the artist to give him a wicked and somber expression. One day, when they were alone, Hume looked at him mockingly and cruelly; Rousseau felt convinced that such a glance could only be that of a wretch; then, in a sudden fit of remorse, he threw his arms about his host's neck, exclaiming in a broken voice: "No, no, David Hume is not a traitor; were he not the best of men, he must inevitably be the worst." Whereupon, Hume, nonplused, politely returned Rousseau's embrace and, while patting him on the back, repeated several times quietly (as we might ourselves have done): "What, my dear sir? . . . Eh! my dear sir? . . . What now, my dear sir? . . ." And Rousseau's other grievances are of the same character.

Besides, I think that Hume, at the beginning, was wanting in delicacy—and that, later, he was wanting in indulgence. And for so strange an invalid, much indulgence was necessary.

Rousseau left Wootton in May, 1767. During three more years,—restless, full of fears, ill,—going to the length of imagining that two inoffensive verses in a tragedy by Du Belloy, were aimed at him;—leaving Grenoble suddenly because a good soul of a President, after having showered attentions upon him, confessed in all simplicity that he had not read his works;—writing on inn doors thoughts inspired by his pride;—getting, now and then, glimmerings of his own madness, as when he wrote to M. de Saint-Germain: "Had I found a heart in which mine might have confided . . . it would have been better for my reason," or to d'Ivernois: "I begin to fear that, after so many real sorrows, imaginary troubles may act upon my brain" (March 28, 1768); then, seized upon by his usual visions;—having by way of books nothing but Plutarch, Astrée and Tasso,—incapable, says he, of thinking,—incapable of remaining long in the same place,—he took up once more, old already, the wandering life of his adolescence and youth, causing himself to be called "Renou" (the family name of mother Lavasseur); went to Fleury-sous-Meudon, at the Marquis de Mirabeau's place; then to Trye, with the Prince de Conti; from which place he fled, says he, on account of disagreeable servants, who refused to let him have vegetables and fruit from the garden; then to Lyons, then to Grenoble, then to Bourgoin, where he was married to Thérèse in the presence of God, of nature and of two virtuous citizens; then to Monquin, which he was obliged to leave on account of quarrels between Thérèse and a servant; then (once more) to Lyons—and finally to Paris, where he took up his old lodging, Rue Plâtrière, and where he once more donned a French dress.

This is where he lived for eight years, like a sensible man—at last. He was no longer—at last—beholden to anyone. He paid his rent—at last—like everybody. He renounced—at last—great lords and fine ladies. He no longer read, and wrote but little. But botany amused him, he took long walks and gathered specimens. He possessed an annuity of about twelve hundred francs, to which he added some five hundred more by copying music, which he did willingly. (In six years, six thousand pages of music, at ten sous a page.)

We possess, on this latter-day Rousseau, plenty of testimony, among which are included the (unfinished) "Essai sur Jean-Jacques Rousseau" of Bernardin de Saint-Pierre; the six letters of Corancez in the "Journal de Paris," (*An* VI); and "Mes visites à Jean-Jacques Rousseau," by M. Eymar, son of a merchant of Marseilles, who went to Paris to see his idol.

For this new generation Rousseau was a sort of lay saint. Saint-Pierre, Corancez, Eymar, saw but his virtues, which were real and which, at the time when they knew Rousseau, were nearly free from all dross.

Rousseau has often been accused of ingratitude; unjustly, I think, except in two or three evil moments of his youth. Only, he did not know how to guard his liberty against benefactors who, out of vanity, imposed their kindness upon him and when, at last, exasperated, he shook them off, he seemed ungrateful. But he was ungrateful neither toward Thérèse, nor toward Mme de Warens, nor toward M. and Mme de Luxembourg, nor toward Malesherbes, nor toward the Lord Marshal, nor toward the Roguins, Dupeyrous, the Moultous, the Corancez, etc. . . .

During those last years, he showed to the best possible advantage. Rousseau, it must be remembered, was extremely disinterested. Another than he would, with his books (even at that period) have made a little fortune. Poor, we see him quietly refuse a pension from the King of England, because it would have to come to him through Hume. He was very charitable, very generous. He was sober. He was charmingly simple in his way of life. He was gentle, polite, amiable. He was pious. He was indulgent. He never said harm of anyone,—(with the exception, toward the end, of those by whom he fancied that he was persecuted, and that only while they were persecuting him; and it is noteworthy that in his "Confessions," he is not bitter except toward Grimm and a little toward Mme d'Epinay). Sometimes, it is true, he had fits of mistrust and of somber susceptibility: but his friends of the last hour knew this and forgave it; and always he returned to them. Usually, he was a simple man, gentle and resigned, a veritable sage, passively good, a little after the fashion of a Brahmin. Thérèse, speaking of his death, said with ingenuousness: "If my husband was not a saint, who then could be one?"

And yet, this sage was a madman. Between 1772 and 1776, this sage from time to time spent some hours writing in copybooks, his madman's vagaries, his visions of a monomaniac, who believed himself to be the victim of a universal conspiracy; he wrote the "Dialogues," where a Frenchman converses with Rousseau about Jean-Jacques, whom he does not know to be Rousseau; and that forms the matter of three dialogues; and it takes up five hundred and forty pages; and it is full of repetitions and sinister twaddle; but it was often tragic and magnificent, and never was Rousseau a greater writer than in certain passages of those somber imaginings.

They do not greatly astonish one who has followed his correspondence, especially after 1762. September 28, 1762, he writes to Mme Latour-Franqueville (the most ardent of his admirers):

"Whoever is inspired with a passion for me is unworthy of me. . . . Whoever does not love me on account of my books is a rogue."

The prologue of book xii. of the "Confessions," the superb letter of forty-five pages, addressed to M. de Saint-Germain (Monquin, February 26, 1770) which is both an apology and an examination of conscience, already ring with madness. After February 9, 1770, he adopted, one cannot say why, a singularly useless mode of dating, and he headed all his letters with these four lines, by way of epigraph (I do not know where he found them; they may be his):

Pauvres aveugles que nous sommes!
Ciel, démasque les imposteurs,
Et force leurs barbares cœurs
A s'ouvrir aux regards des hommes.[1]

In the "Dialogues," madness reigns supreme. I should have liked to cull for you, in a few of the arguments of this work, the most unmistakable signs of an un-

[1] Poor blind creatures that we are!
Heaven, unmask the impostors
And force their savage hearts
To open before men's eyes.

hinged mind. But, for that, time is wanting. I can only tell you what Rousseau fancied he saw. This is it:

. . . Around him, walls were so built that, through them, through the floor, through the keyholes, he could be seen. . . . He was surrounded by detectives, prostitutes, trained beggars, all his letters were opened. . . . If he went into some public place, everyone surrounded him and stared at him, but at a certain distance and without speaking to him. . . . In the pit of a theater, they would be careful to place a guard or a policeman next to him. . . . Everywhere he was designated to postmen, clerks, guards, spies, Savoyards, peddlers, booksellers. . . . If he lacked a book, a calendar, none were left in Paris. . . . The shoe-blacks refused to clean his boots. . . . Did he wish to cross the water opposite the Quatre-Nations, no one would take him, even if he offered to pay for the whole boat. . . . Every day, spies were sent to him under the pretext of solicitations. . . . Beggars were ordered to throw his alms back in his face. . . . Every time it could be done, unnoticed, the passers-by spat on him in the street. He was, each day, the victim of hatred, disguised under sickening compliments. . . . In Dauphiny, he was deprived of all black ink; that which was given him turned white on the paper. . . . False news was imparted to him. . . . During eight years, simply for the spiteful pleasure of others, he and his companion were forced to travel and to spend large sums of money. . . . There was a conspiracy by which, in shops, he was forced to pay less than others, so as publicly to intrude alms upon him and mortify him. . . . He was almost driven to suicide. . . . He was accused of crimes of which he could not defend himself, since he did not know his accusers. What crimes? That, he did not know, except that it was noised abroad that he was a debauchee . . . and that he cheated as to the price of the music he copied—for the rest, he did not know, but that of which he was sure was that he was accused, etc., etc. (All this is repeated twenty times in the "Dialogues" for he wrote them without reading them over afterward.)

Who inflicted these miseries on him? "They." Who were "they"? Everybody: the powerful authors, doctors, men in office, women of evil life, Europe, the whole universe, and particularly Grimm, Mme d'Epinay, Diderot, Hume, d'Alembert and all the philosophers—with Choiseul at their head.

(The truth is that the philosophers began by treating him pretty well, and gently enough as an "original" being, an invalid; then, they began to find him insupportable and, when he publicly declared himself their enemy, ended by hating him and looking upon him as a dangerous lunatic: that is all; it is true that it was something, but nothing out of the way, or extraordinary or mysterious.)

As to the supposed persecutions which he so dramatically enumerates, you will notice that nearly all can be explained by the public curiosity he excited and the precautions taken by the police to protect him from it. The provisions sold to him at a lower rate than to others, is a reminiscence of a delicate attention on Mme. de Luxembourg's part; she knew Thérèse to be extravagant, and had ordered the Montmorency greengrocer to make special bills for her, agreeing to pay the difference. . . . And so on, I fancy, for all.

"They," plot against him. Who, again, are "they"? "Those gentlemen," that is, the philosophers, the "philosophical sect"—"Those gentlemen!" Jean-Jacques treats the philosophers exactly as the "liberals," later on, will treat the Jesuits. He writes in the second "Dialogue":

"Great imitators of the Jesuits' tactics, they [the philosophers] were their most violent enemies, doubtless through professional jealousy; and now they govern minds with the same despotism, the same dexterity with which the others governed consciences . . . and, little by little, substituting *philosophical intolerance* for the other, they became, unconsciously, as dangerous as their predecessors."

And he comes back to this idea indefatigably in the third "Dialogue," speaks of "philosophical inquisition," of the "missionaries of materialism and of atheism," and of the plots of the philosophical sect against all religion and all morality. And this should be read in connection with a very curious page of book ix. of the "Confessions":

". . . I remember the synopsis of Grimm's ideas on morality which Mme d'Epinay told me she had adopted. This synopsis consisted in a single article, that is, that the *only duty* of man consisted in following *entirely* the feelings of his heart. This code of morals, when I learned it, troubled me greatly, though I then took it as a paradox. But I soon perceived that this principle was really his rule of conduct, and, later on, I had proofs of this, to my sorrow. It was the *interior doctrine* of which Diderot so often spoke to me, but which he never explained. . . ."

And thus Jean-Jacques furnished arguments to some future Catholic historians of the Free-Masons.

These judgments of Rousseau's on the Encyclopedists were, perhaps, not those of a madman. There, where he raves, it is on the subject of the organized plot and the special persecutions of which he thought himself the victim. Yes, in that much, he was certainly out of his mind.

But after all, was he mad only on that point?

THE RÊVERIES—RECAPITULATION AND CONCLUSIONS

CHAPTER X

THE RÊVERIES—RECAPITULATION AND CONCLUSIONS

When Rousseau had finished the disorderly and painful composition of the five hundred and forty pages of his "Dialogues," he asked himself how he should make this apology known to men.

The simplest mode would have been to take his manuscript to his publisher, Duchesne, or to the publisher, Pissot, who would gladly have accepted such a windfall. But Jean-Jacques distrusted the whole world. The misprints sprinkled through his books, he attributed to the malice of his foes; he complained loudly that "they" disfigured his works so as to ruin him.

He was in a thoroughly mystical state of mind. He looked upon himself as another Job, seated on his dunghill, abandoned by all, and having no refuge save in God. But, in the midst of his sufferings, thanks to his incredible optimism—born of his dreams—he did not even argue with God, as did Job. It would seem as though, at that time, the virtues sown in him by nature had flowered, and that others had been added to these: gentleness, charity, resignation, simplicity, unselfishness, love of holy poverty: all, in fact, except humility. But, at least, his submission to God and his detachment from the world, were complete.

"I doubt," writes he, "whether ever mortal more entirely or more sincerely said to God: 'Thy will be done;' and this resignation, doubtless, had no great value, coming from one to whom this earth could offer nothing to tempt him."

And that is why he entertained the thought of confiding his manuscript to God. He copied it in his best handwriting and with all his skill of apprenticed engraver; then he resolved—he, a Calvinist, but who communed with God above all religions—to deposit the parcel on the high altar of Notre Dame "hoping that the noise made by this act might cause his manuscript to fall under the King's notice."

Saturday, February 24, 1776, after having wrapped up the manuscript of the "Dialogues," addressing it thus: "Deposit confided to Providence," he went to Notre Dame at about two o'clock, and directed his steps toward the high altar.

But the choir railing was closed. Rousseau was terribly moved by this seeming refusal on God's part. He rapidly left the church "resolved," said he, "never more to enter it."

A third time he copied his five hundred and forty pages, sought sure hands in which to place them, found none. He then reached perfect resignation:

"I therefore completely made up my mind; detached from all that concerns this world and the mad judgments of men, I am resigned to be forever calumniated by them. . . . *My happiness must be of another order*, it is not among them that that I must seek for it. . . . *Freed even from the disturbance of hope* here below, I see no means by which they can again trouble my heart's peace."

He lived thus two more years, meditating, botanizing, copying music—somewhat consoled by a few patient adorers. But his physical sufferings increased. Thérèse fell ill. Rousseau could not afford to hire a servant. His annuity of twelve or fourteen hundred francs (he varies as to the sum) and what he earned as copyist, might have enabled him and Thérèse to have boarded in some decent establishment. But that would have been too simple. A little earlier, according to a known phenomenon among monomaniacs of his kind, he had written and distributed two circulars to the "French nation," one to protest against the falsifying of his books by the publishers, the other to proclaim his innocence and the wickedness of his enemies. He wrote a third one in which he described his distress in consequence of Thérèse's illness and asked, for him and for her, board and lodging of any who would offer them, promising in return, "all he possessed in money, effects and stocks."

It was then that he consented to settle at Ermenonville, on the estate of the Marquis de Girardin—an excellent man, who forced his children to find their breakfast on a mast-top, and ended as an adept in mesmerism. And, at

Ermenonville, Jean-Jacques died forty-two days later. And we shall never know whether he committed suicide or whether he died a natural death; for doctors' certificates in such matters prove but little; and one of his best friends, Corancez, believed in the suicide; and M. Berthelot who held Rousseau's skull in his hands (December 18, 1897) concluded that there was no pistol shot in the head, but could not disprove either poison or a bullet through the heart. Rousseau's piety leads me to believe in a natural death; but at that time he was no longer master of his actions. . . . Therefore, I do not know.

So during those last two years, that is, during the time when he showed most evident marks of lunacy, he wrote the ten chapters of the "Rêveries d'un promeneur solitaïre";[1] that is, with the "Confessions," the most original, the most eternally young of his works.

They are composed of impressions, reminiscences, accounts of walks, descriptions, examinations of conscience, often of a kind of religious soliloquy:

"Let me give myself up entirely to the sweetness of conversing with my soul, since it is the only one [the sweetness] that men cannot take from me."

In the course of these lectures, I have already often quoted from the "Rêveries." Here, even more than in the "Dialogues," we find perfect detachment, total trust in God.

"For me all is ended on earth. None can do me either

[1] "Meditations of a solitary rambler."

good or harm. . . . I am at peace at the bottom of the abyss, a poor victim, but as *impassible as God Himself.*"

"As God Himself?" This is an awakening of pride. When will he become humble? Will he ever understand that humility is not only the most religious but also the most philosophical of virtues? To resign oneself to be the poor creature one really is, to fear exaggerating that nothingness, is not that the perfection of wisdom?

Yet, he was on the right road. . . . He had become less self-indulgent. Close upon death—of all his past faults which surge up in his memory, two only trouble him: and we know what were, in his eyes, his two greatest sins, those which caused him the most remorse. In the first place, the desertion of his children, and also, after fifty years, the lie by which he had accused poor Marion of having stolen the ribbon. . . .

And thereupon follows a penetrating and strict dissertation on lying, as of a penitent who has often been guilty of lies, and who suffered at the thought of them. And that—for the first and only time in his life—brought with it a feeling which is, at last, humility, or something very like it:

"What renders me still more unpardonable, is the motto which I had chosen (*Vitam impendere vero*). This motto obliged me, above all other men, to a strict adherence to truth. . . . That is what I ought to have said to myself when I adopted this proud motto, what I ought to have repeated unceasingly as long as I *dared* to use it. Falseness never prompted my lies, they all came from *weakness*, but that is a *very lame excuse*. With a *weak soul*, one can barely fight off vice, but it would be arrogant and bold to dare profess great virtues."

Here, really, he begins to know himself. However, he as yet only sees and condemns the lies of his life—not the more dangerous lies of his books. Those, he died without having known, for they were his very soul, where blind emotion reigned supreme.

Finally, it was in the fifth "Promenade," still more than in Saint-Preux' journey to the Valais mountains ("Nouvelle Héloïse," I., 23d Letter), still more than in the pilgrimage of Saint-Preux and Julie to Meilleraye (IV., 17th letter), that Rousseau, in very truth brought, with a new manner,—new by the degree, new by the persistency,—a new fashion of seeing, of feeling, of loving, of describing nature.

Whereupon, one may ask: How could he be mad, yet at the same time write such perfect things, so full of emotion, so beautiful? I answer: Perhaps because he may always have been half mad—intermittingly, but always after the same fashion and at every epoch of his life.

In what really consisted the averred folly of his declining years? He was sensitive, tender, credulous. He would take violently to a man to whom he attributed every virtue, and of whom he believed himself to be adored. Then, he would perceive that his new friend was not up to the image he had formed of him, and also that his friend was more loved than loving. Cruelly bereft of his illusions, he fancied himself deceived; and out of this supposed treason of a few persons, he concluded that this treason was universal and that a vast plot had been hatched against him. Deformation of things by sensitiveness and hasty generalization, such was Rousseau's case, most evident in his "Dialogues."

But did he not, likewise, in his other writings, twist and turn reality?

To believe that nature is good because he felt virtuous in following the dictates of nature, that is, in doing all that tempted him; to believe that society is evil because he had suffered from society, and to conclude from all this, that society has corrupted nature;—or else because he loved virtue, especially when it was exceptional, or because of dulled senses, and because he had never tasted of passion more than a certain languor, ardent but ineffectual; to believe that a husband, a wife, that wife's former lover, and a tenderly attached friend of that lover, could all live quietly and openly together, three of the personages, besides, having no other occupation than loving, tenderly caring for and curing the lover (who is Rousseau himself, under the name of Saint-Preux); or else, because he had retained a lively remembrance of some cordial municipal festivity of his little republic, and because he wept with emotion at feeling himself in communion with his dear, recovered Genevese; to believe that the happiness of man consists in being handed over bodily to the State;—or else because, through his life, he loved virtue, to think himself virtuous, and because he was emotional, to believe himself the best of men, and to believe it *mordicus*, as he did believe it;—or else, at last, as in his "Dialogues," to consider himself as persecuted by the whole universe because he had met with a few unfaithful friends:—does not all that, after all, come from the same exorbitant triumph of emotion over reason? And, if Rousseau can be called insane in the last of the cases I have enumerated, who would dare to affirm, except for the degree, that he was not equally mad in the others? He was. . . . Oh! I know, so would be many men in our eyes, if we knew them, if they wrote books and if, in the midst of their unreasonableness, they showed some genius.

Add to all this, Rousseau's ailments, of which it is not necessary once more to give the lamentable list. His illnesses did not cause his sensitiveness; but they made it more acute and tyrannical, by giving it frequent occasions of manifesting itself. They often condemned him to solitude. They forced him to retire within himself. No writer ever, less than he, went out of himself, or more constantly brought all things back to self, or even believed, in fact, in the perversity of more individuals than did this friend of humanity, so intimately persuaded of man's instinctive goodness.

This unreason, this total subordination of judgment to emotion, give him a unique place in literature. Compare him, I do not say with the great writers of the seventeenth century, but with Voltaire, with Montesquieu, with Buffon, even with the fantastical Diderot. Oh! how full of common sense will they seem to you! Why not say it? Innumerable pages by Jean-Jacques are full of ingenuously insolent absurdities. I have pointed out to you that his most determined admirers are themselves often obliged to interpret him and to acknowledge that they do so; we should not, affirm they, consider what he says, but what he understands thereby, which is profound and sublime. Now, Rousseau is the only one of our classical authors (if it be that we are justified as yet in bestowing on him that appellation) who requires so complacent and so radically transforming an interpretation. The others may make mistakes: but what they say, they say, and nothing else. Amidst their caprices or their audacities, their reason stands firm. They remain in the French tradition: Rousseau, that interrupter of traditions, that alien, introduces into our literature a phenomenon, a "monster" (which by way of progeny, will have all the unpoised, great and small, of the nineteenth century).

Hence, perhaps, his fascination. Beside real genius, he possessed and, to the highest degree, the gift of expression; but humanity is so made that it is perhaps the element of absurdity in his books which permitted Rousseau to exercise so prodigious an influence. People went to him on account of his brilliant and emotional folly as poet-dialectician, on account of the singularities and contradictions of his person and of his life, on account of the delirious vibration his suffering soul communicated to his books. Yes, Rousseau's fascination was often the mysterious "fascination of the absurd." For absurdity attracts all the more that it offers to the senses the sudden and gross image of a facile compensation for what is painful in real life.

Shall I now sum up his work and what is called his system? Others have done this, and so well that I should not venture to follow in their traces. Faguet, first of all, and with what penetration in his "Dix-huitième siècle!" Only, he confesses that, in spite of all his efforts, he was not able to place, with any show of logic, the "Contrat social" in Rousseau's system. M. Gustave Lanson has been more fortunate. You should read in his history of the "Littérature française," his chapter on Rousseau, if you love Rousseau unflinchingly, if you desire to believe in the coherency and unity of his work, and in his inexhaustible benevolence. It is, moreover, a model of subtle interpretation and ingenious reconstitution.

I cannot submit it to you as a whole; but a text book used in the schools sums up thus M. Lanson's own synopsis:

"Rousseau's system. First: The state of nature is good, the social state is bad—such is his thesis. Second: But, as one cannot return to the state of nature, one must be resigned to the social state as a necessary makeshift—such is the antithesis. Third: Besides, one can improve the social state by bringing it back, through different means, to the state of nature—such is the synthesis.

Hence one perceives how the development of the first and third points is distributed through his works. The goodness of the state of nature and the vices of the social state, these are the subjects of the two "Discours" and of the "Lettre à d'Alembert." To counteract the evils of the social state for the individual by an education in harmony with nature, this is the subject of "Emile";—counteract them for man as head of a family by the practice of family virtues according to nature, which are capable of cleansing the worldly passions of both sexes, that is the subject of the "Nouvelle Héloïse";—counteract them finally, for men subjected to a government, by a fair observance of the conditions formally stipulated with regard to that submission and which were dictated by nature (so it is supposed), that is the theme of the "Contrat social."

And thus:

"Man in society will be reconciled to natural man, as individual, as husband, as citizen."

Schoolboys will read this, and will be satisfied with it, no doubt, considering Rousseau as the most rectilineal, the most geometrical, among the great writers. I fear these innocents will be far from the truth.

First, a system which means this: "My instincts and my good pleasure are sacred, and I call them nature," and which is contained in these two lines, "Nature is good, society is corrupted; therefore let us return as much as possible to nature," is a rather poor system, and which reposes, besides, on the most arbitrary and vague of postulates. It is not a system, it is a sentimental state of being. The perpetual repetition of a single principle, and of so doubtful a principle, does not suffice to form a system, nor a social philosophy. A single principle, yes, but from which Rousseau draws, according to his fancy, consequences, many of which are in contradiction one with the other,—without mentioning the formal disavowals that his correspondence inflicts upon his works,—(and without counting the contradictions, excusable perhaps, but really too frequent, between his acts and his writings).

But even that principle (the goodness of nature, the evil of society)—which is, at bottom, nothing but a convenient formula of revolt—would he have met with it, if, already thirty-eight years of age, absorbed by music and light dramatic works, the question of the Dijon Academy had not suggested it to him? And was not most of his work suspended, as it were, on that incident? Would he have conceived the superstition of equality, without a new question of that fatal Academy? Would he have written the "Nouvelle Héloïse" if he had not known Mlle de Breil, then Mme d'Houdetot and Saint-Lambert? etc., etc. . . . One might, you would object, put *similar* questions with regard to all writers and all books. No; only with regard to "works of imagination," novels or poems; and Jean-Jacques is always both novelist and poet. And I think that I have proved that all his works were inspired by private circumstances, and that they can, above all, be explained thereby—and also by his temperament, his physical state, by this or that event of his past life, and, I might even say, by that one of his divers souls which, at such and such a moment, acted in him: Genevese soul, Protestant soul, Catholic soul, soul of a vagrant and of a rebel, soul of a would-be lover, soul of a simulator through desire for emotion, soul of a dreamer and almost of a fakir, soul of an invalid. It is not to be wondered at that the work, written under the influence of such different souls, should be wanting in unity; and one will therefore not be surprised at the contradictions between all these books and his letters. Where, then, can we see any unity? Not at all, according to me, in the system, but in the fact that all the disturbed souls of which Rousseau's personality is composed have this in common: a morbid sensitiveness, generally quite distinct from judgment and all critical sense. Or rather, let us simplify yet more. Let us amalgamate the vagrant, the stray waif, the dreamer, the plebeian, the physical sufferer, and also the Protestant,—that is, the man of a religion founded on free interpretation (and all these elements might perhaps form an anarchist)—and on the other hand . . . what? The man who, in spite of all, remains to a certain extent of one country and one tradition; a Protestant bearing the impress of Catholic tenderness; and let us conclude: an exasperated individualism, with, here and there, some vestige of traditionalism, thanks to the religious feeling: there, perhaps, might be the unity, secret and murky, of Rousseau's works, if it be anywhere. And even thus his unity remains a duality.

It is now left for me to point out what novelties Rousseau brought and what was his double influence, political and literary.

Among the novelties, I see, first of all, his style. This novelty seems to me an ancient thing, rediscovered and enriched. I have already said, with regard to the first "Discours" that, as prose writer, Jean-Jacques took up a tradition. Fed, away from Paris and fashion, on the great writers of the seventeenth century, he adopted their harmonious, complex and periodic phrase. It has been said of him that he had recreated Bossuet's style: he at least adopted its grandeur and movement. He used fewer images than Bossuet and his are less original; but he found some that were very beautiful and borrowed from new objects. His construction is more closely knit together, of a less free syntax, more strictly correct, than that of the great orator. He seeks, more than Bossuet, antitheses and the music of words. While, as a usual thing, he preserves the broad rhythm, he endeavors to be more concise; but, as he likes to repeat the same idea several times with different words, it happens that his pages may appear both concise in the detail and prolix as a whole. His is a singularly sensitive ear. One of the peculiarities of his style is the care with which, in the same phrase, he avoids the repetition of words—replacing the substantive, as much as possible, by the personal pronoun, demonstrative or possessive, according to the case, —and that, so frequently, as to render the sentence difficult to follow. He prefers obscurity to the merest appearance of negligence. So as not to seem myself obscure, I shall give you an example, which I have had no difficulty in finding. It is in the "Nouvelle Héloïse" (Part II., letter 25), with regard to Julie's portrait, which Saint-Preux does not consider as sufficiently modest:

"Yes, your face is too chaste to justify your bosom's disorder; one feels that *one of those two objects* should prevent the *other* from showing itself; only love's frenzy could accord them; and, when *his* ardent hand dares to unveil *that which* modesty covers, the rapture and confusion in your eyes then proclaim that you forget rather than expose *it*."

(The "Confesssions" are rather an exception, for, there, the style is more simple, less constantly strained, more varied, freer, truer, more savory, more "sensual," and its vocabulary is enriched with familiar words and even with dialect.)

In a word, Rousseau's style is very beautiful. It contains that of Bernardin de Saint-Pierre, that of George Sand, that of Lamennais and the "argumentative" writers of the nineteenth century, and much more than in germ Chateaubriand's style. It contains also, unfortunately, that of many a journalist and orator of the wearisome type. It matters little. One must certainly acknowledge that Rousseau's style gave elevation to French prose. But others have said that better than I could do.

What other novelties did Rousseau bring? I shall speak

in the first place of those which acted directly on his contemporaries.

It has been said that he was a great reformer of manners; that he restored individual morality in causing it to rest on conscience ("Conscience . . . divine instinct . . . sure guide . . .") and domestic morality by branding adultery, and by preaching the respect of marriage and of paternal and maternal duties.

There is truth in all this; but, all the same, a little exaggeration. One would really imagine that morality had ceased to exist in France, that there was no more religious instruction, that nearly all the middle-class wives and mothers of Paris and the provinces were depraved and forgetful of all their duties. . . . In truth Rousseau (and that after Marivaux, Destouches, La Chaussée, who were moral writers) had some influence, not over much, only on a circle very much depraved but very circumscribed. Because he persuaded a few young women to nurse their babies and to remain a little longer in the country, it must not be supposed that he transformed and regenerated French society. License in the upper classes, unless I am much mistaken, continued to reign up to the Revolution, and likewise licentious literature. Only, it became the fashion to show emotion, and redundant phrases on virtue were more frequent. What Roussau, especially, developed among his contemporaries was a horrible sentimentalism, extraordinarily different from goodness. It seems to me excessive to affirm, as has been done, that "he changed the moral atmosphere of France."

It has also been said that he taught women to feel "passion," great, true passion, quite forgotten, it seems. Oh, it yet might be proved that Mlle de Lespinasse, Mlle d'Aïsse—and others, doubtless, who did not confide their secrets to the world—had not the slightest need of his lessons!

It is true that he influenced even his contemporaries by his deism. He was really a religious man, and that I have shown most abundantly. He took position as the declared antagonist of the atheistical encyclopedists, and that is why they so hated him. His free Protestantism, softened by twenty-six years of Catholicism, is not far removed from Chateaubriand's sentimental Catholicity. And, at a certain moment during the early years of the nineteenth century, one could say that "if Rousseau's influence had led to a Jacobite republic, it contributed, soon after, to the Catholic restoration" (Lanson).

As compared with the Encyclopedists' doctrine, Rousseau's way of looking on progress is likewise a novelty. He had not their beatified faith in that idol. He did not, like them, believe that material and intellectual progress could insure man's happiness. He had by no means the superstition of science. Rousseau is, besides, nearly always excellent on all points where he is in direct antagonism with the Encyclopedists. It might be possible—and interesting—to compose a whole volume of conservative and traditionalistic maxims and reflections culled from the liberty-loving Jean-Jacques Rousseau, and that is why we must give up looking for any formula that could entirely express him. All we can do is to seek for his ideas and his predominant instincts.

But where Jean-Jacques, most indisputably, was a novator, where he was a novator most fully, brilliantly, and with, I think, great profit to others, was in his love for nature (and, in connection with this, for simple and rustic life) a novator, also, in his description of it. Oh, I do not forget the ancient poets, nor those of the French Renaissance, nor Théophile nor Tristan,[1] nor Mme de Sevigné, nor La Fontaine. I do not say that before Rousseau our forbears were not capable of being greatly moved by this earth's beauties. But they did not apply themselves much to the enjoyment of them, and their emotions, in that order of things, even their most lively emotions, were described by them either with extreme artifice (as with Théophile, if you will), or with extreme sobriety (as with La Fontaine); and then, at last, fields, and woods, and mountains were reflected in Rousseau's melancholy eyes.

It is certainly since Rousseau, and thanks to his example, that we have educated ourselves to see, to taste, to relish the different images of the cultivated or wild earth, and that we have wished deeply to enjoy them. The general tenor of novels and lyrical poetry has, through him, been transformed. I should even say that civilized man has been, since Rousseau, more really moved by natural beauty than he had been during thousands of years.

And Rousseau went, at one bound, extremely far in

[1] Poets of Louis XIII's time.

the art of seeing nature, of being moved by it, and of painting it. Since, that art has become more subtle; more minute paintings have been attempted of rarer scenes; words have been tortured, sometimes happily, not always. . . . I confess, for my part, that Rousseau's art, his broad, yet precise, mode of painting satisfies me even to-day. Add to this, that his landscapes are always vivified by the soul, that they are the expression of a sentiment, as well as of a vision. And, in his "Cinquième promenade," he expressed, and most completely, something that was even newer at that time than his landscapes themselves: meditation *in the midst* of nature.

That was his great originality. Through it, he still keeps his grasp on us. I was quite surprised to find in a page written by me long since (more than twenty years ago, certainly) reminiscences undeniable, but probably unconscious, and, on my sensations, a kind of impress from that Rousseau whom, at that time, I rarely read:

"Love of nature," said I, "excites a sort of reverie which brings peace to us, and renders us more gentle, as it is composed of a vague and floating sympathy with all the innocent forms of universal life. . . . It causes us to feel that we are surrounded by the unknown, and awakens in us that feeling of mystery which might otherwise be lost through the abuse of science, and the foolish confidence inspired by that science. It bestows upon us that sweetness of losing ourselves, consciously and voluntarily, in that kingdom of life where thought is unexistent, and from which we sprang. It insinuates into us a fatalistic serenity which is a great boon; it hushes to sleep our dolorous supersensitiveness; and what is charming is that we feel that it is being thus soothed, and that we can remember it without any suffering. It would be a fine spectacle, some day, to see humanity, grown old, disgusted with sterile agitations, exasperated by its own civilization, desert towns, return to natural life, and make use of all its intelligence, all its delicacy, and the sensitiveness acquired by innumerable centuries of culture, the better to enjoy it. Humanity, thus, would end as it began. The last men, like the first, would be inhabitants of forests, but much more highly educated, and subtler than members of the French Academies, and, also, much more philosophical. . . . In reality, the final happiness toward which the human race aspires, and toward which it fancies it is going, could be more easily conceived after that fashion, than after that of an industrial and scientific civilization."

The thought which, that day, thus confusedly took possession of me, was it not the dream on which the absurd "Discours sur les sciences et les arts" and the nebulous "Discours sur l'inégalité" are built? Thus, through certain developments of our sensibility, we are all, more or less, unconsciously disciples of Rousseau.

Besides the love of the different aspects of nature, besides reverie, he brought (especially in the "Confessions"), a sort of cordial and smiling realism. Jean-Jacques was not, like the other writers of his day, a gentleman fashioned by the schools. With him, fresh and pure air burst into literature. His charm is very great. This persists, and is still felt, whenever his rhetoric does not smother it.

I have shown the happy innovations. What remains for me to explain is his posthumous influence.

First, in politics. Neither Voltaire nor Montesquieu and his disciples gave form to the Revolution; but Rousseau did. The theory of absolute democracy and of the divine right of numbers dates from him. The Terror was (as I have shown) the adaptation to a great and old kingdom of a governmental theory imagined by a sophist for a small community. . . . And the breviary of Jacobinism was still the "Contrat social."

Rousseau was the Revolution's god. It carried him to the Pantheon and voted his statue; it pensioned Thérèse, remarried after fifty to a hostler. You remember how, already, in 1788, Marat, in the streets and squares, commented upon the "Contrat social." The revolutionary jargon was Rousseau's tongue, disfigured. Rousseau delighted the people by his affirmations as to the goodness of the poor and the wickedness of the rich and the great. He was worshiped. I possess a collection of pamphlets composed on Rousseau from 1787 to 1793, which show how thoroughly man is a religious animal. There is an account of rustic festivities celebrated at Montmorency in honor of Jean-Jacques. There were seven speeches—and what speeches!—and songs, and emblems, and allegories. Such were the merry-makings he pictured in his "Lettre sur les spectacles." There was also an "Éloge de Rousseau, qui a concouru pour le prix de l'Académie française" (1790);[3] and "L'Éloge de Rousseau, citoyen de Genève, par Michel Edme Petit, citoyen français" (1793).[2] One here sees to what Rousseau's ideas can turn in a fool's brain. It is extraordinarily stupid and of a stupidity akin to ferocity. And there were finally (I cannot mention everything) the "Réflexions philosophiques et impartiales sur J. J. Rousseau et Mme de Warrens,"[3] where Rousseau is not only excused, but glorified, for having deserted his children, and compared to Brutus and Manlius sacrificing their sons to their country! Rousseau, in the eyes of the idiots and knaves of the day, was neither more nor less than the savior, the redeemer of humanity. Without him, without some phrases of this stranger in his "Discours sur l'egalité," especially without his "Contrat social" (for which he himself did not much care), it is possible that, in 1792, no one would have thought of proclaiming the Republic.

What Rousseau left in literature to future ages was romanticism, that is (at bottom, and in reality, and

[1] Panegyric of Rousseau, presented for the prize of the French Academy (1790).

[2] Panegyric of Rousseau, citizen of Geneva, by Michel Edme Petit, French citizen (1793).

[3] Philosophical and impartial considerations on J. J. Rousseau and Mme de Warens.

though many poems or books of the romantics do not fall under that definition), once more, individualism, literary individualism, the complacent exhibition of self—and useless and solitary musings, and the desire for, and the pride in, and the spirit of revolt: all that expressed either directly or through transparent masks to which the poet communicates his soul. (But, after all, the best would be to refer you to M. Pierre Lasserre's fine book, "Le romantisme français.")

At the pitch where Rousseau carried this literary individualism (especially in the "Confessions" and the "Rêveries") it was new, unknown till then; and in it one might observe an abnormal and indecent use of literature. Evidently that was not its aim. Originally, the poet sang or recited, to assembled men, stories, songs, or panegyrics of heroes, or moral precepts. It is evident that no intimate confidences were expected. Such was primitive and "natural" literature, the only one that should have been adopted by Rousseau, priest of nature. Later, after the invention of writing, after that of printing, it was instinctively felt that it would not be fit to expose to the public—multiplied by manuscript or printed copies—anything but thoughts, narratives, and images that might interest everyone; that it was scarcely likely that the intimate and secret being of the writer could touch other men, and that, on the other hand, it would not be modest to show his being to the public. Individualism in literature, antiquity ignored (except for a few elegiac stanzas or couplets). The Middle Ages, the sixteenth, seventeenth and eighteenth centuries, up to Rousseau scarcely knew it. Montaigne himself, for example, is indiscreet only after the fashion of Horace. He does not confess all things, nor entirely (far from it); and his avowals are made in connection with general observations on human nature.

Rousseau, in his "Confessions," really inaugurated this sort of literature, and, at once, gave it its full meaning. No one more will ever open his heart as did Jean-Jacques.

In my first lecture, I spoke to you of this unique book. I must add an observation. Rousseau began the "Confessions" at Motiers, in 1762, at the request of a publisher, and, especially, with an apologetic intention. Had he not been persecuted, he might never have written them. Had he not written them, he would, in the first place, be less famous, and, then, we should know him less well; we should be ignorant of his shame, of the desertion of his children, or, at least, we should not be sure of these things; and, finally, his masterpiece would be wanting, and, consequently, the strange fascination of his reputation being less, the influence of his writings would not have been so powerful. These, will you say, are but vain hypotheses. Wait. As in Rousseau's life there are many adventures and unforeseen events, and as it is self-evident that his works were closely allied to his life, there is much of all this, therefore, in the causes which led him to write this or that book. (I have noticed this full twenty times.) Except for some fortuitous chance, he might never have written certain fatal and terrible things—and things of which he himself was not absolutely sure. He is especially known and influential through two books which he might very easily not have written—the "Contrat social" and the "Confessions." Joseph de Maistre would (I fancy) have said on that subject, that what we call chance in a human life is but the result of the Divine will, and that, thus, Rousseau's destiny, more than that of any other celebrated writer, was directed, ordained, by an irritated Providence, whose blind tool he was. I, for my part, shall simply say, that what he wrote having had so powerful an action on whole generations of men—and not being certain that he believed all he wrote, or that he would have written it but for accidental circumstances—Rousseau appears to me, on that account, in the series of our great writers (in whose ranks he, an alien, takes his place), strange, mysterious, tragically predestined, and far more than he to whom Renan applied this formula, "created by a special and nominative decree of the Eternal." [1]

I close my parenthesis. Therefore, the literary progeny of Jean-Jacques comprises Chateaubriand, Mme de Staël, Senancour, Lamartine, Hugo, George Sand, Michelet, . . . without Rousseau, they would not have been what they were.

Can I, while enumerating such glorious names, regret romantic individualism? Oh, no, for they have too often charmed me—and how deeply! And then, can one say that the romantic poets and writers only gave us personal con-

[1] Feuilles détachées (Victor Hugo, au lendemain de sa mort.)

fidences? Are they entirely romantic? Have you, in Chateaubriand, Hugo, or Vigny, met many personal sentiments which were not general after some fashion or other? What is perhaps true is that the best, the most solid of the nineteenth century literature would yet remain, were romanticism to be taken from it, and that, in reality, the most ancient, the most necessary, and the most powerful is, after all, objective, impersonal literature (philosophy, history, psychological novels, and even theatrical work).

But, how fascinating the other often is! and how exquisitely do the faults and the most intimate sentiments of a writer, who has genius enough to express them, act on our sensibility! A man of this kind, when he examines and describes himself, plunges more deeply into his own soul than he could plunge into that of others. . . . And I know very well that personal literature is but the glorification of mortal sins, but, without it, many things would never have been said, and what a pity that would have been! Let us acknowledge, if you will, that that sort of literature is something irregular, something which is outside of all order. . . . But all the same, it would have been sad had not romanticism—which for the last fifty years has been declining—come into the world.

Shall I follow up the influence of Rousseau on strangers? Here I feel my incompetency; I can only refer you to Joseph Texte's excellent book [1]—and repeat what

[1] "Jean-Jacques Rousseau et les origines du cosmopolitisme littéraire."

has so often been said, that Rousseau's influence is felt with Goethe, Schiller, Byron; with Kant, Fichte, Jacobi, Schleiermacher; and most brilliantly with Tolstoï.

"I have read Rousseau from beginning to end," said Tolstoï, to one of our compatriots, "I have read his twenty volumes, even his dictionary of music. I admired him with something more than mere enthusiasm; I worshiped him. At fifteen I carried around my neck, instead of the usual cross, a medallion with his portrait. There are certain of his pages so familiar to me that it seems to me that I wrote them."

And, finally (and I have often thought as much during this long pilgrimage through his works), either through himself, or through the writers influenced by him, he acts upon us, even without our knowledge. He acts upon the most unconscious part of us, on our sensitiveness; for he himself was a prodigiously sensitive being, of an unruly sensitiveness, that is, quite apart from goodness, often at war with reason, and, often, too, teacher of error and instigator of revolt.

Before taking leave of him, let us consider him in the most flattering of the numberless portraits he left of himself in his four "Lettres à M. de Malesherbes. (And this mania of eternally "explaining his character" is really scarcely a manly trait and is a sign, already, of mental weakness.) When he composed these letters he was at his very best; he had written "Julie," the "Contrat," and "Emile"; and his madness was but incipient. Now, how did he see himself? and how did he explain himself?

In this portrait, which, however, he wished to make as sympathetic as possible, he forgot, or neglected, the healthiest parts of himself, those wherein his Parisian and Catholic ancestors might have recognized themselves; he forgot the Jean-Jacques who wrote such reasonable things on patriotism, (for example in the essay on "Economie politique," or on the Abbé Saint-Pierre's ingenuous "Projet de paix perpétuelle"[1] he forgot him who wrote the admirable third part of the "Nouvelle Héloïse," and, in "Emile," the "Profession de foi du vicaire Savoyard," and the delightful chapters on Sophie's education, and certain pages of the "Lettres de la montagne," and, in his private correspondence, so many letters full of reason (for it was especially for the public that he composed his insanities).

He forgot, as I said, what was best in him; and he painted himself thus:

After having expressed his "disgust for men," he sought for the cause of this disgust: "It is neither more nor less," says he, "than that indomitable spirit of liberty which nothing could conquer" (for, naturally, he gave the most favorable names to things). He went on to say that "*no one in the world but himself knew him.*" He affirmed that he was well aware of his faults and vices, but, immediately, he added, "With it all, I am intimately

[1] "A project for perpetual peace."

persuaded that of all the men whom I have known in my life none was ever better than I."

He painted himself as "an indolent soul, afraid of all trouble, easily alarmed, and excessively sensitive as to what touches it." He proclaimed his absolute contempt for public opinion. (Now "public opinion," as he understood it, could be that of fools, but could also be the most respectable and necessary of traditions.) He wrote proudly, "I hate the great," he who so long seemed unable to do without them. His chief pleasure was to dream. He tells us of the silent revels of his sensibility and imagination in the woods of Montmorency:

"And yet, in the midst of it all, the *nothingness of my chimeras* sometimes arose before me and saddened me. Even had all my dreams turned to realities, they would not have satisfied me; I should still have imagined, dreamed, desired. I found within myself an inexplicable void which nothing could fill, a certain longing of the heart toward another kind of happiness which I could not even conceive, and of which I yet felt the need."

What is all that, if not the brilliant portrait of a lyrical poet, and of a rebel? (And it is that second trait, especially, which seduced men, for revolt pleases above all things.)

Poet, great poet, a soul full of desires, a temperament *of the same order* as that of Byron, of Leopardi, of Musset, but whose poetry, full of individualism, happened to be mainly used for objects which are not of poetry's domain, which especially require observation and reason. And the terrible part of it is that, thanks to these theories, born of his imagination and his sensitiveness, nourished by a brilliant and deceptive dialectic, these theories which, after him, were to prove so fatal, he, according to his own account, did not really believe in them—he dreamed them; and it is by these "chimeras," of which he confessed the "nothingness," that he was destined to lay waste the future.

For, in his "Lettres à M. de Malesherbes," it was not only the lyrical poet his portrait represented, it was also, the dreamer intoxicated and dazed with reveries, the proud hermit, the insolent self-taught man, the instinctive revolutionary, the unsociable man who, every day of his life, tried to mend society, the man from whom, according to himself, dated all things, who brought everything back to himself, and subordinated everything to his dream and his caprice; who eternally swept away the work of ages, and who fancied he caused humanity to advance by breaking the chain which unites generations one to the other; the man capable of associating the anthropoids or the Spartans to his utopias, but who, in reality, held for nought the dead of his race, "more numerous than the living"; in one word the very reverse of a Bossuet or an Auguste Comte.

I once adored romanticism, and I believed in the Revolution. And now, greatly troubled, I reflect that the man who, not alone assuredly, but more than any other,

I believe, was the cause of the Revolution and romanticism, or, at least, prepared them, was a stranger, a perpetual invalid, and, finally, a madman.

But he was greatly loved. Many still love him, because he was a master of illusions and the apostle of the absurd; others, because he was, among the illustrious writers, a being of quivering nerves, of weakness, of passion, of sin, of suffering, and of dreams. And I myself, after this long intimacy from which I have often derived pleasure, I wish to leave him without repulsion for his person—with an acute disapprobation of some of his most notable ideas, the most lively admiration for his art, which was so strange a novelty, with the most sincere pity for his lamentable life—and a "sacred horror" (in the Latin sense) as to the great mystery of his action on humanity.

THE END